Shakespeare-ience
Macbeth

Dr. Robert D. Strickland

Perfection Learning® Corporation
Logan, Iowa 51546-0500

Editorial Director	Julie A. Schumacher
Editorial Research and Feature Writer	Wim Coleman
Design	Kay Ewald, Michelle Glass
Art Research	Lisa Lorimor
Cover Art	Michael Aspengren

1000 North Second Avenue, P.O. Box 500
Logan, Iowa 51546-0500
Tel: 1-800-831-4190 • Fax: 1-800-543-2745

Printed in the United States of America.

Paperback ISBN 0-7891-5687-3
Cover Craft ISBN 0-7569-0736-5
1 2 3 4 5 6 VH 07 06 05 04 03 02

Table of Contents

Introductory Material

The Play

Background Information

Dr. Robert D. Strickland is Executive Director in the Division of Life Skills and Special Projects for all of the arts disciplines in the Miami-Dade County Public Schools. He received a BS in Music Education from the University of Tennessee, a MA and MFA in Theatre from the University of Miami, and an Ed.D in Educational Leadership from Nova Southeastern University. He is a past President of the Florida Association for Theatre Education and a member of the Florida Department of Education writing team for the theatre teacher certification examination, theatre curriculum frameworks/ standards, and theatre course descriptions. He was a senior consultant for developing and writing a high school textbook that received the 1999 Distinguished Book Award from the American Alliance for Theatre Education.

Dr. Strickland has taught at the elementary, secondary, college, and university levels. He received the 1997 Administrator of the Year awards from both the Florida Association for Theatre Education and the Dade Association for Theatre Education. In 2000, Dr. Strickland was awarded the Herbert A. Drew, Jr., Memorial Award for Excellence in Education from Nova Southeastern University.

Dr. Strickland participated in the conceptualization of *Shakespeare-ience,* as well as the writing and editing of the program.

Wim Coleman, a freelance novelist and playwright, has frequently written about Shakespeare for students. Mr. Coleman holds a MA in Teaching in both English and education from Drake University. Coleman has worked as an actor, director, set designer, and scene shop manager. He has taught, directed, and performed in numerous Shakespeare productions and has edited several Shakespeare plays in Perfection Learning's popular *Parallel Text* series. His most recent book for Perfection Learning is *Nine Muses,* a collection of one-act plays based on classical mythology.

Mr. Coleman wrote several background essays for *Macbeth* as well as the informational notes found at the bottom of most pages.

About This Program

This program was designed to help you discover the world of Shakespeare and in particular the story of Macbeth. Shakespeare's plays were meant to be seen and heard. In his day, rowdy audiences responded to them with applause, tears, and jeers. Playwrights were more interested in audiences than in readers, so students did not study the plays as they do today.

This book takes the fear out of studying Shakespeare and puts back the fun. Our approach to *Macbeth* is different in several important ways.

- First, you will create a character or persona that will live within the context of the play. You will participate every day, not just on the days you are reading the part of one of the characters with lines in the text.

- You will find that Shakespeare is not that difficult, contrary to what you might have heard. We have provided you with a number of guiding features, such as on-page plot summaries, word and phrase definitions, and historical insights, to help you with the places that might be troublesome.

- By examining the thoughts of the characters through improvisation and then applying your understanding of the character's actions to the script, you will speak and hear the words of Shakespeare as he intended. You'll find that the words on these pages come to life when the art of theatre is used to study them.

Have fun with this program. While you probably won't mount a full production of *Macbeth,* you *will* learn to use hand and body gestures, expressive speech, and blocking (stage movements) as you read. If you trust yourself and jump into examining this world through the eyes of Shakespeare's characters and your own personas, you will truly have a Shakespeare-ience.

The Gunpowder Plot

Imagine a plot to blow up the Capitol while the president makes a speech to both branches of Congress. Then suppose that the president himself foils the conspiracy. Americans would breathe a huge sigh of relief — but fear of terrorists would linger. According to historian Garry Wills, *Macbeth* was influenced by a similar situation, known as the Gunpowder Plot.

In 1605, conspirators planned to blow up the English Parliament when all of its members and the royal family were inside.

English Catholics had hoped that King James I would remove the ban on practicing their religion. Instead, restrictions on Catholics were tightened. Catholics who refused to attend the Church of England services were fined. Skipping church could cost as much as 20 pounds — a whole year's wages for some families. Continued refusal to participate in the official state religion resulted in jail sentences. This ongoing persecution fueled the Gunpowder Plot.

Before this plot could be carried out, a mysterious letter fell into the King's hands. The letter warned its recipient (a member of Parliament) to stay away from the House of Lords on November 5. According to legend, the letter's deeper meaning was revealed to James in a flash of divine inspiration. The would-be assassin, Guy Fawkes, was captured in the cellar below the House of Lords as he waited to ignite a barrel of gunpowder.

As details of the plot were revealed, the whole business seemed increasingly monstrous. For example, the conspirators had participated in a Black Mass (a ceremony used to summon Satan) to ensure the success of their plot. This news intrigued the King, who was fascinated with witchcraft.

Like any good politician, King James turned his brush with disaster into a public relations coup. And he was in need of good public relations. Since James was not comfortable with large crowds, he was not as popular a ruler as his aunt, and predecessor, Queen Elizabeth I.

Macbeth makes many flattering references to the King, who was considered a hero for thwarting the conspiracy. The noble Banquo (who historically never existed) is presented as the King's direct ancestor. And in Act IV, King Edward miraculously heals people by the touch of his hand — a feat which James I was also reputedly able to perform.

Macbeth is clearly one of the most powerful of a group of plays in which Shakespeare explores the nature of evil. In these plays, he appears to be seeking some answer to the ancient riddle of why there is so much evil in the word and why even good people fall prey to it.

The Story of *Macbeth*

Scotland is at war!

King Duncan of Scotland is faced with an invading army from Norway, and also rebellious subjects at home. Fortunately, he's got a valiant nobleman among his ranks—Macbeth, the Thane of Glamis. Helped by his friend Banquo, Macbeth leads Duncan's forces to victory.

After the battle, Macbeth and Banquo meet three witches. The witches greet Macbeth by his title, the Thane of Glamis. But they predict that he will soon be Thane of Cawdor—and later King of Scotland. As for Banquo, the witches promise that he will be the father of kings, even though he'll never be king himself.

The witches disappear without telling them more.

Just then, a messenger arrives, bringing Macbeth and Banquo amazing news. The traitorous Thane of Cawdor is about to be executed. King Duncan has declared Macbeth the new Thane of Cawdor. The witches' first prediction has come true!

To celebrate the victory, King Duncan decides to visit Macbeth's castle in Inverness. Macbeth arrives at Inverness ahead of the King. He and his wife, Lady Macbeth, talk about the witches' prophecies.

Lady Macbeth urges Macbeth to kill Duncan during his visit. Reluctant at first, Macbeth agrees to her plan.

Duncan and his followers arrive at the castle, then eat and drink until the King is ready for bed. Lady Macbeth drugs the King's guards, putting them in a deep sleep. Then, while Duncan sleeps, Macbeth creeps into his room and murders him with the sleeping guards' daggers.

Macbeth is immediately horrified by his own deed, and hears a voice telling him that he will never sleep again. Deeply shaken, he leaves the room, forgetting something very important—to make it appear that the guards committed the murder. Lady Macbeth takes the daggers back to Duncan's room and smears the sleeping guards with the King's blood.

Morning has dawned. Macduff, the Thane of Fife, arrives at the castle and goes to Duncan's chamber to wake the King. To his horror, he discovers the murder and alerts the castle.

Macbeth returns to the King's room and kills the guards. He tells his guests that he did it out of rage over their obvious guilt.

Fearing for their lives, the King's sons, Malcolm and Donalbain, flee the country. This makes them look guilty of having plotted their father's murder. So Macbeth and Lady Macbeth become King and Queen of Scotland. The witches' second prediction has come true.

But Macbeth is troubled. He rightly guesses that Banquo suspects him of the murder. Moreover, the witches predicted that Banquo's descendants would become Kings. So Macbeth decides to do away with both Banquo and his son, Fleance.

Macbeth persuades some men to meet Banquo and Fleance on a road and murder them both. The murderers kill Banquo, but Fleance escapes.

That very night, Macbeth holds a feast. All goes well—until Macbeth sees Banquo's bloody ghost sitting at the banquet table!

Macbeth panics and rages at the ghost, which nobody else sees. Once the ghost has disappeared, Lady Macbeth persuades the banquet guests to go home. But Macbeth's ravings have convinced some of his subjects that he's a murderer.

Meanwhile, Duncan's son Malcolm has fled to England. There he seeks military aid from the English King Edward to overthrow Macbeth.

Constantly fearing plots against him, Macbeth rules the kingdom with an iron fist. Scotland is ready to explode into civil war. Desperate for advice, Macbeth seeks out the witches in their lair.

This time, the witches summon up spirits to hint at things to come. They warn Macbeth to beware of Macduff, the Thane of Fife. But they also assure Macbeth that no man born of a woman can kill him. Macbeth gloats with joy.

The witches then tell Macbeth that he will never be defeated in battle until Birnham Wood moves toward his castle in Dunsinane. Macbeth is even more delighted. A moving forest? Impossible!

But before the witches disappear, they present a parade of eight kings, all descendants of Banquo. Macbeth sorrowfully realizes that the witches' third prediction will prove true: Banquo's offspring will someday rule Scotland.

After meeting the witches, Macbeth hears that Macduff, the Thane of Fife, has gone to England, unwisely leaving his wife and children behind. Enraged, Macbeth sends murderers to Macduff's castle to slaughter Macduff's entire family.

Not knowing of this horrible deed, Macduff arrives in England and meets with the exiled Malcolm. He describes how Scotland is on the verge of rebellion. He urges Malcolm to invade Scotland, depose Macbeth, and become king.

At first, Malcolm doesn't trust Macduff. He suspects that Macduff is really on Macbeth's side. But after testing Macduff's loyalty, Malcolm tells him that an English army is ready to march against Macbeth.

At that very moment, Ross, another thane, arrives to tell Macduff of his family's terrible fate. Sorrowful and enraged, Macduff vows vengeance against Macbeth.

Back in Scotland, Lady Macbeth has been sinking into madness. One night, a doctor and a servant stay awake to watch her sleepwalking, trying to rub a spot of imaginary blood off her hand and raving about her crimes.

Malcolm's English army marches into Scotland, where it unites with Scottish rebels. The friendless Macbeth can no longer trust anyone, and many of his followers are joining the rebels.

Before marching toward Macbeth's castle, Malcolm orders his soldiers to cut down boughs from Birnham Wood to camouflage themselves.

As the army approaches, Macbeth receives word of Lady Macbeth's suicide. Then a messenger brings impossible news—Birnham Wood appears to be approaching Dunsinane! Macbeth senses his impending defeat.

In the field, he meets the vengeful Macduff. Macbeth warns Macduff that he cannot be killed by a man born of a woman. Macduff retorts that he was not born at all, but ripped from his mother's womb. Macbeth now realizes that he is doomed, but fights on ferociously until Macduff kills him.

Macduff carries Macbeth's severed head to Malcolm, whom he declares King of Scotland. Macbeth's violent reign has ended, and Scotland looks forward to times of peace and order.

Working with Shakespeare's Language

When you first begin reading Shakespeare, you may find his language intimidating and confusing. You will discover, however, that the more Shakespeare you read and the more you know about his writing, the easier it becomes.

Keep in mind that language is a living thing, constantly growing and changing. New words are invented and new definitions for old words are added. Since Shakespeare wrote over 400 years ago, it is not surprising that his work seems challenging to today's readers. To help you with the meaning of the text, unfamiliar words and phrases have been defined for you in the side margins of this book. You may also find a dictionary helpful for this purpose. Beyond the meaning of the words, however, there are stylistic devices that can help you understand Shakespeare.

Blank Verse and Iambic Pentameter

Like most dramatists of his time, Shakespeare frequently used blank verse in his plays. In **blank verse**, the text is written in measured lines that do not rhyme. Look at the following example.

> Then live, Macduff: what need I fear of thee?
> But yet I'll make assurance double sure
> And take my bond of fate. Thou shalt not live,
> That I may tell pale-hearted fear it lies …

u /	u /	u /	u /	u /
Then LIVE	MacDUFF	what NEED	I FEAR	of THEE?

u /	u / u /	u /	u /
But YET	I'll MAKE asSUR	ance DOU	ble SURE …

The length of a line of verse is measured by counting the stresses. This length is known as the **meter,** and when there are five stresses, as in the preceding lines, the pattern is known as **pentameter**. When the rhythm follows an unstressed/stressed pattern, it is called **iambic**. Much of Shakespeare's work is written in **iambic pentameter**.

Of course, Shakespeare was not rigid about this format. He sometimes varied the lines by putting accents in unusual places, by having lines with more or fewer than ten syllables, and by varying where pauses occur. An actor's interpretation can also add variety. (Only a terrible actor would deliver lines in a way that makes the rhythm sound obvious or repetitious!)

Prose

In addition to verse, Shakespeare wrote speeches in **prose**, which is language without rhythmic structure. Look at the Porter's speech on page 67. If you try beating out an iambic rhythm to this and the Porter's other lines, you'll discover that it doesn't work at all, because they're in prose. But once Macbeth enters on page 69, everybody starts speaking iambic pentameter again, and you'll be able to find that rhythm. Shakespeare often uses prose for comic speeches, to show madness, and for characters of lower social rank such as servants. His upper-class characters generally do not speak in prose. But these weren't hard-and-fast rules as far as Shakespeare was concerned. Many of his servants speak in verse, and some of his noble characters (Hamlet, for example) occasionally speak in prose.

Imagery

Imagery refers to vibrant, colorful language that allows readers or listeners to picture things in their mind's eye and to make an emotional connection with the writing. This highly descriptive language appeals to one or more of the five senses—touch, taste, hearing, smell, and sight. How many sensory images can you find in the following speech?

> Come, thick night,
> And pall thee in the dunnest smoke of hell,
> That my keen knife see not the wound it makes,
> Nor heaven peep through the blanket of the dark,
> To cry 'Hold, hold!'

In addition to sensory words, images are often conveyed through the use of **figures of speech** such as simile, metaphor, or personification.

A **simile** is a comparison between two unlike things that uses the words *like* or *as.* Look at the following examples.

> Now does he feel his title
> Hang loose about him, like a giant's robe
> Upon a dwarfish thief.

> Your face, my Thane, is as a book where men
> May read strange matters.

In the first quote, Macbeth's title of king is compared to a loose-fitting robe upon a "dwarfish thief." In the second, Lady Macbeth compares Macbeth's face to a book, too easily read by the people around him.

A **metaphor** is also a comparison between two unlike things, but the words *like* or *as* are left out. In the following quotes, eyes are fools, an owl is a bellman [town crier], and life is wine.

> Mine eyes are made the fools o' th' other senses
> Or else worth all the rest.

> It was the owl that shriek'd, the fatal bellman,
> Which gives the stern'st good-night.

> The wine of life is drawn …

Another type of imagery used extensively by Shakespeare is **personification**, or giving human qualities to inanimate objects or ideas. In the following lines, earth is personified as being able to hear; a bell "invites" Macbeth; and sleep "knits" a skein of cloth.

Thou sure and firm-set earth,
Hear not my steps, which way they walk, for fear
Thy very stones prate of my whereabout ...

The bell invites me.

Sleep that knits up the ravell'd sleave of care ...

Contractions

As you know, contractions are words that have been combined by substituting an apostrophe for a letter or letters that have been removed. Contractions were as common in Shakespeare's time as they are today. For example, we use *it's* as a contraction for the words *it is.* In Shakespeare's writing you will discover that *'tis* means the same thing. Many other examples can be found in the list of Frequently Used Words on pages 14-15.

Shakespeare often used the apostrophe to shorten words so that they would fit into the rhythm pattern of a line. This is especially true of verbs ending in *-ed.* Note that in Shakespeare's plays, the *-ed* at the end of a verb is pronounced as a separate syllable. Therefore, *walked* would be pronounced as two syllables, *walk•ed,* while *walk'd* would be only one. We have added accent marks (walkèd) to help you remember to pronounce *-ed* aloud.

You will learn about other elements of Shakespeare's language such as **puns** and **irony** as they occur in the text.

Finally, if you can't figure out every word in the play, don't get discouraged. The people in Shakespeare's audience couldn't either. At that time, language was changing rapidly and standardized spelling, punctuation, grammar, and even dictionaries did not exist. Besides, Shakespeare loved to play with words. He made up new combinations, like *fat-guts* and *mumble-news.* He often changed one part of speech for another, as in "cursing claims and deep *exclaims.*" To make matters worse, the actors probably spoke at a rate of 140 words per minute. But the audience didn't strain to catch every word. They went to a Shakespeare play for the same reasons we go to a movie—to get caught up in the story and the acting, to have a great laugh, an exciting adventure, or a good cry.

Strategies for Reading Shakespeare

You will find many features in this book designed to help you understand Shakespeare's language. In addition, there are some basic reading strategies that active readers use for all types of text. As you prepare to read *Macbeth*, you may find the following strategic plan useful.

Preview. First, to get a general idea of the events in the play, "read the edges" of the text. Read the summaries at the top of each page. Then skim the definitions and questions in the side margins and examine any images that appear. This will give you a general idea of what the text is about before you actually begin to read it.

Visualize. Try to put yourself into the world of the play by picturing the setting in your mind's eye. Envision how the characters might look and sound as they move within their surroundings. Studying images and reading through the setting and stage directions will help to fire up your imagination.

Read. Read a page using the side notes to help with difficult words and phrases. Go back and reread the page a second time or as many times as necessary until you can understand the text without using the side notes. This may be more difficult in the beginning and take more time than reading modern writing, but don't be discouraged. Most students find that comprehension becomes easier and easier as the play goes on.

Connect. Active readers often make connections with the text. An event in their reading might remind them of something that happened to them or a friend, or they might see similarities between the text and a movie, book, or TV show they have seen. Also, because Shakespeare is quoted so frequently, readers are likely to come across familiar phrases and sayings.

Evaluate. As you read, evaluate the characters' words and actions and form opinions about them. Do you approve or disapprove of how they act? What are their motives? What are their strengths and weaknesses? Do certain actions make you change your mind about a character?

Enrich. Surround your study of *Macbeth* with humor and high-interest material. The notes at the bottom of most pages and the essays in the front and back of the book provide background information. The Tales from the Stage feature contains colorful theatrical anecdotes. The suggestions for props and in-class staging will also help to immerse you in Shakespeare's world.

Frequently Used Words

The following words and phrases are found frequently in Shakespeare's plays. The more of them you know, the easier your reading will be.

afore . . . . . . before

alack . . . . . . expression of sorrow or regret

alas . . . . expression of unhappiness, pity, or concern

anon . . . . . . at once, immediately

an't . . . . if it

art . . . . are

ay, aye . . . . . . yes

bawdy . . . . . . indecent

beseech . . . . . beg

betimes . . . . . at times, occasionally

bid . . . . ask

by my troth . . . truly

coz . . . . cousin; relative

dost . . . . you do (second-person singular of the verb "do")

doth . . . . he, she, it does (third person singular of the verb "do")

e'en . . . . even

e'er . . . . ever

enow . . . . enough

ere . . . . before

exeunt . . . . . . theatre term meaning "everyone leaves the stage"

fain . . . . willingly

fay . . . . faith

fie . . . . O

foresworn . . . . denied

hadst . . . . you had (second person singular past tense of the verb "have")

hap . . . . perhaps

hark you . . . . listen

hast, hath . . . . you have; he, she, it has (second and third person singular of "have")

hence . . . . away from this place

hie . . . . hurry

humor . . . . . . mood

humour . . . . . liquid

is't . . . . is it

knave . . . . rascal

late . . . . recently

marry . . . . . . I swear

mine . . . . . . my

nay . . . . no

ne'er . . . . . . never

o'er . . . . over

oft . . . . often

perchance . . . perhaps

pray . . . . invite

rest you merry . have a good day

saucy . . . . . . rude

scurvy . . . . . disgusting

shalt . . . . you shall (second-person singular of "shall")

shrift . . . . . . confession of sins

sirrah . . . . . . sir (a form of address implying inferiority)

soft . . . . wait

spake . . . . . . said

stay . . . . stop

straight . . . . . at once

sup . . . . to eat (often the evening meal)

thee, thou . . . you

thence . . . . . from that time (or place) on

thine . . . . . . yours

thither . . . . . there; to that place

thrice . . . . . . three times

thy . . . . your

'tis . . . . it is

tut, tush . . . . mild expression of disapproval

'twixt . . . . . . between

wast, wert . . . . were

whence . . . . . where (from what place)

wherefore . . . why

whither . . . . . where (to what place)

wilt . . . . will, must

writ . . . . written

ye . . . . you

yea . . . . yes

yon, yond . . . . that

Preparing for Speaking Parts

At least once during your study of *Macbeth,* you will be assigned a speaking part to perform for an upcoming class. In order to feel comfortable in this role and to respect the efforts of other students reading with you, you will need to prepare beforehand. If you are unsure about how to do this, try using the following plan.

Comprehend. Make sure you understand the meaning of what your character says. If you are unsure, use the reading strategies on page 13.

Analyze. Determine your character's attitude during the scene. What mood is he in? Does this mood change during the scene? Are her thoughts and what she says the same? Or does she say one thing and mean another? What is your character's motivation? What does he want? What is his attitude toward other characters in the scene? Is there a conflict? What is it?

Plan. Decide how you will use your body and voice to create your character. What gestures will you use? Where and when will you move? How will you use your voice? Changes in the tempo (fast, slow); pitch (high, low); and quality (nasal, raspy, etc.) of your voice can help the audience understand your character. If needed, you can put sticky notes in your text to remind you of where you want to change your voice or move.

Practice. You probably won't have a chance to rehearse with others in your scene, but you should still practice your own part. Ask a friend or family member to read lines with you and/or videotape you. You can also practice reading your part into a tape recorder.

Warm Up. Here are a few exercises to make your voice and body more flexible and responsive.

- Stand tall and inhale on a count of four; hold your breath for a count of four; and then exhale on a count of eight. Make sure that your shoulders are relaxed and do not rise up as you breathe. Your lower stomach area should be slowly moving out as you inhale, and in as you exhale.
- Next, repeat the same exercise and while you are exhaling, hum the letter M. You will feel a tingle in your face from the vibration of the sound. After you have done this several times, try a few tongue twisters. Here is one to start with:

  Amidst the mists and coldest frosts,
  With stoutest wrists and loudest boasts,
  He thrusts his fists against the post
  And still insists he sees the ghosts.

- Stand tall with your feet shoulder-width apart. Bend over slowly and reach for or touch the floor. Relax and breathe. Bend your knees more and then straighten your legs slowly. Slowly round up your body to a standing position. Repeat the whole exercise twice.

Act and React. As you present your scene, remember to face the audience and speak loudly enough to be heard throughout the room. Holding your book and your head up as you read will help your voice project out to the audience. Finally, listen, really listen, to what the other characters are saying so that you can respond realistically and pick up cues promptly.

How to Have a Shakespeare-ience

There is an old saying that to really understand someone you need to walk a mile in his or her shoes. This study of *Macbeth* borrows from that old adage by asking you to study the play by becoming a character from 11th-century Scotland. You will "walk" for many days in that person's "shoes."

By seeing the world of 11th-century Scotland through eyes other than your own, you will gain a new perspective and interact with other characters that shape that world. Not all of the characters that you create actually speak within the text of the play, but all are affected by the circumstances and actions of the speaking characters. So you may not be Macbeth, but you may be his attendant or one of his spies. You may not be Lady Macbeth, but you may be a cook or one of Lady Macbeth's waiting gentlewomen.

Each of you will be part of the action of the play, and from time to time will be called upon to be one of the traditional speaking characters as well. In addition, you will be creating events and situations that are only implied by the action of the play. For example, there is a banquet to honor King Duncan at Macbeth's castle. If you were a servant to the Macbeth's, what would your duties be in preparing for the festivities? And if you were to create a scene that happens just before or just after the banquet with the other servants, what do you think would be the focus of that scene? And, as the story of the play unfolds, how do the various events that take place affect you and your world?

You will be discovering what life was like in Scotland hundreds of years ago. The creation of your character, or **persona**, as we will call it throughout the rest of the book, will be based on elements in the text, historical information, human nature, and your imagination. You will discover the events that influenced the lives of the people in Macbeth's Scotland and ultimately played important roles in the unfolding of this story. By being immersed this way in the story and the play, you will be experiencing *Macbeth* as if you were there. This is what we mean by having a **Shakespeare–ience**.

Choosing Your Persona

As you can see by the following list, there were many kinds of people that made up the population of 11th-century Scotland. Your teacher will either assign one of these personas to you or ask you to chose one from the list. In either case, you will begin with only a name or occupation. It will be your job to develop your persona and turn him or her into a complete character. You will begin by answering questions and developing a personality profile. As the play progresses, you will find questions and directions, labeled **Persona Journal** and **Persona Action**, which will guide you. Remember that you are always to respond and react as your persona would.

Your stay in 11th-century Scotland will be ruled by the following assumptions. 1) Assume that almost all characters listed below can be either male or female. Therefore, it is not necessary to limit persona choices to traditional gender roles. 2) Assume that all members of a clan travel with their leader or someone appointed by him. 3) To avoid crowding the acting area, some Persona Action directions will call for **representatives** from clans. Either in a clan meeting, or as your teacher directs, decide how representatives can be chosen so that everyone has equal time on stage. 4) Some directions will call for "in place" reactions which means that you will react, but stay in your "clan homeand."

Citizens of 11th-Century Scotland

Cook
Guard
Watchman
Attendant
Messenger
Secretary
Copyist
Maid
Physician
Seamstress
Laundress
Weaver
Embroiderer
Musician
Artist
Ink Maker
Wine Maker
Stable Keeper
Potter
Farmer
Ox-goad
Mule Train Driver
Tailor
Furrier
Shoemaker
Tanner
Mill Worker
Ale/Mead Maker
Roofer
Stone Mason
Iron/Lead Worker
Wood Carver
Candle Maker
Serf/Peasant/Slave
Carpenter
Blacksmith
Beekeeper
Shepherd
Hunter
Tax Collector
Rent Collector
Jeweler
Goldsmith
Scribe
Soap Maker
Fishmonger
Fisherman
Cabinet Maker
Merchant
Dye Worker
Hosier
Oar & Boat Maker
Craftsman
Baker
Soldier
Officer
Lord
Nobleman
Noblewoman
Sheriff
Servant
Priest
Abbess
Nun
Monk
Abbot
Clerk
Landowner
Grain Dealer
Armor Maker
Cooper
Butcher
Porter
Estate Manager
Ploughman
Reaper

Understanding Improvisation

It is possible that you have heard the word improvisation in connection to theatre, music, stand-up comedy, or dance. Improvisation may sometimes be referred to as role-playing. In this study of *Macbeth,* improvisation exercises before each scene will be used as a discovery tool to explore the characters and the events in the play.

Literally, to improvise is to speak or act out a situation without a script or preconceived way of presenting the scene. You are given the framework of the situation such as the conflict and the characters, and without advanced planning, you make up the scene's dialogue spontaneously. You must find a way to resolve conflicts and overcome obstacles in order to accomplish the objectives of the characters. Direct your concentration toward the situation and the other participants while keeping an open mind about what your character is experiencing. In addition, be receptive to any new information introduced by your partner(s). React honestly.

Improvisation trains people to think on different levels. It helps develop imagination, concentration, self-esteem, self-confidence, observation skills, listening skills, problem-solving skills, and thinking skills.

The following exercises will introduce you to the process of improvisation.

Partner Activities

- A fortune teller says that you are going to achieve great things; try to get him/her to tell you more.
- You think your husband/boyfriend could be more of an achiever by breaking some rules; try to convince him of this.
- Try to persuade someone you know that it's in his/her best interests to betray a mutual acquaintance.
- You've committed a crime, and a police detective seems to suspect you; try to convince him/her of your innocence.
- You're a wartime general. Someone wants to join your army, but you think he/she might be a spy for the other side; test his/her loyalty.

Group Activities

With a group of seven to ten students, improvise waiting in an express checkout line (only ten items) at a grocery store. One customer has more than ten items, and his/her friend keeps bringing more items as you wait. This is the checkout person's first day after completing training.

With a group of ten to fifteen students, improvise a situation where a local radio station is doing a remote location set-up, and as a promotion is giving away tickets to an upcoming concert. There are only three pairs of tickets to give away, and more than ten people show up to win them. Each person must convince the DJ to give him or her the tickets.

Macbeth Warm-ups

- Macbeth and Lady Macbeth talk for the first time about their desire to be King and Queen—and how they might achieve this.
- Just before his execution, the Thane of Cawdor confesses his treachery and asks the King's forgiveness.
- Banquo confides in his son, Fleance, that he thinks Macbeth might be a murderer.
- Malcolm, son of the slain King Duncan, asks the King of England for help in overthrowing Macbeth.
- Macduff turns down Macbeth's invitation to his banquet.
- A messenger brings Lady Macbeth news of the slaughter of Macduff's family; what is her reaction?

A Gathering of the Clans

Just as Shakespeare took liberties with historical facts to write *Macbeth* (see Life in 11th-century Scotland, page 175), the following improvisation takes historical liberties to establish an environment for this introductory exercise. These conditions will allow you to experience as a group, certain aspects of life in Scotland during the 11th-century. Before the exercise, your teacher will assign you to one of four clans – Clan Macbeth (headed by Macbeth), Clan Macduff (headed by Macduff), Clan Stuart (headed by Banquo), or Clan Canmore (headed by King Duncan). You will also receive a clan history and current status report.

Scotland is at war with the King of Norway as well as the traitorous Macdonwald and his clan. The other Scottish clans have gathered in Forres at the command of King Duncan. It is a cloudy, overcast late morning as you enter the large courtyard of the castle. Keep in mind the occupation and/or social status of your persona, and remember, that although you have joined forces to fight a common enemy, as a rule, each clan is highly independent, territorial, and suspicious of other clans. In fact, the word *clannish* means "tending to associate only with a select group of similar background or status." As the clans begin to gather and talk, a series of four messengers arrive with news from the battlefront. (The messages will be supplied by your teacher.)

As you hear the news from each messenger, improvise a reaction and enter into conversations with other members of your clan as well as people from other clans. You look around to see what is taking place, and "in persona," you begin to move and join with your specific clan members to celebrate. Gradually, four distinct groups begin to form – Clan Macbeth moves to the side of the classroom closest to the door, Clan Canmore goes to the opposite side of the room, Clan Macduff groups at the back of the classroom, and Clan Stuart locates at the front of the classroom. Finally, the King arrives. Safe within the protection of your clan, you hear what the King says, and you talk with other members of your clan—commenting on how the news impacts you.

When the activity ends, answer the following questions in your **Persona Journal**.

- How did you react to the news from the first three messengers?
- How does the King's message impact you and your clan?
- Which other clan do you now feel closest to and why?

Were you surprised by the reactions of others in your clan? In the other clans?

Macbeth Act I

Orson Welles in his 1948 film of *Macbeth*.

"Stars, hide your fires, let not light see my black and deep desires..."

Cast of Characters

IN SCOTLAND

DUNCAN, King of Scotland
MALCOLM, his elder son
DONALBAIN, his younger son
CAPTAIN, in the King's army
MACBETH, Thane of Glamis,
then Thane of Cawdor,
then King of Scotland
SEYTON, his armor bearer
LADY MACBETH, wife of Macbeth
A GENTLEWOMAN,
servant to Lady Macbeth
PORTER, servant at Macbeth's castle
BANQUO, a Thane
(nobleman of Scotland)

FLEANCE, his son
MACDUFF, Thane of Fife
LADY MACDUFF, wife of Macduff
SON, to the Macduff's
LENNOX, ROSS, MENTEITH, ANGUS, CAITHNESS — Other Thanes
A DOCTOR
AN OLD MAN
THREE MURDERERS
LORDS, SOLDIERS, SERVANTS,
MESSENGERS

IN ENGLAND

SIWARD, Earl of Northumberland
YOUNG SIWARD, his son
DOCTOR

FROM THE SUPERNATURAL WORLD

WITCHES
HECATE
APPARITIONS

TIME the 11th century

PLACE Scotland and England

Setting the Scene

MACBETH

Act I, scenes i and ii *or* Who's Fair, Who's Foul?

Critical Query: What do you learn about Macbeth in these scenes?

From the Prop Box

- "Blood-stained" rag for Captain's head
- Crown for Duncan
- Swords (plastic or foam — in general main actors will be armed throughout the play)
- Ribbons of four different colors (plaid if possible). Each clan wears its own color.
- Beards and/or fright wigs for the witches
- Clan banners on poles

(NOTE: All props are optional, based on your teacher's instruction.)

Special Effects

- Thunder
- Lightning
- Call to Arms

Behind the Scene: The Tragic Hero

A **tragedy** is a serious work of literature that narrates the events leading to the downfall of a **tragic hero**, who is usually of noble birth and in almost every way displays noble qualities. His downfall is a result of a **tragic flaw** or fatal character weakness. As the play progresses, consider whether Macbeth fits this definition and what his fatal flaw might be.

Classroom Set Design

Move desks back to allow space for an acting area. The classroom should be divided into four sections, one for each clan. These clan "homelands" should remain the same throughout the play. Clan banners may be created and put on the walls to identify each area.

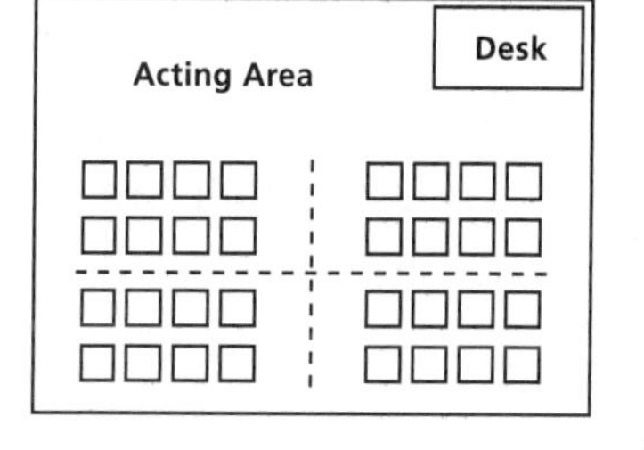

Warm-up Improv 1	Warm-up Improv 2
You and a friend decide to call a future predicting hotline for advice. You are given very good news, but your friend is given very bad news. Help him/her deal with this news.	(Use after page 24) You are a member of a sports team or squad. During the event you are injured and helped to the locker room. Several members of your team bring you the news that your team has won.

Three witches gather amidst the crack of thunder and the flash of lightning. A fierce battle rages nearby. The witches plan to seek out one of the generals, a Scottish nobleman named Macbeth. They exit muttering ominous chants.

ACT I.

Scene i. Scotland. An Open Place

[Thunder and lightning. Enter three WITCHES.*]*

FIRST WITCH. When shall we three meet again
In thunder, lightning, or in rain?

SECOND WITCH. When the hurlyburly's done,
When the battle's lost and won.

THIRD WITCH. That will be ere the set of sun.

FIRST WITCH. Where the place?

SECOND WITCH. Upon the heath.

THIRD WITCH. There to meet with Macbeth.

✱ **FIRST WITCH.** I come, Graymalkin!

SECOND WITCH. Paddock calls.

THIRD WITCH. Anon.

ALL. Fair is foul, and foul is fair,
Hover through the fog and filthy air.

[Exeunt.]

1-2 When...rain: Witches were thought to have been more active in stormy weather.

3 hurlyburly: commotion or turmoil

5 ere: before

7 heath: barren land, covered with small shrubs

9 Anon: right away

PERSONA JOURNAL

Assume that you have seen the witches previously. Tell where you saw them and what they looked like. What were they doing?

✱ **Witches' "Familiars"** witches were said to keep "familiars"—animal companions that helped them with their magic. The first witch's familiar is "Graymalkin"—a gray cat. The second witch's is "Paddock"—a toad. Later in the play we learn that the third witch's familiar is named Harpier. Some scholars believe that Harpier is an owl, others a raven.

King Duncan enters a military camp with his two sons, Malcolm and Donalbain. The King asks for a battle report from a wounded soldier who tells of the intense fighting between the rebellious forces of the traitor Macdonwald and the brave Macbeth.

SCENE ii. A Camp Near Forres

[Alarum within. Enter DUNCAN, MALCOLM, DONALBAIN, LENNOX, *with* ATTENDANTS, *meeting a bleeding* CAPTAIN.*]*

DUNCAN. What bloody man is that? He can report,
As seemeth by his plight, of the revolt
The newest state.

MALCOLM. This is the sergeant
Who like a good and hardy soldier fought
'Gainst my captivity.—Hail, brave friend!
Say to the King the knowledge of the broil
As thou didst leave it.

CAPTAIN. Doubtful it stood,
As two spent swimmers that do cling together
And choke their art. The merciless Macdonwald—
Worthy to be a rebel, for to that
The multiplying villainies of nature
Do swarm upon him—from the Western Isles
Of kerns and gallowglasses is supplied;
And fortune, on his damn'd quarrel smiling,
Show'd like a rebel's whore. But all's too weak;
For brave Macbeth—well he deserves that name—
Disdaining Fortune, with his brandish'd steel,
Which smoked with bloody execution,
Like valour's minion carved out his passage

Stratford Festival (Canada) production of *Macbeth*, 1983

PERSONA ACTION

Representatives from the Canmore clan enter with Duncan. All other Canmores stand and react to events in this scene.

1-3 He can...state: He can tell us the latest news (**newest state**) from the battlefront.

3 sergeant: soldier or officer, during this time period meaning the same as captain

6 broil: battle

? How serious are the captain's injuries? How would you convey this to the audience?

8 spent: tired

9 choke their art: prevent each other from swimming

10-19 Macdonwald was well suited for the role of traitor because of his evilness (**multiplying villainies**). His troops consisted of light infantry (**kerns**) and more heavily-armed soldiers (**gallowglasses**) recruited from Ireland and the Hebrides (**Western Isles**). At first it seemed that luck smiled on his cause, but then, like a fickle woman, luck abandoned him. And Macbeth, waving his blood-stained sword, fought his way through to the front and challenged Macdonwald.

PERSONA JOURNAL

What do you know about the battle?

As the captain continues, he describes how Macbeth killed Macdonwald and caused the rebel troops to turn back. A fresh attack from the Norwegians was also defeated by Macbeth, with the help of another general, Banquo.

Till he faced the slave;
Which ne'er shook hands, nor bade farewell to him,
Till he unseam'd him from the nave to th' chops,
And fix'd his head upon our battlements.

DUNCAN. O valiant cousin, worthy gentleman!

CAPTAIN. As whence the sun 'gins his reflection
Shipwrecking storms and direful thunders break,
So from that spring whence comfort seem'd to come
Discomfort swells. Mark, King of Scotland, mark:
No sooner justice had, with valour arm'd,
Compell'd these skipping kerns to trust their heels,
But the Norweyan lord, surveying vantage,
With furbish'd arms and new supplies of men,
Began a fresh assault.

DUNCAN. Dismay'd not this
Our captains, Macbeth and Banquo?

CAPTAIN. Yes,
As sparrows eagles, or the hare the lion.
If I say sooth, I must report they were
As cannons overcharged with double cracks,
So they doubly redoubled strokes upon the foe.
Except they meant to bathe in reeking wounds
✱ Or memorize another Golgotha,
I cannot tell—
But I am faint; my gashes cry for help.

DUNCAN. So well thy words become thee as thy wounds:
They smack of honour both. Go get him surgeons.

[Exit CAPTAIN, *attended.] [Enter* ROSS *and* ANGUS.*]*

Who comes here?

22-23 Till...battlements: Macbeth cut him open from his stomach (**nave**) to his jaw (**chops**) and set his head on the castle wall.

24 cousin: Macbeth and Duncan were first cousins; however, this term can also be used for friends.

25-33 A sunrise, though beautiful, can signal storms and thunder and a bubbling spring can turn into a dangerous torrent. In the same way, just as one enemy retreated and things seemed calm, the King of Norway saw an opportunity and attacked with fresh troops and new weapons.

? Why might the King of Norway be fighting in Scotland?

? **35 As sparrows...lion:** What does the Captain mean by this?

36 say sooth: speak truthfully

37 cracks: charges or explosives

39 Except: whether; **reeking:** bleeding

40 memorize: make memorable as

PERSONA JOURNAL

You've heard about Macbeth before now. What do you know about him?

✱ **Golgotha** According to the New Testament, Golgotha was the place where Christ was crucified. The word means "skull" in Aramaic—perhaps because it was a hill that looked like a skull, or else because crucified bodies were left there to be picked clean by animals. The word *Golgotha* was translated as "Calvary" in Latin. In this scene, the Captain wonders if Macbeth and Banquo sought to make the battleground as infamous for bloodshed as the place where Christ was slain.

Ross and Angus enter and relate that Macbeth was able to win a glorious victory against Norway and the traitorous Thane of Cawdor. The Norwegian King requested a peace treaty and paid a $10,000 ransom. Duncan sentences the Thane of Cawdor to death and names Macbeth the new Thane of Cawdor.

MALCOLM. The worthy Thane of Ross.

LENNOX. What a haste looks through his eyes! So should he look
That seems to speak things strange.

ROSS. God save the King.

DUNCAN. Whence cam'st thou, worthy Thane?

ROSS. From Fife, great King,
Where the Norweyan banners flout the sky
And fan our people cold.
Norway himself, with terrible numbers,
Assisted by that most disloyal traitor
The Thane of Cawdor, began a dismal conflict;
Till that Bellona's bridegroom, lapp'd in proof,
Confronted him with self-comparisons,
Point against point, rebellious arm 'gainst arm,
Curbing his lavish spirit; and, to conclude,
The victory fell on us.

DUNCAN. Great happiness!

ROSS. That now
Sweno, the Norways' king, craves composition.
Nor would we deign him burial of his men
Till he disbursèd at Saint Colme's Inch
✱ Ten thousand dollars to our general use.

DUNCAN. No more that Thane of Cawdor shall deceive
Our bosom interest. Go pronounce his present death,
And with his former title greet Macbeth.

ROSS. I'll see it done.

DUNCAN. What he hath lost, noble Macbeth hath won. *[Exeunt.]*

45 Thane: the chief of a clan

46 What...eyes!: How anxious he looks!

? Ross eagerly arrives with news from the battle. How would you read these lines?

49 flout: mock

50 And fan...cold: and chill our troops with fear

51 Norway himself: the King of Norway

53 dismal conflict: ferocious battle

54 Bellona: the sister of Mars, the Roman god of war; **Bellona's bridegroom:** refers to Macbeth; **lapp'd in proof:** dressed in battle-tested armor

55-56 Confronted...point: met him face to face, sword to sword

57 lavish spirit: overconfidence

59 craves composition: asks for terms of peace

60 deign: permit

61 Saint Colm's Inch: St. Columba's Island

63-64 deceive/Our bosom interest: betray our friendship; **present:** immediate

? From what you know at this point, how would you describe Macbeth?

✱ **Anachronisms** An **anachronism** is a mistake of historical chronology. Shakespeare allowed many anachronisms to creep into his plays. For example, a clock strikes in *Julius Caesar*—more than a thousand years before clocks were invented! And in this scene of *Macbeth*, Ross mentions dollars. This form of currency did not exist until 1518, about five hundred years after the play takes place.

TALES FROM THE STAGE

The *Macbeth* Curse

Did you know that *Macbeth* is a cursed play, much feared and dreaded by theatre folk? Just when this tradition started is anybody's guess, but according to one rather unlikely story, the boy actor playing Lady Macbeth died on the very day of the play's premiere in 1606.

John Gielgud as Macbeth, with Gwen Ffrangcon-Davies, Piccadilly, 1942. John Vickers Theatre Collection

Awful accidents are said to plague productions of the play, causing injuries and even deaths. Actor and director John Gielgud states, "Certainly Macbeth is an unlucky play. We had a terrible time with a wartime production of it. Several people died during the long provincial tour. One dear old Cornish actress...died during the night while we had been involved in a dress rehearsal. A fine actor who played Duncan died some weeks later; Macduff had to be replaced; and when we at last arrived in London, Gwen Ffrangcon-Davies [Lady Macbeth] walked into a lamp post in the black-out and got a bruised eye."

Some actors and directors are so afraid of the *Macbeth* curse that they refuse to do the play altogether. Even to say the play's name in a theatre is thought to be unlucky. It is all right to call it "The Scottish Play," "The Scots Tragedy," "The Bard's Play," or just *"That* Play." But to actually say *Macbeth* aloud is to really ask for trouble.

If one slips up and says "Macbeth" in a theatre, one must perform a little exorcism ritual. One should step outside the theatre, turn around three times, spit, say a vulgar curse word, and wait for permission to come back inside. A simpler way to repair the damage is to repeat this line from *Hamlet:* "Angels and ministers of grace defend us."

Why is *Macbeth* cursed? According to one theory, it is because Shakespeare put real spells in the mouths of his witches. But there is a more likely explanation. *Macbeth* contains a lot of dim lighting and onstage violence, including the climactic sword fight between Macbeth and Macduff. Accidents, injuries, and even fatalities can happen in such a play.

Setting the Scene

MACBETH

Act I, scene iii *or* Strange Predictions

Critical Query: What effect will the witches' predictions have?

**Time Capsule:
What About the Danes?**

Macbeth was probably performed for King James I, who ruled England when the play was written. James' brother-in-law was King Christian of Denmark, who may actually have attended a performance of *Macbeth.* So in this scene, Shakespeare is careful not to mention the historical fact that the Danes were among the forces fighting against the good King Duncan.

On Location: Where Are We?

You might find yourself confused by all the place names you'll find in *Macbeth*—including Forres, Inverness, Glamis, and Cawdor. The following information might help. See also the map on page 175.

- Forres is a Scottish town; its castle is traditionally said to have been a hunting lodge for ancient Scottish kings like Duncan and Macbeth. That's why Shakespeare shows both of them living there. Actually, today's Forres Castle does not date back to their time.
- Inverness is a region in northern Scotland. It includes the town and castle of Glamis. Macbeth is traditionally said to have lived in Glamis Castle when he was Thane of Glamis. But once again, the existing castle does not date back to his time.
- The town of Cawdor and its castle are also in the Inverness region.

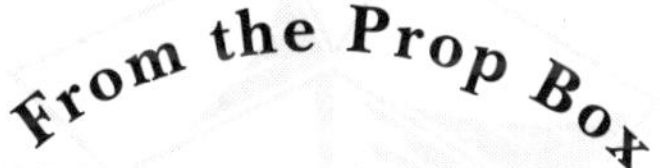

Pouch with thumb of ship's pilot (the "thumb" could be a piece of carrot)

Special Effects

- Thunder
- Drum

Warm-up Improv

You just learned that you have been accepted into a prestigious university on a full scholarship. Your best friend is still waiting to hear about his/her options. Tell your friend about your news and encourage him/her to be optimistic and patient.

Classroom Set Design

Acting Area

Desk

The three witches meet again. The first tells a story of a woman who refused to share the chestnuts she was eating. The witch plans revenge on the woman by tormenting her husband, who is the skipper of a ship at sea. The other witches offer their support.

SCENE iii. A Heath Near Forres

[Thunder. Enter the three WITCHES.*]*

FIRST WITCH. Where hast thou been, sister?

SECOND WITCH. Killing swine.

THIRD WITCH. Sister, where thou?

FIRST WITCH. A sailor's wife had chestnuts in her lap,
And munch'd, and munch'd, and munch'd. 'Give me,' quoth I:
'Aroint thee, witch!' the rump-fed ronyon cries.
Her husband's to Aleppo gone, master o' th' Tiger;
But in a sieve I'll thither sail,
* And, like a rat without a tail,
I'll do, I'll do, and I'll do.

SECOND WITCH. I'll give thee a wind.

FIRST WITCH. Thou'rt kind.

THIRD WITCH. And I another.

FIRST WITCH. I myself have all the other,
And the very ports they blow,
All the quarters that they know
I' the shipman's card.
I will drain him dry as hay:
Sleep shall neither night nor day
Hang upon his penthouse lid;
He shall live a man forbid.

6 'Aroint thee: Get away from me; **rump-fed ronyon:** fat-bottomed ugly creature

7 Aleppo: a city in northern Syria; **Tiger:** the name of the ship

10 I'll do: I'll cause bad things to happen to him.

14 the other: the remaining winds

15 And the very... blow: and the ports they blow from

16 quarters: directions

17 card: compass

18 drain him: keep him out at sea so that his fresh water supply is all used up

20 penthouse lid: eyelid

21 a man forbid: a cursed man

* **A Tale of a Tail** Witches were thought to be able to take the shapes of animals—but only the limbs and body parts that they shared with animals. For example, a witch's hand or foot could become a paw, and the lower part of her face could become a snout. But women don't have tails, so a witch who took the form of a rat would be "a rat without a tail."

The first witch continues to plan her revenge when a drum suddenly announces the arrival of Macbeth. The three witches begin to chant and cast a spell. Macbeth and Banquo enter. Banquo is alarmed by the witches' appearance and wonders what or who these creatures might be.

Weary sev'nights, nine times nine,
Shall he dwindle, peak, and pine.
Though his bark cannot be lost,
Yet it shall be tempest-toss'd.
Look what I have.

SECOND WITCH. Show me, show me.

FIRST WITCH. Here I have a pilot's thumb,
Wrack'd as homeward he did come.

[Drum within.]

THIRD WITCH. A drum, a drum!
Macbeth doth come.

ALL. *[Dancing in a circle.]*
✱ The Weïrd Sisters, hand in hand,
Posters of the sea and land,
Thus do go about, about,
Thrice to thine, and thrice to mine
And thrice again, to make up nine.
Peace! The charm's wound up.

[Enter MACBETH *and* BANQUO.*]*

MACBETH. So foul and fair a day I have not seen.

BANQUO. How far is't call'd to Forres? What are these
So wither'd and so wild in their attire,
That look not like th' inhabitants o' the earth,
And yet are on't? Live you or are you aught
That man may question? You seem to understand me,
By each at once her choppy finger laying
Upon her skinny lips. You should be women,

22 sev'nights, nine times nine: 81 weeks

23 dwindle, peak, and pine: shrink, fade, and waste away

24 bark cannot be lost: ship cannot be sunk. (It was thought that the witches could not actually sink the ship, just make the voyage hazardous.)

28 pilot: helmsman of a ship

29 Wrack'd: shipwrecked

? How would you choreograph the witches' dance?

33 Posters: swift travelers

35 Thrice: three times

37 wound up: all set to work

? **38** Where have you heard these words before? From Macbeth's perspective, why is the day both fair and foul?

39 is't called: do they say it is; **Forres:** a town in northern Scotland

42 aught: anything

44–45 By each...lips: because each of you signals to me by putting a chapped finger to her skinny lips

✱ **The Weïrd Sisters** The word *weird* didn't come to mean strange or bizarre until the early 1800s, about two hundred years after Shakespeare wrote *Macbeth*. The word came from the Old English *wyrd*, having to do with fate or destiny. So Shakespeare's "Weïrd Sisters" are spirits or goddesses of fate, like the three Fates of Greek or Scandinavian mythology.

Macbeth asks the witches to speak. They greet him with his current title, the Thane of Glamis, but also refer to him as both the Thane of Cawdor, and as the future king of Scotland.

✱ And yet your beards forbid me to interpret
That you are so.

MACBETH. Speak, if you can: what are you?

FIRST WITCH. All hail, Macbeth! Hail to thee, Thane of Glamis!

SECOND WITCH. All hail, Macbeth! Hail to thee, Thane of Cawdor!

THIRD WITCH. All hail, Macbeth, that shalt be king hereafter!

49 **hail:** greetings; **Glamis:** a castle and village in eastern Scotland.

PERSONA JOURNAL

Do you believe in superstitions and witches? Why or why not?

1949 production of *Macbeth* at Stratford-upon-Avon (England), Shakespeare Centre Library

✱ **Bearded Ladies** Some women's roles, like Lady Macbeth and Lady Macduff, were played by teenage boys in Shakespeare's theater. But the witches were played by grown men, which may explain Banquo's remark about their beards. Also, in Shakespeare's time, female witches were thought to have beards.

Banquo wonders why Macbeth seems stunned by such favorable predictions and asks the witches to tell his fortune as well. They reply that even though Banquo will not be a king himself, he will be the father of kings. Macbeth then asks the witches for an explanation. Instead of answering, the witches disappear.

BANQUO. Good sir, why do you start, and seem to fear
Things that do sound so fair? I' th' name of truth,
Are ye fantastical, or that indeed
Which outwardly ye show? My noble partner
You greet with present grace and great prediction
Of noble having and of royal hope,
That he seems rapt withal. To me you speak not.
If you can look into the seeds of time
And say which grain will grow and which will not,
Speak then to me, who neither beg nor fear
Your favours nor your hate.

FIRST WITCH. Hail!

SECOND WITCH. Hail!

THIRD WITCH. Hail!

FIRST WITCH. Lesser than Macbeth, and greater.

SECOND WITCH. Not so happy, yet much happier.

THIRD WITCH. Thou shalt get kings, though thou be none.
So all hail, Macbeth and Banquo!

FIRST WITCH. Banquo and Macbeth, all hail!

MACBETH. Stay, you imperfect speakers, tell me more:
By Sinel's death I know I am Thane of Glamis;
But how of Cawdor? The Thane of Cawdor lives,
A prosperous gentleman; and to be king
Stands not within the prospect of belief,
No more than to be Cawdor. Say from whence
You owe this strange intelligence? Or why
Upon this blasted heath you stop our way
With such prophetic greeting? Speak, I charge you.

[Witches vanish.]

? Why do you think Macbeth is so startled?

55 fantastical: a figment of our imagination

57 grace: title

58 noble having...hope: future nobility and the hope of becoming king

59 rapt withal: stunned by all you've said

60 seeds of time: the future

68 happy: fortunate

70 get: father

72 Stay: wait

73 Sinel: Macbeth's father

76 Stands...belief: not within the realm of possibility

77-78 Say from...intelligence: Tell me where you received this startling information.

79 blasted: barren

? How could you create the illusion of the witches vanishing?

Macbeth and Banquo marvel at their encounter with the witches. Ross and Angus enter and tell how grateful the King is for Macbeth's bravery and success on the battlefield.

BANQUO. The earth hath bubbles, as the water has,
And these are of them. Whither are they vanish'd?

MACBETH. Into the air, and what seem'd corporal melted,
As breath into the wind. Would they had stay'd!

BANQUO. Were such things here as we do speak about?
Or have we eaten on the insane root
That takes the reason prisoner?

MACBETH. Your children shall be kings.

BANQUO. You shall be king.

MACBETH. And Thane of Cawdor too. Went it not so?

BANQUO. To th' selfsame tune and words.—Who's there?

[Enter ROSS *and* ANGUS.*]*

ROSS. The King hath happily received, Macbeth,
The news of thy success, and when he reads
Thy personal venture in the rebels' fight,
His wonders and his praises do contend
Which should be thine or his. Silenced with that,
In viewing o'er the rest o' the selfsame day,
He finds thee in the stout Norweyan ranks,
Nothing afeard of what thyself didst make,
Strange images of death. As thick as hail
Came post with post, and every one did bear
Thy praises in his kingdom's great defence,
And pour'd them down before him.

ANGUS. We are sent
To give thee, from our royal master, thanks,

83 corporal: to have a physical body

86 insane root: an herb or root that causes insanity (probably henbane)

90 selfsame: very

92 reads: considers

93 venture: deeds

94 His wonders...contend: His amazement (**wonders**) alternates with his gratitude.

95 Silenced with that: left speechless

97 stout: brave or strong

98-99 Nothing...death: killing many but not afraid of death

100 post with post: messenger after messenger

Ross tells Macbeth that the King has named him Thane of Cawdor. A startled Macbeth asks how he can have the title of another man and is told that the Thane of Cawdor has been sentenced to die for his treason. Macbeth and Banquo begin to wonder about all that the witches have foretold, now that the first prediction has come true.

Only to herald thee into his sight,
Not pay thee.

ROSS. And for an earnest of a greater honour,
He bade me, from him, call thee Thane of Cawdor,
In which addition, hail, most worthy Thane,
For it is thine.

BANQUO. What, can the devil speak true?

✱ MACBETH. The Thane of Cawdor lives. Why do you dress me
In borrow'd robes?

ANGUS. Who was the Thane lives yet,
But under heavy judgment bears that life
Which he deserves to lose. Whether he was combined
With those of Norway, or did line the rebel
With hidden help and vantage, or that with both
He labour'd in his country's wreck, I know not;
But treasons capital, confess'd and proved,
Have overthrown him.

MACBETH. *[Aside.]* Glamis, and Thane of Cawdor:
The greatest is behind.

[To ROSS *and* ANGUS.*]* Thanks for your pains.

[To BANQUO.*]*

Do you not hope your children shall be kings,
When those that gave the Thane of Cawdor to me
Promised no less to them?

104 herald: accompany

106 earnest: promise

108 In which addition: by which title

PERSONA JOURNAL

What do you know about the Thane of Cawdor? How do you feel about Macbeth being given his title?

111 Who: he who

113 combined: allied

114 line the rebel: supported the rebel troops

117 treasons capital: high treason

? Why does Macbeth now have the title Thane of Cawdor?

119 The greatest is behind: The greatest prophecy is the last one, which is yet to come.

✱ **Costume Imagery** "Why do you dress me / In borrow'd robes?" Macbeth asks. This is the first of many images of borrowed or ill-fitting clothing in the play. Actors have used this image in costuming. Laurence Olivier's Macbeth donned an outsized cloak that was hard to drag around, while Orson Welles wore a huge crown that looked almost as if it might drop down over his head.

Orson Welles as Macbeth

Banquo warns Macbeth to be on guard against the witches. As he turns away to speak with Ross and Angus, we hear Macbeth's innermost thoughts. Now that he has become Thane of Cawdor, he fixates on the witches' third prediction. Will he become king? Should he assist fate by murdering Duncan?

BANQUO. That, trusted home,
Might yet enkindle you unto the crown,
Besides the Thane of Cawdor. But 'tis strange.
And oftentimes, to win us to our harm,
The instruments of darkness tell us truths,
Win us with honest trifles, to betray's
In deepest consequence.—
Cousins, a word, I pray you.

MACBETH. *[Aside.]* Two truths are told,
As happy prologues to the swelling act
Of the imperial theme.—I thank you, gentlemen.
[Aside.] This supernatural soliciting
✱ Cannot be ill, cannot be good. If ill,
Why hath it given me earnest of success,
Commencing in a truth? I am Thane of Cawdor:
If good, why do I yield to that suggestion
Whose horrid image doth unfix my hair
And make my seated heart knock at my ribs,
Against the use of nature? Present fears
Are less than horrible imaginings.
My thought, whose murder yet is but fantastical,
Shakes so my single state of man that function
Is smother'd in surmise, and nothing is
But what is not.

BANQUO. Look, how our partner's rapt.

MACBETH. *[Aside.]* If chance will have me King, why, chance may
crown me,
Without my stir.

123 That, trusted home: that taken to its conclusion

? What warning does Banquo give about the witches?

130–131 As happy...theme: as happy introductions (**prologues**) to the inevitable event (**imperial theme**) that makes me king

132 soliciting: temptation

134 earnest: pledge

136 yield to that suggestion: being tempted to kill Duncan

137 unfix my hair: make my hair stand on end

139–140 Against...nature: In a most unnatural way

140–141 Present fears...imaginings: My real fears are less frightening than my horrible fantasies.

142 function: my normal powers

143 surmise: speculation

144 rapt: lost in thought

? What do you think Banquo, Angus, and Ross talk about while Macbeth thinks out loud during an aside?

146 Without my stir: without me taking any action myself

✱ **Antithesis** In this play, things are never what they seem—or as Macbeth puts it in this scene, "nothing is, but what is not." For example, the kindly-looking Cawdor proves a traitor to Duncan, as will the seemingly loyal Macbeth. Indeed, the contrast between illusion and reality is one of the central themes in *Macbeth*. Consider Macbeth's very first line in the play: "So foul and fair a day I have not seen." A statement that makes such a contrast is called an **antithesis**. You will find other examples as you read.

Banquo remarks that Macbeth seems stunned by his new title. He reminds Macbeth that everyone is waiting for him. Macbeth lies about his thoughts and quietly suggests to Banquo that they think over what has happened and discuss it at a later date.

BANQUO. New honours come upon him,
Like our strange garments, cleave not to their mould
But with the aid of use.

MACBETH. *[Aside.]* Come what come may,
Time and the hour runs through the roughest day.

BANQUO. Worthy Macbeth, we stay upon your leisure.

MACBETH. Give me your favour. My dull brain was wrought
With things forgotten. Kind gentlemen, your pains
Are register'd where every day I turn
The leaf to read them. Let us toward the King.
[Aside to Banquo.] Think upon what hath chanc'd, and at more time,
The interim having weigh'd it, let us speak
Our free hearts each to other.

BANQUO. Very gladly.

MACBETH. Till then enough. Come, friends.

[Exeunt.]

147-149 Like our...use: Like new clothes, they don't fit the body until they've been worn a few times.

149 Time...day: Even the most difficult day comes to an end.

150 Stay upon...leisure: We are waiting for you.

151 wrought: busy

153 register'd: remembered, written down

155 chanced: happened

156 The interim...it: Having thought about it for awhile

? How does Macbeth's reaction to the witches' predictions compare to Banquo's reaction?

PERSONA JOURNAL

What would you think of Macbeth as king?

Setting the Scene

MACBETH

Act I, scenes iv and v *or* The Plot Thickens

Critical Query: How do others' views of the Macbeths compare to the way they really are?

Word Play: Imagery

Imagery refers to an author's use of words for their appeal to the senses of sight, hearing, touch, taste, and smell. Such language carries a powerful emotional impact, providing the reader or listener with vivid mental images. *Macbeth* overflows with images of all kinds, especially of blood and darkness. Be on the lookout for these and other images as you read. (For more about imagery, see pages 190-191.)

Special Effects

- Trumpet fanfare

From the Prop Box

- Crown
- Letter for Lady Macbeth

Classroom Set Design

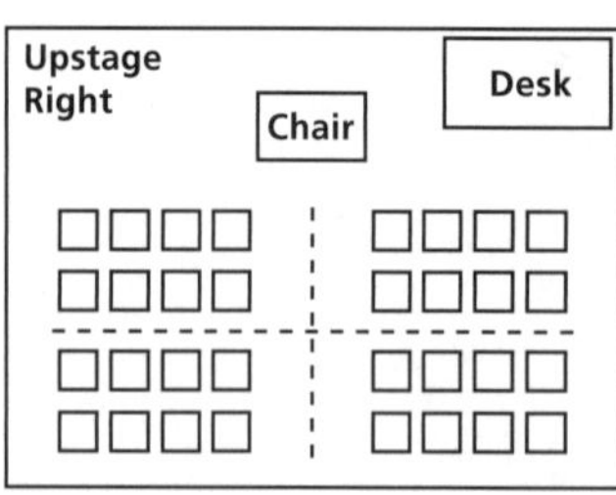

A chair placed in the acting area can be used as a throne in scene iv and a seat for Lady Macbeth in scene v. For future reference, learn the following stage terminology. **Upstage** means away from the audience and **downstage** means toward or closer to the audience. **Stage left** and **stage right** refer to the actor's left and right as he or she faces the audience.

Behind the Scene: Macbeth

"Look like th' innocent flower, but be the serpent under't," says Lady Macbeth to her husband. But now he must tell the truth. After scene v ends, the actor who plays Macbeth will sit in the "hot seat" and answer questions from class members, especially questions regarding his true feelings about Duncan and Lady Macbeth.

Warm-up Improv 1	Warm-up Improv 2
You have been selected as the vice president for a school club. You were vice president last year and worked hard to be president this coming year. The club sponsor's son was selected to be president instead. Talk this over with a good friend.	(Use after page 43) Your daughter will try out for an Olympic team, but she doubts her ability to make it. Give her a pep talk.

King Duncan enters and asks if the execution of Cawdor has been carried out. Malcolm tells him that Cawdor asked for forgiveness for his treason and then died bravely. When Macbeth enters, the King expresses gratitude for his brave service, claiming there is no way to repay him.

SCENE iv. A Room in the Palace

[Flourish. Enter DUNCAN, MALCOLM, DONALBAIN, LENNOX, *and* ATTENDANTS.*]*

DUNCAN. Is execution done on Cawdor? Are not
Those in commission yet return'd?

MALCOLM. My liege,
They are not yet come back. But I have spoke
With one that saw him die, who did report
That very frankly he confess'd his treasons,
Implored your Highness' pardon and set forth
✱ A deep repentance. Nothing in his life
Became him like the leaving it. He died
As one that had been studied in his death
To throw away the dearest thing he owed
As 'twere a careless trifle.

DUNCAN. There's no art
To find the mind's construction in the face.
He was a gentleman on whom I built
An absolute trust.

[Enter MACBETH, BANQUO, ROSS, *and* ANGUS.*]*

O worthiest cousin!
The sin of my ingratitude even now
Was heavy on me. Thou art so far before
That swiftest wing of recompense is slow
To overtake thee. Would thou hadst less deserved,
That the proportion both of thanks and payment
Might have been mine! Only I have left to say,
More is thy due than more than all can pay.

PERSONA ACTION

Representatives from the Canmore clan enter with Duncan. Representatives from all other clans enter with Banquo and Macbeth.

[*stage directions*] Flourish: fanfare of trumpets

2 in commission: ordered to carry out the execution; **liege:** lord

6 Implored: begged for

10 owed: owned

11 careless: worthless

11–12 There's no art...face: There's no point in trying to determine a man's character by the expression on his face.

16–18 Thou art...thee: Your success is so great that the rewards due to you could never be payment (**recompense**) enough or be given too quickly.

18–20 Would thou...mine: I wish that you deserved less so that I could give you more than you deserve.

21 all: all that I own

✱ **Real World Connection** For more than a decade, the Earl of Essex was Queen Elizabeth's favorite courtier; but after raising an unsuccessful rebellion against her in 1601, he was sentenced to death. Before his beheading at the Tower of London, Essex humbly confessed his crimes and apologized to the Queen. When Malcolm says of Cawdor, "Nothing in his life / Became him like the leaving it," Shakespeare's audience probably remembered Essex's graceful death.

Macbeth expresses his loyalty to the King, and Duncan replies that both he and Banquo will be rewarded for their service. The King then names his own son Malcolm as successor to the Scottish throne, conferring on him the title of Prince of Cumberland. The party sets out for Macbeth's castle at Inverness where they will spend the night.

MACBETH. The service and the loyalty I owe
In doing it pays itself. Your Highness' part
Is to receive our duties; and our duties
Are to your throne and state, children and servants,
Which do but what they should, by doing everything
Safe toward your love and honour.

DUNCAN. Welcome hither.
I have begun to plant thee and will labour
To make thee full of growing.—Noble Banquo,
That hast no less deserv'd nor must be known
No less to have done so, let me enfold thee
And hold thee to my heart.

BANQUO. There, if I grow,
The harvest is your own.

DUNCAN. My plenteous joys,
Wanton in fulness, seek to hide themselves
In drops of sorrow. Sons, kinsmen, thanes,
And you whose places are the nearest, know
We will establish our estate upon
* Our eldest, Malcolm, whom we name hereafter
The Prince of Cumberland; which honour must
Not unaccompanied invest him only,
But signs of nobleness, like stars, shall shine
On all deservers. From hence to Inverness,
And bind us further to you.

23 pays itself: is its own reward

27 Safe toward: to safeguard

28 plant thee: reward you (with the new title Thane of Cawdor)

? The King says that Banquo is no less deserving than Macbeth. Speculate as to why the King does not give Banquo a new title as well.

34 Wanton: overflowing

35 drops of sorrow: tears that usually mean sadness, but in this case, joy

37 We will...estate upon: I plan to designate my heir.

38 hereafter: from now on

39 Prince of Cumberland: the title given to the heir to the throne

39-40 which...only: this is not the only honor to be given

? Macbeth must be startled with Duncan's decision to name Malcolm heir to the throne. How can you show that he is upset on the inside while he remains gracious on the outside?

* **If at First You Don't Succeed...** In this scene, Duncan names his eldest son, Malcolm, as his successor. This makes sense to us, and probably did to Shakespeare. After all, isn't the King's oldest son *supposed* to become his heir? But Shakespeare himself may not have known that this was not the practice in medieval Scotland, where kings were elected by the nobility. Historically, Macbeth had a better claim to the throne than Malcolm. So he had good reason to resent Duncan's decision. See page 76.

Macbeth is stunned by the naming of Malcolm as the future king — a serious obstacle to his own ambitions. His thoughts turn dark as he broods over what must be done to achieve his goal.

Duncan anointing Malcolm as Prince of Cumberland, Polanski film, 1971

MACBETH. The rest is labour, which is not used for you.
I'll be myself the harbinger and make joyful
The hearing of my wife with your approach;
So humbly take my leave.

DUNCAN. My worthy Cawdor.

MACBETH. *[Aside.]* The Prince of Cumberland! That is a step
On which I must fall down or else o'erleap,
For in my way it lies. Stars, hide your fires;
Let not light see my black and deep desires.
The eye wink at the hand, yet let that be,
Which the eye fears, when it is done, to see.

[Exit.]

DUNCAN. True, worthy Banquo. He is full so valiant,
And in his commendations I am fed:
It is a banquet to me. Let's after him,
Whose care is gone before to bid us welcome.
It is a peerless kinsman.

[Flourish. Exeunt.]

PERSONA JOURNAL

Are you happy, unhappy, or neutral about Malcolm becoming king? Why?

44 The rest...you: Our leisure time is labor, if it is not used in your service.

45 harbinger: messenger

52 The eye...hand: Don't let the eye see what the hand is doing.

54 full so valiant: very brave

56 after: follow

57 before: ahead

58 peerless: unequaled

PERSONA ACTION

Members of all clans gather to gossip about Malcolm, Cawdor, the battle and anything else that's on their minds.

Dramatic Irony *Irony* is when appearances are somehow at odds with reality. For example, at the end of this scene, Duncan praises Macbeth as a "peerless kinsman," and is expecting splendid hospitality when he visits Macbeth's castle. But the king doesn't know that Macbeth is thinking of killing him. This is an example of *dramatic irony*—in which the audience knows something that a character does not.

At Inverness, Lady Macbeth reads a letter from her husband describing his encounter with the witches and their predictions.

SCENE v. Inverness. Macbeth's Castle

[Enter LADY MACBETH, *reading a letter.]*

LADY MACBETH. 'They met me in the day of success, and I have learned by the perfectest report they have more in them than mortal knowledge. When I burned in desire to question them further, they made themselves air, into which they vanished. Whiles I stood rapt in the wonder of it came missives from the King, who all-hailed me "Thane of Cawdor," by which title, before, these Weird Sisters saluted me and referred me to the coming on of time, with "Hail, King that shalt be!" This have I thought good to deliver thee, my dearest partner of greatness, that thou might'st not lose the dues of rejoicing by being ignorant of what greatness is promised thee. Lay it to thy heart, and farewell.'

2 perfectest report: most reliable source

5 rapt: dazed

6 missives: messengers

9 coming on of time: future

12 lose the dues of rejoicing: be deprived of the joy to which you are entitled

PERSONA JOURNAL

From what you know or have heard, describe Lady Macbeth.

Angela Bassett as Lady Macbeth

Lady Macbeth ponders Macbeth's news. She fears that he will not have the courage to act decisively and attain the greatness the witches have predicted. She wishes for her husband's swift return so that she may counsel him. A messenger enters to announce the arrival of Macbeth and the King.

Glamis thou art, and Cawdor, and shalt be
What thou art promised. Yet do I fear thy nature;
It is too full o' th' milk of human kindness
To catch the nearest way. Thou wouldst be great;
Art not without ambition, but without
The illness should attend it. What thou wouldst highly,
That wouldst thou holily; wouldst not play false,
And yet wouldst wrongly win. Thou'd'st have, great Glamis,
That which cries 'Thus thou must do,' if thou have it,
And that which rather thou dost fear to do,
Than wishest should be undone. Hie thee hither,
That I may pour my spirits in thine ear
And chastise with the valour of my tongue
All that impedes thee from the golden round,
Which fate and metaphysical aid doth seem
To have thee crown'd withal.

[Enter a MESSENGER.*]*

What is your tidings?

MESSENGER. The King comes here tonight.

✱ **LADY MACBETH.** Thou'rt mad to say it.
Is not thy master with him, who, were't so,
Would have inform'd for preparation?

MESSENGER. So please you, it is true. Our Thane is coming.
One of my fellows had the speed of him,
Who, almost dead for breath, had scarcely more
Than would make up his message.

16 fear: worry about

18 catch: take; **wouldst:** wish to

20 illness should: ruthlessness to

20-22 What thou...win: You have high aspirations and you wish to achieve them in an ethical manner. In other words, you want the reward without doing the work.

25 Hie: hasten

26 spirits: strength or power

27 chastise: reprimand you

28 round: crown

29 metaphysical: supernatural

30 withal: already; **tidings:** news

32 were't so: if it were true

33 inform'd for preparation: sent word so that I could have made preparations

35 had the speed of him: outrode him

✱ **Mistaken Identity?** The messenger tells Lady Macbeth that the King is coming, and she replies, "Thou'rt mad to say it." Why does she react so strongly to this news? One critic has made an intriguing suggestion. Lady Macbeth has been thinking of Macbeth as king. Then the messenger enters and announces the King's visit. Perhaps Lady Macbeth briefly imagines the messenger means Macbeth! The messenger would then seem mad, indeed, to speak aloud such a dangerous thought.

The messenger exits and Lady Macbeth continues with her thoughts. She asks the spirits to take away any feminine weaknesses and fill her with the strength and cruelty necessary for murder. Macbeth arrives and is greeted by his wife.

LADY MACBETH. Give him tending.
He brings great news.

[Exit MESSENGER.*]*

The raven himself is hoarse
That croaks the fatal entrance of Duncan
* Under my battlements. Come, you spirits
That tend on mortal thoughts, unsex me here,
And fill me from the crown to the toe top-full
Of direst cruelty! Make thick my blood;
Stop up th' access and passage to remorse,
That no compunctious visitings of nature
Shake my fell purpose, nor keep peace between
Th' effect and it. Come to my woman's breasts
And take my milk for gall, you murd'ring ministers,
Wherever in your sightless substances
You wait on nature's mischief! Come, thick night,
And pall thee in the dunnest smoke of hell,
That my keen knife see not the wound it makes,
Nor heaven peep through the blanket of the dark,
To cry 'Hold, hold!'

[Enter MACBETH.*]*

Great Glamis, worthy Cawdor,
Greater than both by the all-hail hereafter!
Thy letters have transported me beyond
This ignorant present, and I feel now
The future in the instant.

38 raven: a bird often linked to ill-omens and fateful powers

41 mortal: deadly; **unsex me here:** free me of mercy and gentleness

44 remorse: compassion

45 compunctious...nature: natural feelings of conscience

46 Shake my...it: weaken my cruel purpose, nor come between the actual murder and my willing it

48 And take...gall: replacing my milk with bitter bile; **ministers:** agents

49 sightless: invisible

50 wait on: attend to; **mischief:** evil

51 pall thee: cover yourself; **dunnest:** darkest

54 Hold: stop

? What emotions will Lady Macbeth show as she greets her husband? How can you convey this through voice and movement?

55 by the all-hail hereafter: in the future when you are king

58 instant: present

* **The Fourth Witch?** "Come, you Spirits / That tend on mortal thoughts," Lady Macbeth exclaims—and in the lines that follow, she sounds like she's working a magical spell. This has led some critics to suggest that Lady Macbeth herself is a witch—the "fourth witch" of the play. In one production of *Macbeth*, Lady Macbeth actually appeared (unrecognized by her husband) as one of the play's three witches.

Lady Macbeth urges her husband to put on a friendly face that will hide his true intent. She promises to devise a plan for Duncan's murder.

MACBETH. My dearest love,
Duncan comes here tonight.

LADY MACBETH. And when goes hence?

MACBETH. Tomorrow, as he purposes.

LADY MACBETH. O, never
Shall sun that morrow see!
Your face, my Thane, is as a book where men
May read strange matters. To beguile the time,
Look like the time. Bear welcome in your eye,
Your hand, your tongue. Look like th' innocent flower,
But be the serpent under't. He that's coming
Must be provided for; and you shall put
This night's great business into my dispatch,
Which shall to all our nights and days to come
Give solely sovereign sway and masterdom.

MACBETH. We will speak further.

LADY MACBETH. Only look up clear;
To alter favour ever is to fear.
Leave all the rest to me. *[Exeunt.]*

59 What is Lady Macbeth really asking with her question?

63-64 To beguile ...time: To deceive others, behave as they do.

68 dispatch: management

70 solely...masterdom: absolute power and control

71-72 Only...fear: Just look innocent, a troubled expression is always dangerous.

Laurence Olivier and Vivien Leigh as the Macbeths, 1959 Shakespeare Memorial Theatre production at Stratford

Setting the Scene

MACBETH

Act I, scenes vi and vii *or* Decisions, Decisions

Critical Query: How many times does Macbeth change his mind about murdering the King? What causes each change?

From the Prop Box

- Flashlights to be used as torches
- Crown
- Platters and other utensils

Special Effects Oboe music

Classroom Set Design

For scene vi, actors will use the stage right area exiting either out the classroom door or through the created 'doorway'. For scene vii, representatives from each clan sit at the banquet table while other Clan Macbeth members serve the guests. The banquet scene is performed in pantomime as the Macbeths converse in the acting area stage right.

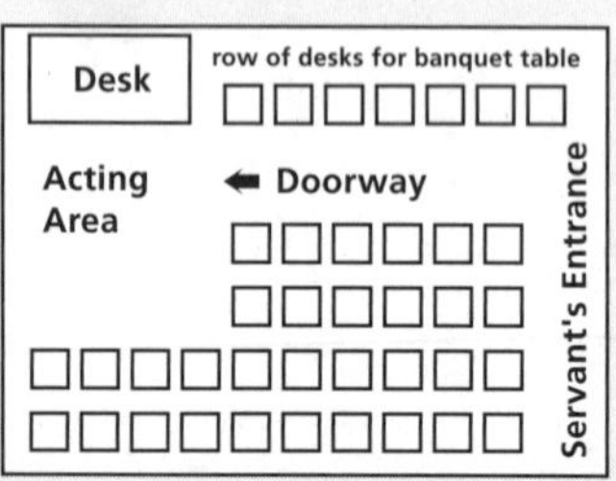

In Character: Lady Macbeth

Lady Macbeth is going to have to work very hard to get Macbeth to do what she wants. What are some methods she might try? Choose three Lady Macbeths. Have each read the lines on pages 50-51 using a different method of persuasion. Possibilities might include anger, sex appeal, tears, and so on.

Time Capsule: Banquet Beverages

In honor of King Duncan's visit, there will be some serious drinking at Macbeth's castle. So what did Macbeth and his guests drink? Today's famous Scotch whisky had not yet been invented. And since grapes were in scant supply, 11th-century Scots were not wine drinkers, either. Instead, they drank ale made from wheat and barley, and cider made from apples. A favorite drink was probably mead—an extremely sweet, spiced beverage made from fermented honey.

Warm-up Improv 1	Warm-up Improv 2
Things are not always what they seem. A friend has been disloyal and betrayed a confidence. They lie and tell you it is not so. Confront them. You know the truth.	(Use after page 48) Your parents want the best for you, but sometimes they push too hard. This is one of those times. Ask them to ease up.

King Duncan and Banquo arrive at Macbeth's castle. They comment on the brisk, fresh air. The King and Lady Macbeth great each other with great courtesy.

SCENE vi. Before Macbeth's Castle

[Hautboys and torches. Enter DUNCAN, MALCOLM, DONALBAIN, BANQUO, LENNOX, MACDUFF, ROSS, ANGUS, *and* ATTENDANTS.*]*

DUNCAN. This castle hath a pleasant seat. The air
Nimbly and sweetly recommends itself
Unto our gentle senses.

BANQUO. This guest of summer,
The temple-haunting martlet, does approve,
By his loved mansionry, that the heaven's breath
Smells wooingly here. No jutty, frieze,
Buttress, nor coign of vantage, but this bird
Hath made his pendant bed and procreant cradle.
Where they most breed and haunt, I have observed,
The air is delicate.

[Enter LADY MACBETH.*]*

DUNCAN. See, see, our honour'd hostess!—
The love that follows us sometime is our trouble,
Which still we thank as love. Herein I teach you
How you shall bid God 'ild us for your pains
And thank us for your trouble.

LADY MACBETH. All our service,
In every point twice done and then done double,
Were poor and single business to contend
Against those honours deep and broad wherewith
Your Majesty loads our house. For those of old,
And the late dignities heap'd up to them,
We rest your hermits.

[*stage directions*] Hautboys: older version of the musical instrument, the oboe

1 seat: setting

3–10 Banquo says that it's obvious that the martin (**martlet**) finds this climate appealing. It 's built it's hanging (**pendant**) nests in every possible niche (**coign of vantage, jutty, frieze, buttress**) of the castle. Where these birds live, he notes, the air seems especially refreshing.

? How does the bird imagery here compare with that on page 44?

11–14 The love...trouble: The love others show us is sometimes inconvenient for them, but we are still thankful for it. And you should ask God to reward (**'ild**) me for coming, because it is my love for you that causes me to visit.

16–19 Were poor...house: would be a poor and feeble effort compared to the honor you do us

19 late dignities: recent honors

20 We rest your hermits: We are in your debt and will repay you with prayers. (Hermits were sometimes hired to pray for the dead.)

DUNCAN. Where's the Thane of Cawdor?
We cours'd him at the heels and had a purpose
To be his purveyor; but he rides well,
And his great love, sharp as his spur, hath holp him
To his home before us. Fair and noble hostess,
We are your guests tonight.

LADY MACBETH. Your servants ever
Have theirs, themselves, and what is theirs in compt
To make their audit at your Highness' pleasure,
Still to return your own.

DUNCAN. Give me your hand. *[Taking her hand.]*
Conduct me to mine host. We love him highly
And shall continue our graces towards him.
By your leave, hostess. *[Exeunt.]*

21 We cours'd: I pursued

22 purveyor: a servant who makes advanced arrangements for his master

23 holp: helped

25-28 Your...own: We are your servants and everything we have is yours, ready to be delivered to you whenever you wish.

30 graces: royal favors

TALES FROM THE STAGE

The Voodoo *Macbeth*

In 1936, Orson Welles directed a famous production of *Macbeth* in Harlem with an all African-American cast. This historically important production opened up new possibilities for black performers, who had seldom been cast in classical plays.

"The Negro has become weary of carrying the White Man's blackface burden in the theatre," wrote Roi Otley, a black journalist. "In *Macbeth* he has been given the opportunity to discard the bandana and the burnt-cork casting to play a universal character ..."

Voodoo *Macb*
produced by Orson Welles, 1

Welles moved the action of the play from Scotland to an imaginary Caribbean country that resembled Haiti. Instead of three witches, there were 43; and Hecate was not female, but a male Voodoo priest wielding a 12-foot bullwhip. A troupe of African drummers—which included an authentic witch doctor—offered musical accompaniment.

All performances sold out, and most New York critics loved the production. But the *Herald Tribune*'s critic Percy Hammond wrote a withering review denouncing the entire enterprise. The night the review appeared, the African musicians performed sinister drummings and chants long after the performance. The next day, a news item announced that Hammond had fallen ill. He died a few days later.

During the banquet for King Duncan, Macbeth leaves the hall and struggles with the decision to murder the King. He lists the arguments against such a monstrous act.

SCENE vii. A Room in Macbeth's Castle

[Hautboys and torches. Enter a SEWER *and divers* SERVANTS *with dishes and service and pass over the stage. Then enter* MACBETH.*]*

✱ **MACBETH.** If it were done when 'tis done, then 'twere well
It were done quickly. If th' assassination
Could trammel up the consequence and catch
With his surcease success, that but this blow
Might be the be-all and the end-all here,
But here, upon this bank and shoal of time,
We'd jump the life to come. But in these cases
We still have judgment here, that we but teach
Bloody instructions, which, being taught, return
To plague th' inventor. This even-handed justice
Commends th' ingredience of our poison'd chalice
To our own lips. He's here in double trust:
First, as I am his kinsman and his subject,
Strong both against the deed; then, as his host,
Who should against his murderer shut the door,
Not bear the knife myself. Besides, this Duncan
Hath borne his faculties so meek, hath been
So clear in his great office, that his virtues
Will plead like angels, trumpet-tongued, against
The deep damnation of his taking-off;
And pity, like a naked newborn babe
Striding the blast, or heaven's cherubim hors'd
Upon the sightless couriers of the air,
Shall blow the horrid deed in every eye,
That tears shall drown the wind. I have no spur
To prick the sides of my intent, but only

***[stage directions]* Sewer:** butler

PERSONA ACTION

As the scene opens, representatives from all clans gather for pre-banquet chatter and then seat themselves at the table where they continue talking and eating in pantomime during Macbeth's speech. Some of the Macbeth clan serve the guests.

3-4 Could...success: If the attempt could take place without any bad consequences and end with Duncan's death, then it would be a success; **trammel up:** catch up in a net; **his surcease:** Duncan's death

7 We'd jump...come: I'd risk the fate of my soul.

10 inventor: teacher

17 Hath borne...meek: has used his power so gently

18 clear: blameless

20 taking-off: murder

22 Striding the blast: riding the wind; **cherubim:** angels

23 sightless couriers: invisible steeds

? What reasons does Macbeth give for NOT killing Duncan?

✱ **Soliloquys and Monologues** are both long speeches delivered by a single actor. So what's the difference between them? A monologue can be delivered to other characters. A soliloquy expresses a character's private thoughts, even if other characters are on stage. Macbeth speaks many soliloquys, including the one on this page. Although Shakespeare didn't invent the soliloquy, he used it more brilliantly than any other writer before or since to reveal the innermost conflicts of his characters.

Macbeth admits that his own ambition is the only real reason to kill the King. Lady Macbeth enters and scolds him for leaving the dining hall. Macbeth tells her he has decided against the King's murder. Lady Macbeth scornfuly berates her husband for his cowardice.

Vaulting ambition, which o'erleaps itself
And falls on th' other—

[Enter LADY MACBETH.*]*

How now, what news?

LADY MACBETH. He has almost supp'd. Why have you left the
chamber?

MACBETH. Hath he ask'd for me?

LADY MACBETH. Know you not he has?

MACBETH. We will proceed no further in this business:
He hath honour'd me of late, and I have bought
Golden opinions from all sorts of people,
Which would be worn now in their newest gloss,
Not cast aside so soon.

LADY MACBETH. Was the hope drunk
Wherein you dress'd yourself? hath it slept since?
And wakes it now, to look so green and pale
At what it did so freely? From this time
Such I account thy love. Art thou afeard
To be the same in thine own act and valour
As thou art in desire? Wouldst thou have that
Which thou esteem'st the ornament of life
And live a coward in thine own esteem,
Letting 'I dare not' wait upon 'I would,'
✱ Like the poor cat i' th' adage?

MACBETH. Prithee, peace.
I dare do all that may become a man.
Who dares do more is none.

27 which o'erleaps itself: like a rider when mounting, jumps too far and falls on the other side of the horse

29 chamber: dining hall

32 bought: earned

35 hope: wish to be king

39 did so freely: decided so easily

42 ornament of life: crown

44 wait upon: always follow

? In this and the speeches that follow, what approach(es) do you think Lady Macbeth uses to get her way?

47 none: not a man

PERSONA JOURNAL

If you are a member of the Macbeth clan, have you heard Macbeth and Lady Macbeth argue? Who usually wins? Why?

✱ **"Like the poor cat i' th' adage ..."** The proverbial "poor cat" that Lady Macbeth refers to is one that wanted to eat fish, but didn't want to get his feet wet.

Lady Macbeth continues to criticize her husband's apparent weakness as well as the fact that he has broken his word to her. She claims that she would kill her own child before she would go back on a promise made to him. She then outlines her plan for killing Duncan.

LADY MACBETH. What beast was't, then,
That made you break this enterprise to me?
When you durst do it, then you were a man;
And to be more than what you were, you would
Be so much more the man. Nor time nor place
Did then adhere, and yet you would make both.
They have made themselves, and that their fitness now
✱ Does unmake you. I have given suck, and know
How tender 'tis to love the babe that milks me.
I would, while it was smiling in my face,
Have pluck'd my nipple from his boneless gums
And dash'd the brains out, had I so sworn as you
Have done to this.

MACBETH. If we should fail—

LADY MACBETH. We fail!
But screw your courage to the sticking place,
And we'll not fail. When Duncan is asleep—
Whereto the rather shall his day's hard journey
Soundly invite him—his two chamberlains
Will I with wine and wassail so convince
That memory, the warder of the brain,
Shall be a fume, and the receipt of reason
A limbeck only. When in swinish sleep
Their drench'd natures lie as in a death,
What cannot you and I perform upon
Th' unguarded Duncan? What not put upon
His spongy officers, who shall bear the guilt
Of our great quell?

48 break this enterprise: reveal this plan

49 durst: dared

52 adhere: agree

53 fitness: convenience

54 unmake: unnerve

60 But screw...place: Lady Macbeth uses a metaphor that refers to tightening (**screw**) either a musical instrument string or an archer's bow string until the point of tautness (**the sticking place**).

61-67 After Duncan is asleep, Lady Macbeth plans to get his bodyguards so drunk they won't remember anything. Memory, thought to be located at the base of the skull, was supposed to guard the brain against unhealthy vapors rising from the body. Drink would turn memory and reason into smoke, which would rise up into the head just like vapors in a laboratory vessel (**limbeck**).

68 drench'd natures: drowned senses

70 put upon: attached blame to

71 spongy: drunk

72 quell: murder

✱ **Lady Macbeth's Children?** Lady Macbeth claims to know "How tender 'tis to love the babe that milks me ..." But later in the play, we will learn that Macbeth has no children. Some critics think Lady Macbeth might be referring to a child from an earlier marriage; according to a historical source, Macbeth was her second husband. But Shakespeare often created such inconsistencies. For him, it probably seemed all right to have Lady Macbeth mention a child, then later describe the Macbeths as childless.

Judi Dench and Ian McKellen as the Macbeths, RSC Warehouse 1977

Macbeth marvels at his wife's strength. He and Lady Macbeth resolve to kill the King, blame it on the King's servants, and then publicly mourn his death.

MACBETH. Bring forth men-children only,
For thy undaunted mettle should compose
Nothing but males. Will it not be received,
When we have mark'd with blood those sleepy two
Of his own chamber and used their very daggers,
That they have done't?

LADY MACBETH. Who dares receive it other,
As we shall make our griefs and clamour roar
Upon his death?

MACBETH. I am settled, and bend up
Each corporal agent to this terrible feat.
Away, and mock the time with fairest show.
False face must hide what the false heart doth know.

[Exeunt.]

73 mettle: spirit; **compose:** produce

74 received: believed as true

? At this point, how do you think Macbeth feels about his wife?

77 other: in any other way

80 settled: determined

80-81 bend up...agent: will exert all my physical energy

82 and mock...show: and fool others by looking and acting innocent

Reacting to Act I

Analysis

1. Do you believe some things are fated to happen, no matter what? Or do you believe that your actions can change the course of your life? Explain your answer.
2. If you were having your fortune told, what questions would you ask the teller?
3. Why do you think Shakespeare used a scene with three witches to begin this play? How might this beginning prepare the audience for what is to come?
4. Why do you think Macbeth and Banquo do not seem afraid of the witches?
5. In your opinion, what is Lady Macbeth's attitude toward her husband? Give examples from the text to support your answer.
6. What is Macbeth's opinion of Banquo?
7. Do you agree with King Duncan that you cannot tell what people are really like just by looking at them? Reread King Duncan's speech in Act I, scene iv, lines 11-21, and discuss why you think Shakespeare had Duncan say this just before Macbeth enters.
8. Using a Venn diagram, select a major character from the first act and compare your persona to that character.

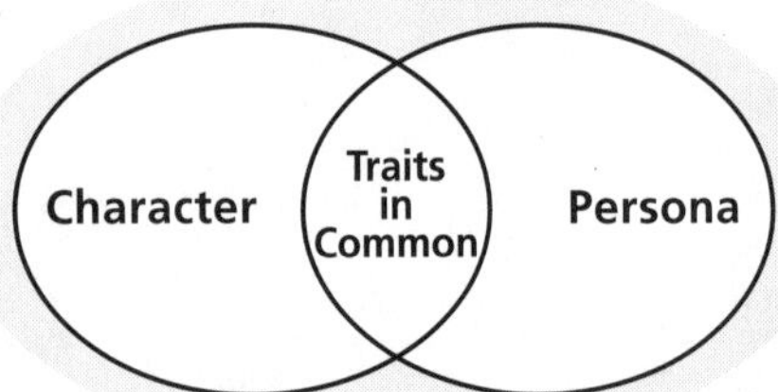

9. Using a graphic organizer like the one at the top of the next column, list the steps of Lady Macbeth's plan to kill King Duncan and blame it on someone else. The first step has been done for you. Next to each step, write possible things that could go wrong.

Steps in the Plan	What Could Go Wrong
Greet Duncan and provide a great banquet. He will sleep well after a large meal with drink.	Duncan decides not to drink.

Literary Elements

1. Shakespeare allows his characters to reveal their innermost thoughts and feelings to the audience through speeches called **soliloquies**. Find an example of this in Act I. Explain why you think Shakespeare wrote the soliloquy for this character in this particular location of the text.
2. **Images** of blood and darkness run through the entire play of Macbeth. Find as many examples of this imagery as possible in Act I.

Writing

1. Write a news report about the recent battles. Refer to the information that was presented to King Duncan by the Captain and Ross.
2. Imagine that you are the sailor's wife or the sailor that the witches refer to in Act I, scene iii. Write your version of the events the witches speak about.
3. Act I, scene v begins with Lady Macbeth reading the ending of a letter from her husband, Macbeth. Keeping true to all of the information you have from the play so far, write the beginning of the letter. Remember to tell Lady Macbeth about the recent battle.

Macbeth Act II

Pat Hingle and Jessica Tandy as Macbeth and Lady Macbeth

"Will all great Neptune's ocean wash this blood clean from my hand?"

Setting the Scene

MACBETH

Act II, scenes i and ii, *or* The Deed Is Done

Critical Query: Who seems more determined to kill Duncan—Macbeth or Lady Macbeth?

Famous Quote from Scene ii

Will all great Neptune's ocean wash this blood clean from my hand?

Special Effects

- Bloody dagger illusion
- Bell
- Owl hoot
- Cricket's chirp
- Knocking
- Optional: Stage blood for hands

Time Capsule: Castles of the Rich and Famous

The real castles of 11th-century Scotland weren't much more than rough forts built on hilltops. But Shakespeare didn't know much about Scottish history. He visualized the kinds of castles that were built later in the Middle Ages. The most important part of a typical medieval castle was the keep. This was a huge tower in which the noble family lived. It often featured numerous rooms, a great hall, a well, and a courtyard.

Classroom Set Design

These two scenes can best be played in the round with chairs and personas situated on all four sides of the room.

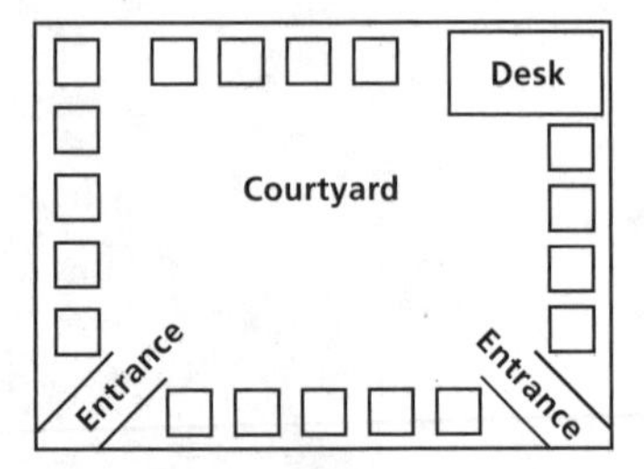

Word Play: Imagery

Are you keeping up with all the blood and darkness imagery? Now add images of sleep and death. You'll find many of them in this act of the play.

From the Prop Box

- Flashlights to be used as torches
- Goblet for Lady Macbeth
- "Diamond," a gift from King Duncan to Lady Macbeth

Warm-up Improv 1	Warm-up Improv 2
The lights have gone out in your home due to a power failure. You stumble around and are suddenly startled by someone you didn't know was inside.	(Use after page 60) You and a good friend have agreed to run the cotton candy booth at the school carnival. The two of you have made your plans and ordered supplies when your friend suddenly wants to back out, which would leave you to do the whole thing by yourself or risk being embarrassed by the carnival committee. Talk to your friend about this.

It is late at night in Macbeth's castle. Banquo and his son, Fleance, are trying to find their way in the dark. Banquo is uneasy and startles at the sudden appearance of Macbeth. Banquo tells him that the King has gone to bed in a very good mood.

ACT II.

Scene i. Court of Macbeth's Castle

[Enter BANQUO and FLEANCE bearing a torch before him.]

BANQUO. How goes the night, boy?

FLEANCE. The moon is down. I have not heard the clock.

BANQUO. And she goes down at twelve.

FLEANCE. I take't, 'tis later, sir.

BANQUO. Hold, take my sword. There's husbandry in heaven;
Their candles are all out. Take thee that too.
A heavy summons lies like lead upon me,
And yet I would not sleep. Merciful powers,
Restrain in me the curs'd thoughts that nature
Gives way to in repose!

[Enter MACBETH *and a* SERVANT *with a torch.]*

Give me my sword.
Who's there?

MACBETH. A friend.

BANQUO. What, sir, not yet at rest? The King's abed.
He hath been in unusual pleasure, and
Sent forth great largess to your offices.
This diamond he greets your wife withal,
By the name of most kind hostess; and shut up
In measureless content.

[He gives Macbeth a diamond.]

PERSONA JOURNAL

You were at the banquet last night. Describe the atmosphere, food, and conversation. Did you notice anything unusual about the Macbeths behavior?

1 How goes...boy?: How late is it, boy?

3 she: the moon

4 husbandry: thrift

5 that: probably his dagger

6 A heavy...me: The desire to sleep (**heavy summons**) is very strong (**like lead**) with me.

7-9 I ask the angels (**merciful powers**) to keep away the nightmares (**curs'd thoughts**) that sometimes trouble sleep (**repose**).

13 unusual pleasure: a good mood

14 largess: gifts; **offices:** servants

? Why has the King given gifts to Macbeth's servants?

15 withal: with

16 shut up: retired to bed

? Why is the King in such a good mood?

Macbeth and Banquo resolve to speak again soon about the witches' prophesies. Macbeth asks Banquo to trust him in this matter, and Banquo agrees as long as his honor and loyalty are not compromised. They wish each other goodnight. Now alone, Macbeth is startled by the image of a dagger floating in the air.

MACBETH. Being unprepar'd,
Our will became the servant to defect;
Which else should free have wrought.

BANQUO. All's well.
I dreamt last night of the three Weïrd Sisters.
To you they have show'd some truth.

MACBETH. I think not of them.
Yet, when we can entreat an hour to serve,
We would spend it in some words upon that business,
If you would grant the time.

BANQUO. At your kind'st leisure.

MACBETH. If you shall cleave to my consent, when 'tis,
It shall make honour for you.

BANQUO. So I lose none
In seeking to augment it, but still keep
My bosom franchis'd and allegiance clear,
I shall be counsell'd.

MACBETH. Good repose the while.

BANQUO. Thanks, sir. The like to you.

[*Exeunt* BANQUO *and* FLEANCE.]

MACBETH. Go bid thy mistress, when my drink is ready,
She strike upon the bell. Get thee to bed.

[*Exit* SERVANT.]

Is this a dagger which I see before me,
The handle toward my hand? Come, let me clutch thee.

18-19 Our will...wrought: Our desire to serve was hampered by lack of time; otherwise, we would have done more.

? Why does Macbeth lie about his thoughts of the witches?

? How do you think Macbeth reacts to Banquo's speech about honor and loyalty?

22 entreat an... serve: find a convenient time

24 At your...leisure: whenever it is good for you

25 cleave...'tis: support me when the time comes

26-28 So I...clear: provided that I lose no honor, that I keep my conscience clear (**bosom franchis'd**), and my loyalty to the King (**allegiance**) secure (**clear**)

? If you were the director, would you have a real dagger "float" in front of Macbeth, or would you let the actor and audience imagine it? Why?

TALES FROM THE STAGE

In an 1882 production of *Macbeth*, the actor playing the title role decided to take a daringly long pause before saying the line, "Is this a dagger which I see before me, / The handle toward my hand?" As if in reply to Macbeth's question, a stray cat walked across the stage looking for mice. Needless to say, the effect of the dramatic pause was rather spoiled.

An agitated Macbeth realizes that the ghostly dagger is much like the one he plans to use to kill Duncan. When he sees blood on the dagger, he is horrified.

I have thee not, and yet I see thee still.
Art thou not, fatal vision, sensible
To feeling as to sight? Or art thou but
A dagger of the mind, a false creation
Proceeding from the heat-oppressèd brain?
I see thee yet, in form as palpable
As this which now I draw.

[He draws his dagger.]

Thou marshall'st me the way that I was going,
And such an instrument I was to use.
Mine eyes are made the fools o' th' other senses
Or else worth all the rest. I see thee still,
And, on thy blade and dudgeon, gouts of blood,
Which was not so before. There's no such thing.
It is the bloody business which informs
Thus to mine eyes. Now o'er the one half-world
Nature seems dead, and wicked dreams abuse
The curtain'd sleep. Witchcraft celebrates
Pale Hecate's off'rings, and wither'd murder,
Alarum'd by his sentinel, the wolf,
Whose howl's his watch, thus with his stealthy pace,
* With Tarquin's ravishing strides, towards his design
Moves like a ghost. Thou sure and firm-set earth,
Hear not my steps, which way they walk, for fear
Thy very stones prate of my whereabout,
And take the present horror from the time,

36-37 sensible...sight: Can you be felt as well as seen?

? As Macbeth, how would you react to the dagger?

39 heat-oppressèd: feverish

40 palpable: real

42 marshall'st: lead

44 o' th': by the

45 all the rest: more than all the other senses

46 dudgeon: handle; **gouts:** large drops

48 informs: gives false information

50 abuse: deceive

51 curtain'd sleep: refers to a sleeping area with curtains

52 Hecate: goddess of magic and witchcraft

52-56 Murder is personified as a shriveled ghost who, wakened **(alarum'd)** by the howls of his bodyguard **(watch)** the wolf, moves stealthily towards his victim.

58 prate: talk foolishly

59 take the...time: take away the horror of the moment

* **Tarquin** Roman legend tells of a virtuous wife named Lucretia who was raped by Sextus Tarquinius (Tarquin), the son of the king of Rome. More than ten years before writing *Macbeth*, Shakespeare told her story in his narrative poem *The Rape of Lucrece*. When Macbeth speaks of "wither'd murder" moving with "stealthy pace," Shakespeare may have been borrowing from his earlier poem, in which "Lust and Murder wakes to stain and kill."

Despite his hallucinations, Macbeth strengthens his resolve to kill Duncan.

Which now suits with it. Whiles I threat, he lives.
Words to the heat of deeds too cold breath gives.

[A bell rings.]

* I go, and it is done. The bell invites me.
Hear it not, Duncan, for it is a knell
That summons thee to heaven or to hell.

[Exit.]

? As Macbeth, how would you plot the movements and emotions you will use during this long soliloquy?

60 suits: agrees

61 Words to...gives: Talking destroys the passion that drives the action.

63 knell: the ring of a funeral bell

PERSONA JOURNAL

Many Canmores have observed and gossiped about Macbeth's tendency toward having hallucinations. What have you seen or heard?

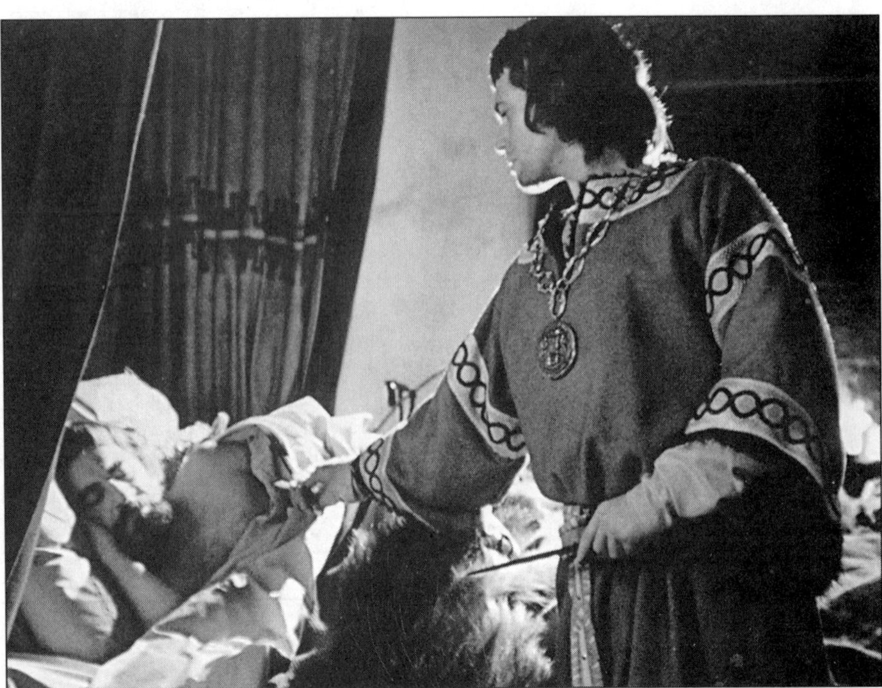

Macbeth preparing to kill Duncan
Polanski film, 1971

* **Murder, He Wrote** When Macbeth hears a bell, he grimly observes that it summons Duncan "to heaven or to hell." This line echoes an earlier Shakespearean murderer, the much more gleeful Richard III. When contemplating the murder of his uncle, Richard remarks, "I do love thee so, / That I will shortly send thy soul to heaven, / If heaven will take the present at our hands."

In the castle courtyard, Lady Macbeth nervously waits for Macbeth's return. She has drugged the King's guards and put their daggers where Macbeth will find them. She fears that the household will wake before Macbeth has finished. Macbeth, shaken and bloody, enters with the daggers and announces that the King is dead.

Scene ii. Court of Macbeth's Palace

[Enter LADY MACBETH.*]*

LADY MACBETH. That which hath made them drunk hath made me bold;
What hath quench'd them hath given me fire.
Hark! Peace.
✱ It was the owl that shriek'd, the fatal bellman,
Which gives the stern'st good-night. He is about it.
The doors are open, and the surfeited grooms
Do mock their charge with snores. I have drugg'd their possets,
That death and nature do contend about them
Whether they live or die.

MACBETH. *[Within.]* Who's there? What, ho!

LADY MACBETH. Alack, I am afraid they have awak'd,
And 'tis not done. Th' attempt and not the deed
Confounds us. Hark! I laid their daggers ready;
He could not miss 'em. Had he not resembled
My father as he slept, I had done't.

[Enter MACBETH *with bloody daggers.]*

My husband?

MACBETH. I have done the deed. Didst thou not hear a noise?

LADY MACBETH. I heard the owl scream and the crickets cry.
Did not you speak?

MACBETH. When?

1 That: the wine

2 quench'd: extinguished — in this case, put to sleep

3 owl: According to superstition the owl's cry foretells death.

4 He: Macbeth

5 surfeited grooms: drunken guards

6 mock...snores: abandon their duty to watch over Duncan (**their charge**) by falling asleep; **possets:** a hot drink taken before bedtime made from curdled milk, ale, wine, etc.

7 contend about: happen around

? How would you describe Lady Macbeth's mood? How could you show it to the audience?

11 Confounds us: will ruin us

? Why didn't Lady Macbeth kill Duncan herself?

✱ **"The Fatal Bellman"** In 1605, a wealthy tailor named Robert Dow bequeathed a rather morbid gift to London's Newgate Prison. He paid for a man to ring a bell at midnight outside the cells of prisoners condemned to die the next day, chanting a rhyme calling for them to repent and pray. Lady Macbeth is probably referring to this bellman, who did indeed give "the stern'st good-night."

While Macbeth was in the King's chamber, he heard someone cry out from another room. Lady Macbeth informs him that the King's sons are asleep in the second bedroom. They apparently woke briefly during the murder, said some prayers, and went back to sleep. Macbeth is haunted by his inability to say "Amen" to their prayers.

LADY MACBETH. Now.

MACBETH. As I descended?

LADY MACBETH. Ay.

MACBETH. Hark!
Who lies i' th' second chamber?

LADY MACBETH. Donalbain.

MACBETH. This is a sorry sight.

[Looking on his hands.]

LADY MACBETH. A foolish thought, to say a sorry sight.

MACBETH. There's one did laugh in's sleep, and one cried
'Murder!'
That they did wake each other. I stood and heard them.
But they did say their prayers, and address'd them
Again to sleep.

* **LADY MACBETH.** There are two lodg'd together.

MACBETH. One cried 'God bless us!' and 'Amen' the other,
As they had seen me with these hangman's hands,
List'ning their fear. I could not say 'Amen'
When they did say 'God bless us.'

LADY MACBETH. Consider it not so deeply.

MACBETH. But wherefore could not I pronounce 'Amen'?
I had most need of blessing, and 'Amen'
Stuck in my throat.

LADY MACBETH. These deeds must not be thought
After these ways; so, it will make us mad.

19 chamber: bedroom

20 sorry: miserable

? What do you think woke up the two sleepers?

27 As: as if

28 List'ning: listening to

30 wherefore: why

32-33 thought/After these ways: regarded in this way; **so:** if so

? Why is Macbeth so upset about his inability to say 'Amen'?

* **Which Two?** When Lady Macbeth says, "There are two lodg'd together," she is referring to Donalbain and his brother Malcolm, who are sleeping in a room across the hall from their father, King Duncan. Macbeth hears *them* laugh, cry out, and pray—not the two grooms guarding the King.

Macbeth is distraught over what he has done. Lady Macbeth scolds him for returning with the daggers, which were supposed to have been left with the drunken guards. Macbeth refuses to return them, so Lady Macbeth impatiently says that she will do it and that she will also smear blood on the guards' faces to insure they appear guilty.

MACBETH. Methought I heard a voice cry 'Sleep no more!
Macbeth does murder sleep'—the innocent sleep,
Sleep that knits up the ravell'd sleave of care,
The death of each day's life, sore labour's bath,
Balm of hurt minds, great nature's second course,
Chief nourisher in life's feast.

LADY MACBETH. What do you mean?

MACBETH. Still it cried 'Sleep no more!' to all the house.
'Glamis hath murder'd sleep, and therefore Cawdor
Shall sleep no more. Macbeth shall sleep no more.'

LADY MACBETH. Who was it that thus cried? Why, worthy Thane,
You do unbend your noble strength to think
So brainsickly of things. Go get some water
And wash this filthy witness from your hand.
* Why did you bring these daggers from the place?
They must lie there. Go carry them and smear
The sleepy grooms with blood.

MACBETH. I'll go no more:
I am afraid to think what I have done;
Look on't again I dare not.

LADY MACBETH. Infirm of purpose!
Give me the daggers. The sleeping and the dead
Are but as pictures; 'tis the eye of childhood
That fears a painted devil. If he do bleed,
I'll gild the faces of the grooms withal,
For it must seem their guilt.

[Exit LADY MACBETH. *Knocking within.]*

36–39 Macbeth says the healing power of sleep smoothes out (**knits up**) the tangled threads (**ravell'd sleave**) of the day's worries just as a warm bath refreshes the body. Sleep is the remedy (**balm**) for the troubled mind. It is the second and most nourishing part of each day, just like the main course of a meal.

? Why do you think Macbeth is so obsessed with sleep?

44 unbend: sap

45 brainsickly: insanely

46 witness: evidence

51 Infirm of purpose!: weak-willed creature!

55 gild: smear; **withal:** with it

? Compare Macbeth and Lady Macbeth's feelings about each other in this scene.

* **Time Lapse** Shakespeare didn't always make things easy for his actors. Consider Lady Macbeth's alarm when she asks, "Why did you bring these daggers from the place?" Actually, Macbeth has been standing there for more than 30 lines. Has he been hiding the daggers behind his back this whole time? If not, how is the actress playing Lady Macbeth supposed to make her surprise believable?

TALES FROM THE STAGE

Lady Macbeth Takes Charge

In an age when women weren't even allowed to appear on the stage, Shakespeare penned some extraordinarily strong and memorable female characters, such as Portia from the *The Merchant of Venice,* Juliet, and Cleopatra. One of the most powerful female roles is Lady Macbeth, and most actresses would give a month's pay or more to have a shot at playing her. There have been many memorable Lady M's, with each actress developing her own unique interpretation. Vivien Leigh (page 45) played her with equal parts sexual intensity and evil; Judith Anderson's performance (page 79) featured a cold woman driven by ambition and greed. No matter how she is characterized, however, it is hard to deny her strength of purpose in this scene. When Macbeth refuses to return the daggers to the bodyguards' room, Lady Macbeth impatiently takes them from him and does the deed herself.

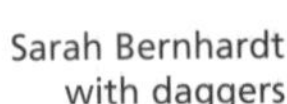

Sarah Bernhardt with daggers

Mr. and Mrs. Charles Kean, 1858

David Garrick and Hannah Pritchard in a 1768 Drury Lane production, Victoria and Albert Museum

A half-mad Macbeth stares with terror at his bloody hands. Lady Macbeth shows her own bloody hands to Macbeth. At her urging, they go to their room to wash and prepare for playing their roles as sleepy, innocent hosts.

MACBETH. Whence is that knocking?
How is't with me when every noise appals me?
What hands are here? Ha! they pluck out mine eyes.
Will all great Neptune's ocean wash this blood
Clean from my hand? No, this my hand will rather
The multitudinous seas incarnadine,
Making the green one red.

[Reenter LADY MACBETH.*]*

LADY MACBETH. My hands are of your colour, but I shame
To wear a heart so white. *[Knocking]* I hear a knocking
At the south entry. Retire we to our chamber.
A little water clears us of this deed:
How easy is it, then! Your constancy
Hath left you unattended. *[Knocking]* Hark, more knocking.
Get on your nightgown, lest occasion call us
And show us to be watchers. Be not lost
So poorly in your thoughts.

MACBETH. To know my deed, 'twere best not know myself.

[Knocking within.]

Wake Duncan with thy knocking! I would thou couldst.

[Exeunt.]

59 Neptune: Roman god of the sea

60-62 will rather...red: will turn the vast (**multitudinous**) oceans blood red (**incarnadine**), making the green waters red.

63 shame: would be ashamed

? What does Lady Macbeth mean by "A little water clears us of this deed"?

67-68 Your constancy...unattended: Your sanity (**constancy**) has abandoned you (**left you unattended**).

69 occasion: circumstances

70 show us to be watchers: we are discovered to be awake.

PERSONA JOURNAL

You were wakened by a noise last night. What did you think it was?

Setting the Scene

MACBETH

Act II, scene iii *or* Whodunit?

Critical Query: How is the murder plot working so far?

Famous Quote from Scene iii
There's daggers in men's eyes.

Special Effects

- Knocking
- Bell

Time Capsule: Miracle Plays

During the Middle Ages and early Renaissance, plays based on biblical stories were performed outdoors for common people. These were called miracle or mystery plays, and Shakespeare probably saw them when he was young. Some of these plays featured scenes in hell, where a comical porter welcomed dead sinners to their damnation. In the scene that follows, the Porter is pretending to be this familiar character.

In Character: Banquo

It's Banquo's turn for the hot seat. At the end of scene iii, the actor playing him must answer questions from the audience such as the following:
Is he just too good to be true or is he the real deal?
What is his opinion of the Macbeths?
Has it changed since he heard about Duncan's murder?

Classroom Set Design

Use the same courtyard setting that was arranged for scenes i and ii, but add a gate as shown, where Macduff and Lennox wait until the Porter opens it. The Porter should enter the courtyard from the opposite corner of the room which will give him time and space to perform his long rambling speech.

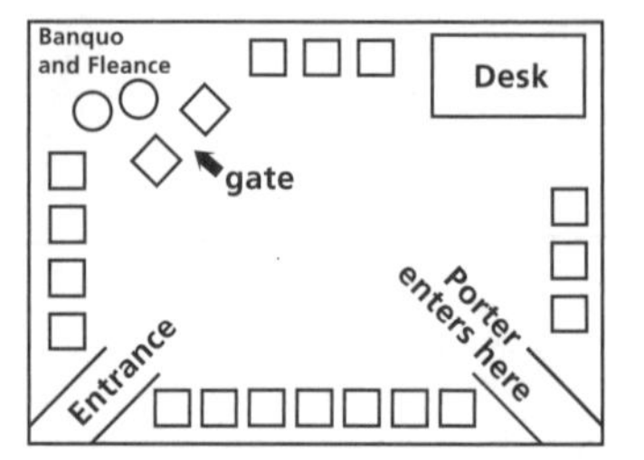

Warm-up Improv

You had an accident with your mom's car. It was the other driver's fault, but you know she'll blame you. Call a friend and discuss ways of explaining your innocence to your mom.

Early the next morning, insistent knocking arouses Macbeth's porter. As he makes his way to the gate, he drunkenly describes himself as the gatekeeper of hell, who welcomes the greedy, the liars, and the thieves. He opens the gate for Macduff and Lennox, who ask why the household is still asleep.

Scene iii. Court of Macbeth's Palace

[Knocking within. Enter a PORTER.*]*

PORTER. Here's a knocking indeed! If a man were porter of hell gate, he should have old turning the key. *[Knocking within.]* Knock, knock, knock! Who's there, i' th' name of Beelzebub? Here's a farmer that hang'd himself on the expectation of plenty. Come in time! Have napkins enough about you; here you'll sweat for't. *[Knocking within.]* Knock, knock! Who's there, in the other devil's name? Faith, here's an equivocator that could swear in both the scales against either scale, who committed treason enough for God's sake, yet could not equivocate to heaven. O, come in, equivocator. *[Knocking within.]* Knock, knock, knock! Who's there? Faith, here's an English tailor come hither for stealing out of a French hose. Come in, tailor. Here you may roast your goose. *[Knocking within.]* Knock, knock! Never at quiet.—What are you?—But this place is too cold for hell. I'll devil-porter it no further. I had thought to have let in some of all professions that go the primrose way to th' everlasting bonfire. *[Knocking within.]* Anon, anon! *[Opens the gate.]* I pray you, remember the porter.

[Enter MACDUFF *and* LENNOX.*]*

MACDUFF. Was it so late, friend, ere you went to bed,
That you do lie so late?

PORTER. Faith, sir, we were carousing till the second cock, and drink, sir, is a great provoker of three things.

[*stage directions*] Porter: gatekeeper

? What kind of movements and speaking voice would you use during this long, humorous speech?

2 should...old: He would grow old turning the key because so many people end up in hell.

3–12 Beelzebub: the devil. The porter pretends to be opening the gates of hell for new arrivals including a farmer who lost his money after trying to manipulate prices, a fast talker **(equivocator)** who deceived others with his doubletalk, but couldn't talk his way into heaven, and a tailor who stole some of the fabric intended for a customer's pants.

13 goose: a tailor's iron

17 primrose way...bonfire: easy, pleasant path to hell

18 Anon: Right away! or Coming!; **remember:** refers to tipping

21 the second cock: second cock-crow or about 3:00 a.m.

PERSONA ACTION

Representatives of the Macduff clan enter with him and react appropriately to both the humor and the horror of the scene.

* **Lie or Die** *Macbeth* was performed soon after the Gunpowder Plot, a failed Catholic conspiracy to destroy the Protestant government of England. When caught and interrogated about their activities, radical Catholics did not consider it sinful to evade the truth. After all, honesty might lead to execution for treason. When Catholics gave testimony that was not entirely true, they called it "equivocation," a practice that the Porter ridicules here. For more about the Gunpowder Plot, see page 7.

TALES FROM THE STAGE

Shakespearean critics can be amazingly stuffy at times. During the 19th century, some scholars insisted that Shakespeare simply *couldn't* have written the vulgar, comical scene with the Porter. Never mind that Shakespeare wrote more than a few vulgar, comical scenes, even in other tragedies.

Today's scholars generally agree that the Porter's lines were written by Shakespeare, and that the character belongs in the play. For one thing, his scene serves a practical theatrical purpose. At the end of Act II, scene ii, Macbeth is fully clothed, and his hands are covered with blood. He needs time offstage to wash his hands and to change into night clothes before making his next entrance—and the Porter supplies the necessary time.

James Swift
Federal Theatre Project
New York Classical
High School Program, 1939

But more than that, the Porter scene is fascinating in its own right. It includes some of the play's most pointed references to the Gunpowder Plot. The alleged mastermind of this conspiracy was the Catholic priest Father Henry Garnet, who sometimes used the name "Farmer" as an alias. And so the farmer, the first of the sinners welcomed by the Porter to hell, is probably Garnet himself.

Garnet also defended the practice of equivocation, which allowed Catholic conspirators to avoid telling the truth under interrogation. So he's probably also the *second* sinner the Porter welcomes—"an equivocator, that could swear in both the scales against either scale ..."

The Porter scene also echoes themes and ideas that recur throughout the play. After all, *Macbeth* is full of equivocations—from Macbeth's pretenses of hospitality toward Duncan to the witches' numerous deceptions and half-truths. In the last act, Macbeth himself will complain that he's been tricked by "the equivocation of the fiend" (page 162).

As in much of the play, nothing in the Porter's speeches is quite what it seems. Drink both "provokes" and "unprovokes" lechery: "it makes him, and it mars him; it sets him on, and it takes him off; it persuades him and disheartens him; makes him stand to, and not stand to; in conclusion, equivocates him in a sleep and, giving him the lie, leaves him". As he does often in this play ("So foul and fair a day I have not seen"), Shakespeare uses antithesis to suggest a conflict between illusion and reality.

There can be little doubt that Shakespeare wrote the Porter scene—and that he would be very unhappy with prudish critics' attempts to banish it from *Macbeth*.

The Porter rambles on, explaining that drink causes three things: a red nose, sleep, and urine. And, he continues, while drink creates sexual desire, it takes away the ability to perform. Macbeth enters. Macduff and Lennox ask if the King is awake.

MACDUFF. What three things does drink especially provoke?

PORTER. Marry, sir, nose-painting, sleep, and urine. Lechery, sir, it provokes, and unprovokes. It provokes the desire, but it takes away the performance. Therefore, much drink may be said to be an equivocator with lechery. It makes him, and it mars him; it sets him on, and it takes him off; it persuades him and disheartens him; makes him stand to and not stand to; in ✱ conclusion, equivocates him in a sleep and, giving him the lie, leaves him.

MACDUFF. I believe drink gave thee the lie last night.

PORTER. That it did, sir, i' th' very throat on me; but I requited him for his lie, and, I think, being too strong for him, though he took up my legs sometime, yet I made a shift to cast him.

MACDUFF. Is thy master stirring?

[Enter MACBETH.*]*

Our knocking has awak'd him. Here he comes.

LENNOX. Good morrow, noble sir.

MACBETH. Good morrow, both.

MACDUFF. Is the King stirring, worthy Thane?

MACBETH. Not yet.

MACDUFF. He did command me to call timely on him:
I have almost slipp'd the hour.

MACBETH. I'll bring you to him.

MACDUFF. I know this is a joyful trouble to you,
But yet 'tis one.

24 nose-painting: getting a red nose from drinking too much

27 mars: hinders

30 giving him the lie: In this and the following lines, Macduff and the Porter trade puns based on the multiple meanings of the word *lie*, "to deceive" and *lie* "to lie down."

33 i' th' very throat on me: I cannot deceive you; **requited:** repaid

34-35 though he...legs: refers to drinking so much that he could not walk straight; **made a ...him:** tricked him and vomited him up

? Find as many interpretations as possible for the word *lie* in lines 30-35.

40 timely: early

41 slipp'd the hour: arrived late

✱ **Very Punny** A **pun** is a humorous play on words such as the title "Very Punny" where the expected word "funny" is replaced by the word "punny." Shakespeare obviously loved puns. His comedies are filled with them. And even in this scene, the only comic relief in the play, he did not miss the opportunity to have some fun with the word "lie." The most common varieties of puns make use of words with multiple meanings (lie, case, pop), or words with different spellings that sound alike (soul/sole, great/grate, pare/pair).

Macbeth directs Macduff and Lennox to Duncan's chambers. Macduff goes to wake Duncan, while Lennox and Macbeth discuss the rough, eerie night that has just passed. Macduff returns aghast over the sight of the murdered king.

MACBETH. The labour we delight in physics pain.
This is the door.

MACDUFF. I'll make so bold to call,
For 'tis my limited service.

[Exit.]

LENNOX. Goes the King hence today?

MACBETH. He does. He did appoint so.

LENNOX. The night has been unruly. Where we lay,
Our chimneys were blown down and, as they say,
Lamentings heard i' th' air, strange screams of death,
And prophesying, with accents terrible,
Of dire combustion and confused events
New hatch'd to th' woeful time. The obscure bird
Clamour'd the livelong night. Some say the earth
Was feverous and did shake.

MACBETH. 'Twas a rough night.

LENNOX. My young remembrance cannot parallel
A fellow to it.

[Reenter MACDUFF.*]*

MACDUFF. O horror, horror, horror! Tongue nor heart
Cannot conceive nor name thee!

MACBETH AND LENNOX. What's the matter?

MACDUFF. Confusion now hath made his masterpiece.
Most sacrilegious murder hath broke ope
The Lord's anointed temple and stole thence
The life o' th' building!

44 physics: is a remedy for

46 limited service: appointed task

47 appoint: intend to do

50 Lamentings: weeping

52 dire combustion: dreadful tumult

53 Just born (**new hatch'd**) out of this terrible (**woeful**) time; **obscure bird:** owl

56 My...it: In my young life, I've never seen a night to equal this.

59 Confusion: distraction

60 ope: open

PERSONA JOURNAL

How do you hear about Duncan's murder?

61 The Lord's...temple: the King's body (The King was believed to be God's representative on earth.)

Macduff sends Macbeth and Lennox to see for themselves and then wakes the castle. Lady Macbeth and Banquo enter and Macduff tells what has happened.

MACBETH. What is't you say? The life?

LENNOX. Mean you his majesty?

MACDUFF. Approach the chamber and destroy your sight
With a new Gorgon. Do not bid me speak.
See and then speak yourselves.

[Exeunt MACBETH *and* LENNOX.*]*

Awake, awake!
Ring the alarum bell. Murder and treason!
Banquo and Donalbain! Malcolm! Awake!
Shake off this downy sleep, death's counterfeit,
And look on death itself! Up, up, and see
The great doom's image! Malcolm, Banquo,
As from your graves rise up and walk like sprites
To countenance this horror.—Ring the bell.

[Bell rings.]

[Enter LADY MACBETH.*]*

LADY MACBETH. What's the business,
That such a hideous trumpet calls to parley
The sleepers of the house? Speak, speak!

MACDUFF. O gentle lady,
✱ 'Tis not for you to hear what I can speak.
The repetition in a woman's ear
Would murder as it fell.

[Enter BANQUO.*]*

O Banquo, Banquo,

PERSONA JOURNAL

How do you feel about Duncan's murder? How will it affect you?

66 Gorgon: a monster with snakes for hair. In Greek mythology, anyone who looked on a Gorgon was turned to stone.

70 death's counterfeit: the imitation of death

72 great doom's image: a sight as terrible as Judgment Day

73 sprites: ghosts

74 countenance: see

PERSONA ACTION

The ringing bell draws representatives from all clans to the courtyard. All other clan members react in place.

76 calls to parley: calls us to gather together

79 repetition: telling

? How does Macbeth react to Duncan's death? Does he give anyone reason to be suspicious?

✱ **Irony** Irony is when appearances are somewhat at odds with reality. *Macbeth* is a play in which nothing is quite what it seems, and so it is full of irony. For example, here Macduff fears telling Lady Macbeth about Duncan's death because such news "in a woman's ear / Would murder as it fell." Little does he know that Lady Macbeth, far from being too frail to hear this news, actually planned the murder and has already seen Duncan's corpse.

As Lady Macbeth, Macbeth, and Banquo lament the tragedy, Malcolm and Donalbain enter and learn of their father's death. Lennox describes the evidence against the guards.

Our royal master's murder'd!

LADY MACBETH. Woe, alas!
What, in our house?

BANQUO. Too cruel anywhere.
Dear Duff, I prithee, contradict thyself
And say it is not so.

[Reenter MACBETH *and* LENNOX, *with* ROSS.*]*

✱ **MACBETH.** Had I but died an hour before this chance,
I had liv'd a blessèd time; for from this instant
There's nothing serious in mortality.
All is but toys. Renown and grace is dead.
The wine of life is drawn, and the mere lees
Is left this vault to brag of.

[Enter MALCOLM *and* DONALBAIN.*]*

DONALBAIN. What is amiss?

MACBETH. You are, and do not know't.
The spring, the head, the fountain of your blood
Is stopp'd; the very source of it is stopp'd.

MACDUFF. Your royal father's murder'd.

MALCOLM. O, by whom?

LENNOX. Those of his chamber, as it seem'd, had done't.
Their hands and faces were all badged with blood.
So were their daggers, which unwip'd we found
Upon their pillows. They stared, and were distracted.
No man's life was to be trusted with them.

83 prithee: beg you

? What might Banquo be thinking about at this point?

85 chance: event

87 serious in mortality: important in life

88 toys: trifles; **grace:** honor

89–90 The best part of life **(wine)** is gone and only the dregs **(lees)** remain in the world **(vault)**.

91 amiss: wrong

92 head: origin

96 badged: marked

98 were distracted: looked confused

PERSONA JOURNAL

Did you know the guards? Do you believe that they killed Duncan?

✱ **Self-Fulfilling Prophecy** "Had I but died an hour before this chance," says Macbeth, "I had liv'd a blessèd time ..." Of course, he says this to convince others of his innocence. But intriguingly, this statement and the lines which follow happen to be true. The rest of his life will be very unhappy, indeed. Does Macbeth fully understand the truth of what he says?

Macbeth says that in his rage for revenge he has killed the guards. Lady Macbeth faints.

MACBETH. O, yet I do repent me of my fury,
That I did kill them.

MACDUFF. Wherefore did you so?

MACBETH. Who can be wise, amaz'd, temp'rate and furious,
Loyal and neutral, in a moment? No man.
Th' expedition of my violent love
Outrun the pauser, reason. Here lay Duncan,
His silver skin lac'd with his golden blood,
And his gash'd stabs look'd like a breach in nature
For ruin's wasteful entrance; there the murderers,
Steep'd in the colours of their trade, their daggers
Unmannerly breech'd with gore. Who could refrain
That had a heart to love, and in that heart
Courage to make's love known?

✱ **LADY MACBETH.** Help me hence, ho!

MACDUFF. Look to the lady.

? Was it necessary for Macbeth to kill the guards? Why or why not?

103 in a moment: all at the same time

104 expedition: haste

107 breach: gap

108 wasteful: destructive

109 Steep'd: soaked

110 Unmannerly breech'd with gore: obscenely clothed in blood

112 make's: make his

? If Lady Macbeth only pretended to faint, why do you think she chose this particular moment?

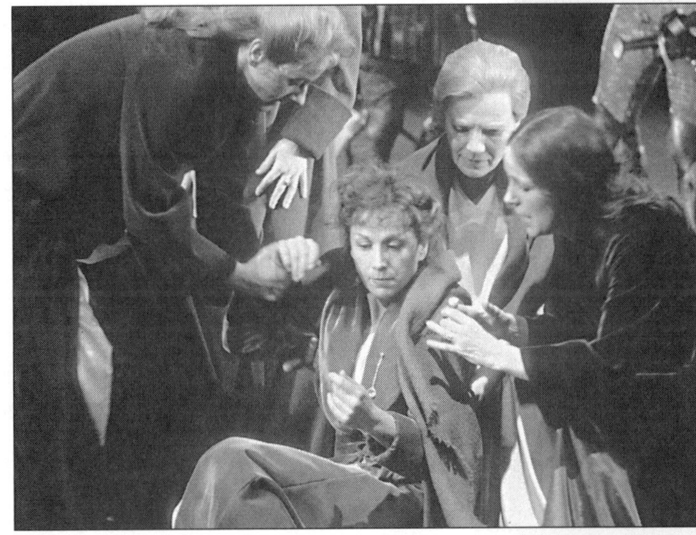

Cheryl Campbell as Lady Macbeth

✱ **Does She or Doesn't She?** "Help me hence, ho!" exclaims Lady Macbeth, and then she faints. Or does she? At this point in the play, she seems stronger than her husband and anything but squeamish. So perhaps her fainting is a sham to persuade her guests of her innocence. On the other hand, perhaps she's not as tough as she seems, and her fainting is genuine—a foreshadowing of her madness later in the play. An actress must decide which way to play this moment.

Malcolm and Donalbain quietly discuss their own safety. Banquo recommends that everyone get dressed and meet to discuss what should be done next. All leave except Malcolm and Donalbain who stay to confer with each other. Malcolm decides to go to England, Donalbain to Ireland.

MALCOLM. *[To* DONALBAIN.*]* Why do we hold our tongues, that most
may claim
This argument for ours?

DONALBAIN. *[To* MALCOLM.*]* What should be spoken
Here, where our fate, hid in an auger hole,
May rush and seize us? Let's away:
Our tears are not yet brew'd.

MALCOLM. Nor our strong sorrow
Upon the foot of motion.

BANQUO. Look to the lady:—

*[*LADY MACBETH *is carried out.]*

And when we have our naked frailties hid,
That suffer in exposure, let us meet,
And question this most bloody piece of work,
To know it further. Fears and scruples shake us.
In the great hand of God I stand, and thence
Against the undivulg'd pretence I fight
Of treasonous malice.

MACDUFF. And so do I.

ALL. So all.

MACBETH. Let's briefly put on manly readiness,
And meet i' th' hall together.

ALL. Well contented.

[Exeunt all but MALCOLM *and* DONALBAIN.*]*

MALCOLM. What will you do? Let's not consort with them.
To show an unfelt sorrow is an office
Which the false man does easy. I'll to England.

114-120 Malcolm wonders why he and Donalbain are silent when Duncan's murder affects them more than anyone else. Donalbain cautions that it is unwise to show tears and emotion here, where the murderer may still be hidden, waiting to harm them. They agree that their deep grief cannot show itself yet.

? Why are Malcolm and Donalbain worried?

PERSONA JOURNAL

You see Lady Macbeth faint and be carried into the castle. In your opinion, did she really faint? Explain.

124 naked frailties hid: get dressed. (They are all still in their nightclothes.)

126 scruples: doubts

127 thence: with His support

129-130 undivulg'd...malice: secret motives of the traitors

131 briefly put...readiness: quickly put on appropriate clothing

PERSONA ACTION

All representatives leave the stage.

133 consort: meet

134 an office: a function

Malcolm and Donalbain quickly and secretly leave the castle.

DONALBAIN. To Ireland, I. Our separated fortune
Shall keep us both the safer. Where we are,
There's daggers in men's smiles. The near in blood,
The nearer bloody.

MALCOLM. This murderous shaft that's shot
Hath not yet lighted, and our safest way
Is to avoid the aim. Therefore to horse,
And let us not be dainty of leave-taking,
But shift away. There's warrant in that theft
Which steals itself when there's no mercy left.

[Exeunt.]

138 The near...bloody: Those closest to Duncan are the most likely to be murdered.

? What does Donalbain mean by "There's daggers in men's smiles"?

142 dainty of: polite in our

143 shift away: leave quickly and quietly

? Do you think Duncan's sons are in danger?

PERSONA ACTION

All clan members move into the courtyard to discuss what has happened and what might happen next. Remember to remain "in persona."

Setting the Scene

MACBETH

Act II, scene iv *or* The King Is Dead, Long Live the King!

Critical Query: Does anyone suspect Macbeth?

Time Capsule: Macbeth's Claim

Why was Macbeth so obsessed with becoming king? It might be that he felt his right to the throne had been stolen from him. Even though Scottish kings did not automatically inherit the throne, lineage and nobility were important factors in their election. As you can see from the family tree on the right, Macbeth had an even stronger claim than Duncan did. Malcolm II had two children. His son, Bethoc, had Duncan, the king in this play. So Duncan's claim to the throne came from being the grandson of Malcolm II. But the family tree shows that Macbeth was also a grandson of Malcolm II. Not only that, he had a second claim through his wife, who was the granddaughter of another high king, Kenneth III.

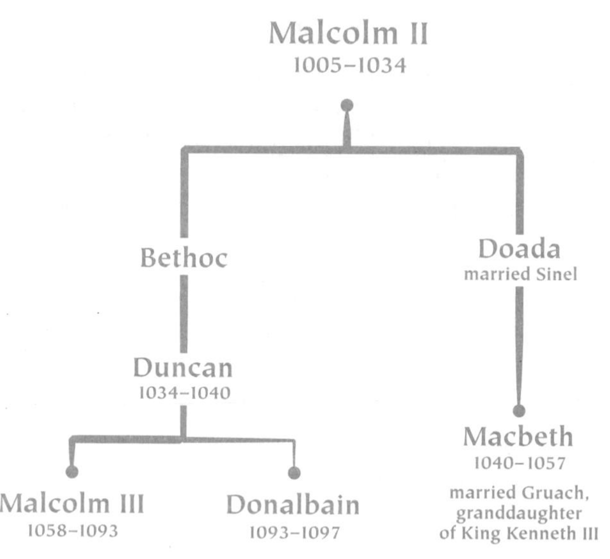

Word Play: Hyperbole

Hyperbole is an exaggeration or overstatement not meant to be taken literally. In the context of the play, do you think Ross and the Old Man in this scene are trying to top each other with exaggerated statements or have they really seen the fantastic things they describe on page 77?

Classroom Set Design

Either keep the courtyard acting space for this brief scene (even though it takes place outside the castle) or use the basic four-clan space as shown in this diagram.

Acting Area

Desk

Warm-up Improv

Several students have cheated on a major exam. Now all students must retake the exam. You think you know who cheated, but you cannot prove it. Discuss this with a friend.

The morning after Duncan's murder, Ross speaks with an old man about the strange, unnatural events of the previous night.

Scene iv. Outside Macbeth's Castle

[Enter ROSS *and an* OLD MAN.*]*

OLD MAN. Threescore and ten I can remember well,
Within the volume of which time I have seen
Hours dreadful and things strange, but this sore night
Hath trifled former knowings.

ROSS. Ah, good father,
✱ Thou seest the heavens, as troubled with man's act,
Threaten his bloody stage. By th' clock, 'tis day,
And yet dark night strangles the travelling lamp.
Is't night's predominance, or the day's shame,
That darkness does the face of earth entomb,
When living light should kiss it?

OLD MAN. 'Tis unnatural,
Even like the deed that's done. On Tuesday last
A falcon, towering in her pride of place,
Was by a mousing owl hawk'd at and kill'd.

ROSS. And Duncan's horses—a thing most strange and certain—
Beauteous and swift, the minions of their race,
Turn'd wild in nature, broke their stalls, flung out,
Contending 'gainst obedience, as they would
Make war with mankind.

OLD MAN. 'Tis said they eat each other.

ROSS. They did so, to th' amazement of mine eyes
That look'd upon't. Here comes the good Macduff.

PERSONA JOURNAL

What strange events did you see or hear during the night?

1 Three score and ten: seventy years

3 sore: painful

4 trifled former knowings: made my earlier experiences seem trivial

6 his bloody stage: this bloody world

7 travelling lamp: the sun

8-9 Is it because night is stronger (**predominance**) than day, or is it because of the day's shame that darkness buries (**entomb**) the face of the earth?

? What "deed" is the old man referring to?

12-13 A falcon, flying (**towering**) at her highest point (**pride of place**), was attacked (**hawk'd at**) and killed by a mouse-hunting (**mousing**) owl.

15 minions: finest

17 as: as if

✱ **A Little Bit of Heaven** When the actor playing Ross spoke of "the heavens" in Shakespeare's original production, he probably pointed to the canopy above the stage, which was painted with the signs of the zodiac (see the theatre diagram on page 182). So when he went on to speak of the "bloody stage," the audience understood him to mean the stage of the Globe Theatre as well as the "stage" of the world.

Macduff joins Ross and explains that although it was Duncan's guards who killed him, they were likely bribed to do so by Malcolm and Donalbain, who have fled. Ross speculates that Macbeth will be crowned king, and Macduff confirms this. Macduff plans to return to Fife. Ross says that he will go to Macbeth's crowning at Scone.

[Enter MACDUFF.*]*

How goes the world, sir, now?

MACDUFF. Why, see you not?

ROSS. Is't known who did this more than bloody deed?

MACDUFF. Those that Macbeth hath slain.

ROSS. Alas the day,
What good could they pretend?

MACDUFF. They were suborn'd.
Malcolm and Donalbain, the King's two sons,
Are stol'n away and fled, which puts upon them
Suspicion of the deed.

ROSS. 'Gainst nature still!
Thriftless ambition, that wilt ravin up
Thine own lives' means! Then 'tis most like
The sovereignty will fall upon Macbeth.

✱ **MACDUFF.** He is already named, and gone to Scone
To be invested.

ROSS. Where is Duncan's body?

MACDUFF. Carried to Colmekill,
The sacred storehouse of his predecessors,
And guardian of their bones.

ROSS. Will you to Scone?

MACDUFF. No, cousin, I'll to Fife.

ROSS. Well, I will thither.

24 What good...pretend?: What benefit could they receive from it?; **suborn'd:** bribed
28 Thriftless ambition... means!: greedy ambition that devours its own parent
30 sovereignty: role of king
31 named: elected; **Scone:** ancient Scottish capital where kings were crowned
32 invested: crowned
33-34 Colmekill: island, now called Iona, where Scottish kings were buried in a crypt **(storehouse)**
36 thither: go to Scone

? Why do you think Macduff does not go to Scone to attend the crowning of Macbeth?

PERSONA JOURNAL

What kind of ruler do you think Macbeth will be?

37

✱ **The Stone of Scone** In the time of *Macbeth*, Scottish kings were crowned in the city of Scone while sitting or standing on the Stone of Destiny, a sandstone rock believed to have been used as a pillow by the biblical patriarch Jacob. This stone was stolen from Scotland by King Edward I around 1300, and for some 700 years was kept under the seat of the coronation throne in London. It was returned to Scotland in 1996, and is now in Edinburgh Castle.

Macduff, Ross, and the old man leave.

MACDUFF. Well, may you see things well done there. Adieu!
Lest our old robes sit easier than our new!

ROSS. Farewell, father.

OLD MAN. God's benison go with you and with those
That would make good of bad, and friends of foes.

[Exeunt.]

Adieu!: Goodbye!

40 benison: blessing

Maurice Evans and Judith Anderson in a 1961 film of *Macbeth* directed by George Schaefer

Reacting to Act II

Analysis

1. Think of a time when you relied on someone who turned out to be untrustworthy. What was your reaction when you found they'd turned against you?
2. Why did Shakespeare begin scene i in Act II with Banquo and Fleance? What purpose did this scene serve dramatically?
3. In Act II, scene ii, Lady Macbeth says, "The attempt and not the deed itself will ruin us." What do you think would happen if the attempt to kill Duncan or the cover-up failed?
4. What went wrong with Lady Macbeth's plan, and how did she fix the situation? Why did she need to correct the error?
5. The killing of King Duncan does not occur onstage. Why do you think Shakespeare choose not to show his death?
6. Do you think Macbeth would have gone ahead with the murder of Duncan if his wife had not encouraged him to do so? Explain your answer.
7. How do Lady Macbeth and Macbeth react differently to the murder of King Duncan?
8. Do you think Macduff believes that Malcolm and Donalbain were responsible for the death of their father? Explain your answer.

Literary Elements

1. Why might **comic relief** such as the Porter scene be found in a tragedy like Macbeth?
2. A **double entendre** is a statement that has two different meanings, one of which is often sexual. Find an example of double entendre in the porter's speeches on pages 67 and 69.
3. **Double entendre** can also be used for darker purposes. What two interpretations can you give to Lady Macbeth's line as she plots the murder of Duncan: "He that's coming/Must be provided for"?
4. **Conflict** is what creates tension and drama in a piece of writing. **External conflict** refers to a struggle between man and an outside force such as nature or another individual. **Internal conflict** refers to a mental struggle within the individual. Find examples of both kinds of conflict in the first two acts.

Writing

1. Some directors have decided to cut the Old Man out of scene iv. As a director, decide whether or not to eliminate this part of the scene and explain your decision in a memo to the producer.
2. Write either a description or a dialogue telling what happened at the meeting where Macbeth was elected to be the new king. Was there dissension? Were other candidates considered?
3. Compose a letter from Malcolm to Donalbain or vice versa after the brothers have escaped to England and Ireland respectively. Utilize the language of Shakespeare in writing the letter.

Macbeth Act III

Orson Welles, as Macbeth, sees Banquo's ghost.
Welles film, 1948

"Thou canst not say I did it; never shake thy gory locks at me!"

Setting the Scene

MACBETH

Act III, scenes i and ii *or* Banquo Must Go

Critical Query: How are the Macbeths enjoying their new status?

Time Capsule: Falconry

"Come, seeling night," says Macbeth at the end of scene ii. This refers to the sport of falconry, in which hawks were trained to hunt. Hawks' eyes were "seeled," or sewn shut, to help tame them. Falconry dates perhaps to the 8th century B.C. It reached the peak of its popularity during Shakespeare's time, and there are several references to it throughout his plays.

From the Prop Box

- 2 Crowns for the Macbeths

Special Effects

- Trumpet fanfare

In Character: Homicide Unit

At the end of scene ii you have a chance to question the two murderers. The actors who played these characters must sit in the hot seat. Feel free to ask them about their backgrounds, what their lives are like, why they agreed to murder Banquo, and what they think the future holds for them.

Classroom Set Design

This design is a variation of the regular four-clan set-up. Desks are pushed together as closely as possible to allow entrance and exit aisles on either side of the room. Two chairs placed in the acting area may be used by either or both of the Macbeths.

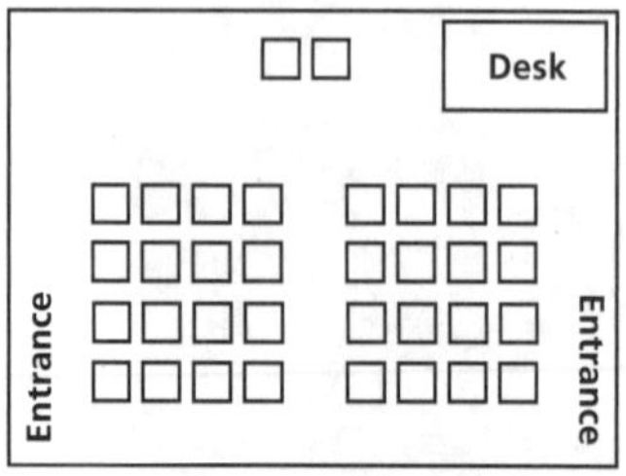

Desk

Entrance

Entrance

Warm-up Improv 1	Warm-up Improv 2
Someone is making moves on your girlfriend/boyfriend. Ask two bullies to "convince" that person to stay away.	(Use after page 90.) You and your spouse won the lottery and life's been nothing but a hassle ever since. You're seriously thinking of giving all the money to charity, but your spouse disagrees.

Banquo fears that Macbeth may have played a part in making himself king. He wonders if the witches' predictions for him will also come true.

ACT III

Scene i. Forres. The Palace

[Enter BANQUO *.]*

* **BANQUO.** Thou hast it now—King, Cawdor, Glamis, all,
As the Weïrd Women promised, and, I fear
Thou play'dst most foully for't. Yet it was said
It should not stand in thy posterity,
But that myself should be the root and father
Of many kings. If there come truth from them
(As upon thee, Macbeth, their speeches shine)
Why, by the verities on thee made good,
May they not be my oracles as well,
And set me up in hope? But hush, no more.

[Sennet sounded. Enter MACBETH, *as King,* LADY MACBETH, *as* QUEEN, LENNOX, ROSS, LORDS, LADIES, *and* ATTENDANTS.*]*

Macbeths entering a hall
Polanski film, 1971

PERSONA JOURNAL

What did you see or hear about Macbeth's coronation ceremony?

PERSONA ACTION

Representatives from all clans except Macduff enter with Macbeth.

4 **It should...posterity:** that the crown would not be passed to your children

? How eager do you think Banquo is to have his sons become kings?

7 **their speeches shine:** their predictions have come true

8-9 **by the verities...well:** Judging by the prophecies that came true for Macbeth, the witches may be predicting the truth about my future as well.

? Does Banquo suspect Macbeth of evil doing?

[*stage directions*] **Sennet:** a trumpet fanfare

* **Banquo—Innocent or Guilty?** According to Shakespeare's source for *Macbeth*, Holinshed's *Chronicles,* Banquo actually took part in the killing of Duncan. Why did Shakespeare portray him as innocent of the deed? Banquo was said to be the direct ancestor of James I, the King of England when *Macbeth* was written. Shakespeare didn't dare portray James' ancestor as a murderous conspirator. (Actually, Banquo was a mythical figure whose story was told so often he became "real.")

Macbeth greets Banquo and insists that he attend a banquet that evening. Banquo replies that he is going riding, but will be back in time for the festivities. Macbeth tells him that Malcolm and Donalbain have not confessed to their father's murder but instead are spreading wild tales.

MACBETH. Here's our chief guest.

LADY MACBETH. If he had been forgotten,
It had been as a gap in our great feast
And all-thing unbecoming.

MACBETH. Tonight we hold a solemn supper, sir,
And I'll request your presence.

BANQUO. Let your highness
Command upon me, to the which my duties
Are with a most indissoluble tie
Forever knit.

MACBETH. Ride you this afternoon?

BANQUO. Ay, my good lord.

MACBETH. We should have else desir'd your good advice,
(Which still hath been both grave and prosperous)
In this day's council, but we'll take tomorrow.
Is't far you ride?

BANQUO. As far, my lord, as will fill up the time
'Twixt this and supper. Go not my horse the better,
I must become a borrower of the night
For a dark hour or twain.

MACBETH. Fail not our feast.

BANQUO. My lord, I will not.

MACBETH. We hear our bloody cousins are bestow'd
In England and in Ireland, not confessing
Their cruel parricide, filling their hearers
With strange invention. But of that tomorrow,

12 It had been as: it would have been like

13 all-thing: totally

14 solemn: formal

16 to the which my duties: your commands are my obligations

18 knit: joined

21 still: always

25-27 Go not...twain: Unless my horse goes faster than usual, I'll still be riding an hour or two after sunset.

? How do the characters on this page feel about each other? As an actor, how will you show these feelings?

29 cousins: Malcolm and Donalbain; **bestow'd:** taken refuge

31 parricide: the killing of a father

31 strange intervention: terrible lies

? What kinds of "lies" might Malcolm and Donalbain be telling?

PERSONA JOURNAL

Do you sympathize with Malcolm and Donalbain? Why or why not?

Macbeth determines that Banquo's son, Fleance, will ride with him. He then orders a servant to bring in two men who have been outside. As he waits, Macbeth expresses concern that the combination of Banquo's integrity and possible suspicions make him dangerous.

When therewithal we shall have cause of state
Craving us jointly. Hie you to horse. Adieu,
Till you return at night. Goes Fleance with you?

BANQUO. Ay, my good lord. Our time does call upon's.

MACBETH. I wish your horses swift and sure of foot;
And so I do commend you to their backs.
Farewell.

[Exit BANQUO.*]*

Let every man be master of his time
Till seven at night. To make society
The sweeter welcome, we will keep ourself
Till suppertime alone. While then, God be with you.

[Exeunt all but MACBETH *and an* ATTENDANT.*]*

Sirrah, a word with you. Attend those men
Our pleasure?

ATTENDANT. They are, my lord, without the palace gate.

MACBETH. Bring them before us.

[Exit ATTENDANT.*]*

To be thus is nothing,
But to be safely thus. Our fears in Banquo
Stick deep, and in his royalty of nature
Reigns that which would be fear'd. 'Tis much he dares;
And to that dauntless temper of his mind
He hath a wisdom that doth guide his valour

33-34 cause of...jointly: official state business that requires both your attention and mine

34 Hie: Hurry.

36 Our time...upon's: It is time that we were on our way.

38 do commend...backs: wish you well on your journey

? Why do you think Macbeth is so interested in the details of Banquo's journey?

PERSONA ACTION

Stuarts leave with Banquo; others leave after line 43.

? Why might Macbeth send everyone away and plan to stay by himself until the banquet?

44 Sirrah: a term used to address someone of inferior social rank

44-45 Attend those...pleasure: Are those men awaiting my orders?

46 without: outside

48 To be thus: to be king

51 to: in addition to; **dauntless:** fearless

PERSONA JOURNAL

What are you doing to prepare for the feast?

Macbeth continues to worry about the prediction that Banquo's sons will become kings. If that happens, Macbeth realizes that his bloody deeds will ultimately have been for Banquo's benefit rather than his own. The servant enters with two men who are, in fact, hired murderers.

To act in safety. There is none but he
Whose being I do fear, and under him,
✱ My genius is rebuked, as it is said
Mark Antony's was by Caesar. He chid the Sisters
When first they put the name of king upon me
And bade them speak to him. Then prophet-like,
They hail'd him father to a line of kings.
Upon my head they placed a fruitless crown
And put a barren scepter in my grip,
Thence to be wrench'd with an unlineal hand,
No son of mine succeeding. If't be so,
For Banquo's issue have I fil'd my mind;
For them the gracious Duncan have I murder'd,
Put rancours in the vessel of my peace
Only for them, and mine eternal jewel
Given to the common enemy of man,
To make them kings, the seed of Banquo kings.
Rather than so, come fate into the list,
And champion me to the utterance.— Who's there?

[Reenter ATTENDANT, *with two* MURDERERS.*]*

Now go to the door, and stay there till we call.

[Exit ATTENDANT.*]*

Was it not yesterday we spoke together?

FIRST MURDERER. It was, so please your Highness.

? Why does Macbeth fear Banquo?

54 under him: next to him

55 genius: spirit; **rebuked:** overwhelmed

56 Caesar Octavius Caesar; **He chid the Sisters:** Banquo scolded the witches

58 bade: ordered

60 fruitless: sterile

? What does Macbeth mean by a "fruitless crown" and "barren scepter"?

62 wrench'd with an unlineal hand: pulled away by someone not of my family

64-71 For Banquo's descendants **(issue)**, I have corrupted **(filed)** myself, murdered Duncan, ruined my peace of mind and given my soul **(eternal jewel)** to the devil **(enemy of man)** all for Banquo's benefit. Rather than this, I'll fight fate to the death **(utterance)**.

✱ **Sheer Genius** When Macbeth says, "My genius is rebuked," he doesn't mean that Banquo has insulted his intelligence. The word "genius" didn't come to signify high mental abilities until some years after *Macbeth* was written. To Shakespeare, the word still referred to a guardian spirit or demon.

Macbeth refers to a conversation he had earlier with the men and asks if they now realize that it is Banquo, not Macbeth, who is to blame for all their troubles.

MACBETH. Well then, now
Have you consider'd of my speeches? Know
That it was he, in the times past, which held you
So under fortune, which you thought had been
Our innocent self. This I made good to you
In our last conference, pass'd in probation with you
How you were borne in hand, how cross'd,
the instruments,
Who wrought with them, and all things else that might
To half a soul and to a notion crazed
Say "Thus did Banquo."

FIRST MURDERER. You made it known to us.

76 he: Banquo

78 made good: proved

79 pass'd in...you: reviewed the evidence with you

80 borne in head: deceived; **cross'd:** double-crossed

81 instruments: legal means

83 To half a soul: even to a half-wit; **a notion crazed:** a mad man

Macbeth speaks to the murderers.
Polanski film, 1971

Macbeth challenges the murderers, asking if they are too cowardly to defend themselves against Banquo's cruel actions. Macbeth claims he has a plan that will help right those wrongs.

MACBETH. I did so, and went further, which is now
Our point of second meeting. Do you find
Your patience so predominant in your nature
✱ That you can let this go? Are you so gospell'd
To pray for this good man and for his issue,
Whose heavy hand hath bow'd you to the grave
And beggar'd yours forever?

FIRST MURDERER. We are men, my liege.

MACBETH. Ay, in the catalogue you go for men,
As hounds and greyhounds, mongrels, spaniels, curs,
Shoughs, water-rugs, and demi-wolves, are clept
All by the name of dogs. The valu'd file
Distinguishes the swift, the slow, the subtle,
The housekeeper, the hunter, every one
According to the gift which bounteous nature
Hath in him clos'd; whereby he does receive
Particular addition, from the bill
That writes them all alike. And so of men.
Now, if you have a station in the file,
Not i' th' worst rank of manhood, say 't;
And I will put that business in your bosoms
Whose execution takes your enemy off,
Grapples you to the heart and love of us,
Who wear our health but sickly in his life,
Which in his death were perfect.

SECOND MURDERER. I am one, my liege,
Whom the vile blows and buffets of the world
Have so incensed that I am reckless what
I do to spite the world.

86 Our point of: the purpose of this

89 issue: children

91 beggar'd yours: impoverished your families; **liege:** Lord

92–108 Yes, in any list (**catalogue**) of humans you would pass for men, just as all the various breeds of dog are still called (**clept**) "dog." But a detailed list (**valued file**) would state the special qualities of each breed. So it is with men. If you have qualities that place you above those at the bottom of the list, I will tell you of a plot that will destroy your enemy and make you much loved by me. My state of mind is fragile while Banquo lives, but would be perfect if he were dead.

? What could have happened to the murderers that would make them so desperate?

✱ **"Are you so gospell'd...?"** Macbeth asks the murderers, "Are you so gospell'd / To pray for this good man...?" The Bible that Shakespeare knew was the Geneva Bible, published in 1560. Here Macbeth refers to Matthew 5:44, which in the Geneva version reads, "Love your enemies: bless them that curse you: do good to them that hate you, and pray for them which hurt you, and persecute you." Macbeth is trying to discourage the murderers from following a Christian example.

Macbeth says that Banquo is his enemy as well, but due to his public office and alliances, he cannot personally take any action. The men agree to murder Banquo and are told to wait for further instructions.

FIRST MURDERER. And I another
So weary with disasters, tugg'd with fortune,
That I would set my life on any chance,
To mend it, or be rid on't.

MACBETH. Both of you
Know Banquo was your enemy.

BOTH MURDERERS. True, my lord.

MACBETH. So is he mine, and in such bloody distance
That every minute of his being thrusts
Against my near'st of life. And though I could
With barefac'd power sweep him from my sight
And bid my will avouch it, yet I must not,
For certain friends that are both his and mine,
Whose loves I may not drop, but wail his fall
Who I myself struck down. And thence it is,
That I to your assistance do make love,
Masking the business from the common eye
For sundry weighty reasons.

SECOND MURDERER. We shall, my lord,
Perform what you command us.

FIRST MURDERER. Though our lives—

MACBETH. Your spirits shine through you. Within this hour at most
I will advise you where to plant yourselves,
Acquaint you with the perfect spy o' th' time,
The moment on't, for't must be done tonight,
And something from the palace; always thought

113 **tugg'd with:** pulled about by

115 **on't:** of it

117 **in such bloody distance:** we are such mortal enemies

119 **my near'st of life:** my heart

121 **bid my will avouch it:** justify it solely because it was my wish

123 **but wail:** but instead I must mourn

? What reasons does Macbeth give for not killing Banquo himself?

125 **to your ... love:** ask you for your help

127 **sundry weight:** various important

129 **spirits:** courage does

131 **the perfect spy o' th' time:** how to do the deed

134 **something from:** at some distance; **always thought:** keep in mind

? Who are the murderers? Are they nobility? Soldiers? Serfs? Choose one possibility and decide how his vocal qualities might differ from other characters.

Macbeth emphasizes that it is just as important to kill Banquo's son, Fleance.

That I require a clearness. And with him—
To leave no rubs nor botches in the work—
Fleance, his son, that keeps him company,
Whose absence is no less material to me
Than is his father's, must embrace the fate
Of that dark hour. Resolve yourselves apart.
I'll come to you anon.

BOTH MURDERERS. We are resolv'd, my lord.

MACBETH. I'll call upon you straight. Abide within.

[Exit MURDERERS.*]*

It is concluded. Banquo, thy soul's flight,
If it find heaven, must find it out tonight.

[Exeunt.]

134 require a clearness: should be kept above suspicion

135 rubs nor botches: flaws or blunders

137 material: important

139 Resolve yourselves apart: decide by yourselves in private

142 straight: immediately

? What do you think the murderers expect to gain from killing Banquo?

PERSONA JOURNAL

Consider what you know and don't know about events involving the nobility of Scotland. If you could, would you change clans and leaders now? Why or why not?

Lady Macbeth wonders if everything she and her husband have done has been worth it, because they are not happy. Macbeth worries that they are not yet safe and that they need peaceful sleep free from nightmares. He says it would be better to be dead with no cares or worries than to live with such torment.

Scene ii. The Palace

[Enter LADY MACBETH *and a* SERVANT.*]*

LADY MACBETH. Is Banquo gone from court?

SERVANT. Ay, madam, but returns again tonight.

LADY MACBETH. Say to the King, I would attend his leisure
For a few words.

SERVANT. Madam, I will.

[Exit.]

LADY MACBETH. Naught's had, all's spent,
Where our desire is got without content.
'Tis safer to be that which we destroy
Than by destruction dwell in doubtful joy.

[Enter MACBETH.*]*

* How now, my lord, why do you keep alone,
Of sorriest fancies your companions making,
Using those thoughts which should indeed have died
With them they think on? Things without all remedy
Should be without regard. What's done is done.

MACBETH. We have scorch'd the snake, not kill'd it.
She'll close and be herself, whilst our poor malice
Remains in danger of her former tooth.
But let the frame of things disjoint, both the worlds suffer,
Ere we will eat our meal in fear, and sleep
In the affliction of these terrible dreams
That shake us nightly. Better be with the dead,
Whom we, to gain our peace, have sent to peace,

PERSONA JOURNAL

How have the Macbeth's been acting lately? Tell what you've seen or heard.

4 Naught's had, all's spent: We've gained nothing, and sacrificed everything.

5 content: happiness

9-11 making terrible thoughts (**sorriest fancies**) that should have died along with those you think about

11 without: beyond

? How does what Lady Macbeth says to herself differ from what she says to her husband?

13 scorch'd: slashed

14 close: heal

14-15 whilst our ... tooth: while our feeble plots (**poor malice**) are still in danger of her poisonous fangs

16-20 better that heaven and earth (**both worlds**) fall apart (**disjoint**) before we eat in fear and sleep with the awful nightmares that terrorize (**shake**) us each night. We'd have more peace if we were dead like those we killed.

* **Marital Problems?** Until this moment, the Macbeths have seemed devoted to each other. But has something gone wrong between them? "How now, my lord," asks Lady Macbeth, "why do you keep alone, / Of sorriest fancies your companions making ... ?" Lady Macbeth is worried that her husband isn't confiding in her as usual. She's also feeling somewhat neglected. All may not be well in the Macbeths' marriage. They will only have one other scene together in the rest of the play.

He agrees to be cheerful at the banquet that evening and then hints at a plan that will solve their problems.

Than on the torture of the mind to lie
In restless ecstasy. Duncan is in his grave.
After life's fitful fever he sleeps well.
Treason has done his worst; nor steel, nor poison,
Malice domestic, foreign levy, nothing,
Can touch him further.

LADY MACBETH. Come on.
Gentle my lord, sleek o'er your rugged looks.
Be bright and jovial among your guests tonight.

MACBETH. So shall I, love, and so, I pray, be you:
Let your remembrance apply to Banquo;
Present him eminence, both with eye and tongue:
Unsafe the while that we
Must lave our honours in these flattering streams,
And make our faces vizards to our hearts,
Disguising what they are.

LADY MACBETH. You must leave this.

✱ **MACBETH.** O, full of scorpions is my mind, dear wife!
Thou know'st that Banquo, and his Fleance lives.

LADY MACBETH. But in them nature's copy's not eterne.

MACBETH. There's comfort yet; they are assailable.
Then be thou jocund. Ere the bat hath flown
His cloister'd flight, ere to black Hecate's summons
The shard-borne beetle with his drowsy hums
Hath rung night's yawning peal, there shall be done
A deed of dreadful note.

LADY MACBETH. What's to be done?

22 In restless ecstasy: in a frenzy of sleeplessness

25 Malice domestic: civil unrest; **levy:** armies

27 Gentle my...looks: My noble Lord, smooth over your furrowed brows.

31 Give (**present**) him special consideration (**eminence**) with both your looks (**eye**) and your conversation (**tongue**).

? Why does Macbeth tell Lady Macbeth to pay extra attention to Banquo at the feast?

32-33 Unsafe the...streams: We are in danger as long as we have to wash our honors in flattery.

34 vizards: masks

38 But in...eterne: But nature hasn't given them a lease on eternal life.

40 jocund: joyful

41 cloistere'd: secluded

42 shard-borne: scaly-winged

43 rung night's yawning peal: announced the coming of sleepy night

✱ **Going Buggy** When Macbeth tells his wife that his mind is "full of scorpions," he may mean it quite literally. According to an old superstition, live scorpions could actually grow inside the brain. This was said to be a consequence of sniffing too much basil.

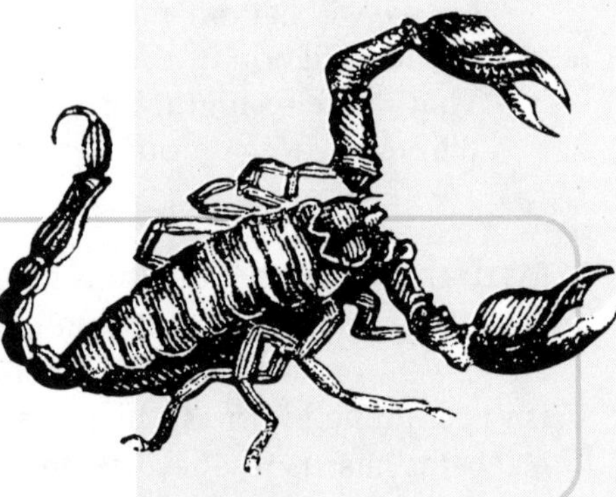

Macbeth thinks it better that Lady Macbeth not know of his plans until after the deed is done. He hopes that he will find peace once Banquo and Fleance are out of the way.

MACBETH. Be innocent of the knowledge, dearest chuck,
Till thou applaud the deed. —Come, seeling night,
Scarf up the tender eye of pitiful day
And with thy bloody and invisible hand
Cancel and tear to pieces that great bond
Which keeps me pale. Light thickens, and the crow
Makes wing to th' rooky wood.
Good things of day begin to droop and drowse,
Whiles night's black agents to their preys do rouse.
Thou marvel'st at my words, but hold thee still.
Things bad begun make strong themselves by ill.
So, prithee, go with me.

[Exeunt.]

45 chuck: chick, a pet name

47 Scarf up: blindfold

50 Light thickens: The day grows dim.

51 rooky: full of rooks or blackbirds

52 droop and drowse: nod and fall asleep

53 to their preys do rouse: awaken to strike their prey

? Why doesn't Macbeth tell Lady Macbeth of his plans to kill Banquo and Fleance?

PERSONA JOURNAL

What have you done in the past when you had to cheer up a depressed relative or friend?

Macbeth Takes Charge A very important change happens in this scene. Until now, Lady Macbeth has had to goad her husband to act. But here, Macbeth not only devises the plan to kill Banquo, he takes care not to tell his wife about it. From this point on, Macbeth will act completely on his own, and Lady Macbeth's role in the tragedy will grow smaller and smaller.

Setting the Scene

MACBETH

Act III, scenes iii and iv *or* A Ghostly Visitor

Critical Query: What is the impact of Banquo's death?

Classroom Set Design

The set consists of a row of chairs upstage against the wall and two "thrones" stage left. An aisle at one side of the room will be used as an entrance and exit for the actors. Scene iii is played on an empty stage, 'tho the chairs and desks could be used as trees. For scene iv, the chairs are pulled forward to become the banquet table.

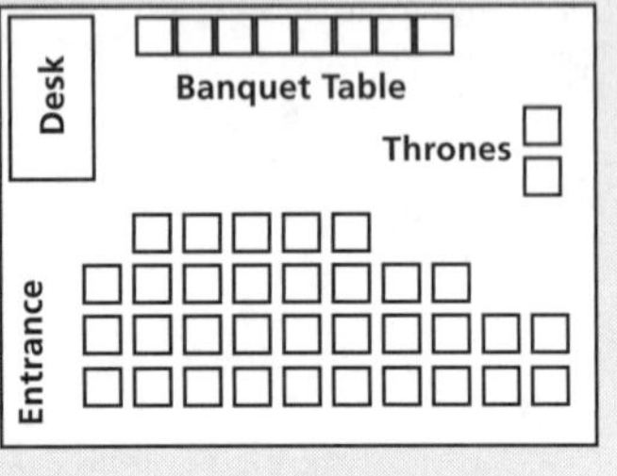

From the Prop Box

- Flashlights to be used as torches
- Goblet for each banquet guest & host
- 2 crowns for Macbeth and Lady Macbeth
- Serving platters for the banquet
- Optional: Bloody rags for Banquo's ghost
- Optional: Blood for murderer's face

Special Effects

- Horse hoofs
- Music

Behind the Scene: Where's Banquo?

Before the start of scene iv, decide whether or not to have an actor play Banquo's ghost. If a real person will be Banquo, determine beforehand how he will "appear" and "disappear" during the scene.

Time Capsule: What's for Dinner?

At an 11th century Scottish banquet, guests we served numerous courses, possibly including r boar smeared with marmalade made from ros hips. Several kinds of porridge might also be p of the fare. The bowls and cups were made fro wood or pottery; nobody used forks or knives. slightly stale loaf of bread might be hollowed to use as a bowl, then eaten after its contents.

Warm-up Improv 1	Warm-up Improv 2
You and your science partner are doing an experiment with two white mice. One escapes. You must find it or risk getting a failing grade and perhaps failing the class.	(Use after page 96.) All the relatives are at the Thanksgiving dinner table. One of them begins acting strangely. All of you try to ignore the outbursts, but finally the host/hostess asks everyone to leave.

It is just past dusk outside a gate leading to the palace. A third murderer has joined the first two. They soon hear Banquo and Fleance approaching.

Scene iii. A Park or Lawn, with a Gate Leading to the Palace

✱ *[Enter three* MURDERERS.*]*

FIRST MURDERER. But who did bid thee join with us?

THIRD MURDERER. Macbeth.

SECOND MURDERER. *[To the* FIRST MURDERER.*]*
He needs not our mistrust, since he delivers
Our offices and what we have to do
To the direction just.

FIRST MURDERER. Then stand with us.—
The west yet glimmers with some streaks of day.
Now spurs the lated traveller apace
To gain the timely inn, and near approaches
The subject of our watch.

THIRD MURDERER. Hark, I hear horses.

BANQUO. *[Within.]* Give us a light there, ho!

SECOND MURDERER. Then 'tis he. The rest
That are within the note of expectation
Already are i' th' court.

FIRST MURDERER. His horses go about.

THIRD MURDERER. Almost a mile; but he does usually,
So all men do, from hence to th' palace gate
Make it their walk.

SECOND MURDERER. A light, a light!

[Enter BANQUO *and* FLEANCE *with a torch.]*

2 He: the third murderer

3 offices: instructions

4 To the direction just: so that we do our job correctly

6–8 Now the traveler rides quickly (**spurs**) to get to the inn before dark and soon, the person (**subject**) we are waiting for will arrive.

9 Give us ...ho!: Banquo is calling to a servant.

10 That are ... expectation: of the other expected guests

11 go about: are taking the long way around

? Read the note at the bottom of the page. As director, if the third murderer in your production is definitely another character in the play, who would it be? Why?

✱ **Three's Company** Why does Shakespeare introduce a third murderer in this scene, when the original two would do the job just as well (or badly)? Critics and scholars have come up with some imaginative answers to this question. In the 18th century, Samuel Johnson said that the third murderer is actually the "perfect spy" mentioned by Macbeth earlier (page 89). In some productions of the play, the third murderer has been the nobleman Ross. In other productions, he has been Macbeth himself in disguise.

THIRD MURDERER. 'Tis he.

FIRST MURDERER. Stand to't.

What happens that allows Fleance to escape from the murderers?

BANQUO. It will be rain tonight.

FIRST MURDERER. Let it come down.

[They set upon BANQUO.*]*

BANQUO. O, treachery! Fly, good Fleance, fly, fly, fly!
Thou mayst revenge— O slave!

[He dies. FLEANCE *escapes.]*

THIRD MURDERER. Who did strike out the light?

FIRST MURDERER. Was't not the way?

THIRD MURDERER. There's but one down. The son is fled.

SECOND MURDERER. We have lost
Best half of our affair.

FIRST MURDERER. Well, let's away, and say how much is done.

[Exeunt.]

Murderers killing Banquo
Polanski film, 1971

The banquet begins; Macbeth circulates, greeting his guests.

Scene iv. A Room of State in the Palace

✱ *[A banquet prepared. Enter* MACBETH, LADY MACBETH, ROSS, LENNOX, LORDS, *and* ATTENDANTS.*]*

MACBETH. You know your own degrees; sit down. At first
And last, the hearty welcome.

LORDS. Thanks to your Majesty.

MACBETH. Ourself will mingle with society
And play the humble host.
Our hostess keeps her state, but in best time
We will require her welcome.

LADY MACBETH. Pronounce it for me, sir, to all our friends;
For my heart speaks they are welcome.

Henry Irving's production of *Macbeth*,
Lyceum Theatre, 1888–9
Victoria and Albert Museum:
The Theatre Museum
from a souvenir program of the production

PERSONA ACTION

Representatives from all clans except Macduff enter the banquet hall laughing and chatting. They quiet down when Macbeth begins to speak and act in pantomime for the rest of the scene.

1 **degrees:** rank, and therefore, where you should sit

3 **Ourself:** I; **society:** our guests

5 **keeps her state:** will remain on her throne; **in best time:** at the proper time

? Why do you think Macbeth circulates among his guests instead of sitting on his throne as Lady Macbeth does?

6 **require:** request

PERSONA JOURNAL

Clan Macduff: How do you feel about the fact that Macduff has chosen not to attend Macbeth's coronation and banquet?

✱ **Fashion Sense** For this royal banquet scene, Shakespeare's original actors would have been dressed in the height of Elizabethan fashion. (They probably made little or no attempt to look like Medieval Highlanders.) Where did they get such elegant clothes? Sometimes servants to aristocrats inherited their employers' clothing, then sold them to theatrical companies.

The first murderer slips into the hall and reports the death of Banquo. Macbeth is upset that Fleance still lives.

[FIRST MURDERER *appears at the door.]*

MACBETH. See, they encounter thee with their hearts' thanks.
Both sides are even. Here I'll sit i' th' midst.
Be large in mirth. Anon we'll drink a measure
The table round.

[Approaching the door.]

✱ There's blood upon thy face.

FIRST MURDERER. 'Tis Banquo's then.

MACBETH. 'Tis better thee without than he within.
Is he dispatched?

FIRST MURDERER. My lord, his throat is cut. That I did for him.

MACBETH. Thou art the best o' th' cutthroats! Yet he's good
That did the like for Fleance. If thou didst it,
thou art the nonpareil.

FIRST MURDERER. Most royal sir,
Fleance is scap'd.

MACBETH. *[Aside]* Then comes my fit again. I had else
been perfect,
Whole as the marble, founded as the rock,
As broad and general as the casing air.
But now I am cabin'd, cribb'd, confined, bound in
To saucy doubts and fears. —But Banquo's safe?

FIRST MURDERER. Ay, my good lord. Safe in a ditch he bides,
With twenty trenchèd gashes on his head,
The least a death to nature.

9 encounter thee: respond to your greeting

11 Enjoy **(mirth)** yourselves fully **(be large)**. Soon **(Anon)** we'll drink a toast **(measure)**.

14 Tis better ... within: It's better that the blood is on your face than in Banquo's body.

? Do the other guests notice the murderer at the door?

19 the nonpareil: without equal

21–22 I had else ... perfect: Except for this, I would feel completely secure.

23 founded: steady

24 As free **(broad)** and open **(general)** as the surrounding **(casing)** air

26 To saucy: with insolent; **safe:** safely dead

27 bides: waits

28 trenchèd: huge, deep

29 The least ... nature: the smallest of which could have killed him.

✱ **"There's blood upon thy face."** A murderer shows up at Macbeth's banquet with blood on his face. This isn't the sort of thing you'd expect to have happen on a rerun of *Columbo* or *Murder, She Wrote*. In a murder story of today, the killer would at least go to the trouble of washing his face before showing up in public. But Shakespeare wasn't nearly as concerned about psychological realism as we are today.

Macbeth consoles himself with the fact that Fleance is not yet a threat. Lady Macbeth reminds him of his duties as host, and Macbeth pretends to fault Banquo for his absence. Banquo's ghost appears and sits in Macbeth's place at the table.

MACBETH. Thanks for that.
There the grown serpent lies. The worm that's fled
Hath nature that in time will venom breed,
No teeth for th' present. Get thee gone. Tomorrow
We'll hear ourselves again.

[Exit MURDERER.*]*

LADY MACBETH. My royal lord,
You do not give the cheer. The feast is sold
That is not often vouch'd, while 'tis a-making,
'Tis given with welcome. To feed were best at home;
From thence, the sauce to meat is ceremony;
Meeting were bare without it.

[Enter the GHOST OF BANQUO *and sits in* MACBETH'S *place.]*

MACBETH. Sweet remembrancer!—
Now, good digestion wait on appetite
And health on both!

LENNOX. May't please your Highness, sit.

MACBETH. Here had we now our country's honour roof'd,
Were the graced person of our Banquo present,
Who may I rather challenge for unkindness
Than pity for mischance.

ROSS. His absence, sir,
Lays blame upon his promise. Please't your Highness
To grace us with your royal company?

MACBETH. The table's full.

LENNOX. Here is a place reserved, sir.

30 worm: small snake (Fleance)

33 hear ourselves: talk

34 cheer: toast

34-38 The feast ... it: A feast is like a paid-for-dinner when the host does not let the guests know how welcome they are. Mere eating can be done at home. When dining out, ceremony is the sauce for every dish; a social occasion is empty without it.

? As director, would you have an actual figure appear or let the ghost be only in Macbeth's imagination?

? If the figure of Banquo's ghost does appear, what would you use for his costume and make-up?

38 Sweet remembrancer!: My Sweet, thank you for reminding me!

39 wait on: follow

41 our country's honour roof'd: all of our country's best men under one roof

43-44 He hopes Banquo's absence is due to mere thoughtlessness and not an accident (**mischance**).

45 Lays blame ... promise: makes one question his promise to be here

Macbeth becomes agitated and shouts at the ghost. Lady Macbeth brushes off the outburst, telling guests that there is no need for alarm. She says Macbeth often has such fits. She then pulls Macbeth aside and demands that he get control of himself.

MACBETH. Where?

LENNOX. Here, my good lord. What is't that moves your
Highness?

MACBETH. Which of you have done this?

LORDS. What, my good lord?

* **MACBETH.** *[To the* GHOST.*]* Thou canst not say I did it,
never shake
Thy gory locks at me.

ROSS. Gentlemen, rise. His Highness is not well.

LADY MACBETH. Sit, worthy friends. My lord is often thus
And hath been from his youth. Pray you, keep seat;
The fit is momentary; upon a thought
He will again be well. If much you note him
You shall offend him and extend his passion.
Feed and regard him not. *[Drawing* MACBETH *aside.]*
Are you a man?

MACBETH. Ay, and a bold one, that dare look on that
Which might appall the devil.

LADY MACBETH. O, proper stuff!
This is the very painting of your fear:
This is the air-drawn dagger which, you said,
Led you to Duncan. O, these flaws and starts,
Impostors to true fear, would well become
A woman's story at a winter's fire,
Authoriz'd by her grandam. Shame itself!
Why do you make such faces? When all's done,
You look but on a stool.

49 moves: disturbs

? As Macbeth, how would you react to the ghost?

54 gory locks: bloody hair

PERSONA JOURNAL

Clan Macbeth servants: What do you think about Macbeth's behavior? Have you ever seen him act this way before?

58 upon a thought: in a moment

59 note: pay attention to

60 extend his passion: make him worse

64 O, proper stuff!: O, how ridiculous!

65 the very ... fear: a figment of your fearful imagination

66 the air-drawn dagger: like the dagger in mid-air

67-70 These outbursts (**flaws and starts**) when compared to real fear, are like an old wife's tale beside a winter fireplace — one passed down from her grandmother (**gramdam**).

* **Critic's Corner** "Thou canst not say I did it," Macbeth exclaims to Banquo's ghost. One critic has suggested that Macbeth has had the "childish notion" that if he didn't commit the murder with his own hands, he wouldn't be haunted by the deed.

Macbeth speaks to Banquo's ghost, but the ghost vanishes. Macbeth tries to explain what he saw to Lady Macbeth, but she chides him again and tells him to take care of his guests. Macbeth makes excuses for his behavior.

MACBETH. Prithee, see there. Behold, look! [*To the* GHOST.] Lo! how say you?
Why, what care I? If thou canst nod, speak too.—
If charnel houses and our graves must send
Those that we bury back, our monuments
Shall be the maws of kites.

[GHOST OF BANQUO *vanishes.*]

LADY MACBETH. What, quite unmann'd in folly?

MACBETH. If I stand here, I saw him.

* **LADY MACBETH.** Fie, for shame!

MACBETH. Blood hath been shed ere now, i' th' olden time,
Ere human statute purged the gentle weal;
Ay, and since too, murders have been perform'd
Too terrible for the ear. The time has been
That, when the brains were out, the man would die,
And there an end. But now they rise again
With twenty mortal murders on their crowns
And push us from our stools. This is more strange
Than such a murder is.

LADY MACBETH. My worthy lord,
Your noble friends do lack you.

MACBETH. I do forget.—
Do not muse at me, my most worthy friends.
I have a strange infirmity, which is nothing
To those that know me. Come, love and health to all.
Then I'll sit down.—Give me some wine. Fill full.

? How could you stage the movement of the ghost to help elicit these words from Macbeth?

76 **charnel houses:** vaults to hold the bones of the dead

77–78 Our graves (**monuments**) shall be the stomachs (**maws**) of birds of prey (**kites**).

78 Has this foolish fear (**folly**) made you a coward (**quite unmann'd**)?

81 Before (**ere**) civilized laws (**human statute**) freed the people (**weal**) of violence and made them gentle

86 **mortal murders:** deadly wounds; **crowns:** heads

89 **lack you:** miss your company

90 **muse:** be amazed

* **Seeing Is Believing** Macbeth obviously sees Banquo's ghost. But does Lady Macbeth, too? The great 18th-century actress Sarah Siddons, who played Lady Macbeth many times, observed, "I have imagined that the last appearance of Banquo's ghost became no less visible to her eyes than it became to those of her husband." She played the scene that way—and critics have been debating her decision ever since.

[Enter GHOST.*]*

I drink to th' general joy o' th' whole table
And to our dear friend Banquo, whom we miss.
Would he were here! To all and him we thirst,
And all to all.

LORDS. Our duties, and the pledge.

MACBETH. Avaunt, and quit my sight! Let the earth hide thee.
Thy bones are marrowless; thy blood is cold;
Thou hast no speculation in those eyes
Which thou dost glare with.

96 thirst: drink

97 And all to all: Let everyone drink to everyone else.

98 Avaunt: Get out. **quit:** leave

100 speculation: perception

PERSONA ACTION

Everyone begins to react to Macbeth's outbursts.

John Gielgud, as Macbeth, sees the ghost of Banquo played by Leon Quartermaine.
Picadilly Theatre, 1942
John Vickers Theatre Collection

Macbeth is tormented by the ghost and continues to shout, claiming that there is nothing else in the world that could frighten him so. He wonders why no one else can see the apparition.

LADY MACBETH. Think of this, good peers,
But as a thing of custom; 'tis no other;
Only it spoils the pleasure of the time.

MACBETH. What man dare, I dare,
Approach thou like the rugged Russian bear,
The arm'd rhinoceros, or th' Hyrcan tiger;
Take any shape but that, and my firm nerves
Shall never tremble. Or be alive again
And dare me to the desert with thy sword.
If trembling I inhabit then, protest me
The baby of a girl. Hence, horrible shadow!
Unreal mock'ry, hence!

*[*GHOST OF BANQUO *vanishes.]*

Why, so, being gone,
I am a man again.— Pray you, sit still.

LADY MACBETH. You have displaced the mirth, broke the good meeting,
With most admired disorder.

MACBETH. Can such things be
And overcome us like a summer's cloud,
Without our special wonder? You make me strange
Even to the disposition that I owe,
When now I think you can behold such sights,
And keep the natural ruby of your cheeks
When mine is blanched with fear.

102 But as...other: but as a recurring condition; it's nothing special

106 Hyrcan: from Hyrcania, an ancient region south of the Caspian Sea where tigers were reported to be fierce.

107 that: of Banquo's

110–111 If I tremble then, you can call (**protest**) me a weak baby.

112 mock'ry: illusion; **hence!:** go away

118 admired: amazing

118–122 Can things like this happen without one being amazed (**special wonder**)? It makes me uncertain (**strange**) of what kind (**disposition**) of man I am when I think that you can see such things without turning pale (**blanched**) as I do.

? How is Lady Macbeth reacting to her husband's swings between sanity and madness?

TALES FROM THE STAGE

Most actors play Macbeth as deeply terrified of Banquo's ghost. For example, Charles Laughton scampered up a flight of stairs to get away from it! But not Laurence Olivier in a 1955 production of the play. When Banquo appeared the second time, Olivier leaped up on the banquet table, drew his sword, and lunged at the ghost defiantly. Critics were impressed by this startling interpretation.

Lady Macbeth sends the guests away, and a shaken Macbeth continues to speak of the ghost.

ROSS. What sights, my lord?

LADY MACBETH. I pray you, speak not. He grows worse and worse.
Question enrages him. At once, good night.
Stand not upon the order of your going,
But go at once.

LENNOX. Good night, and better health
Attend his Majesty.

LADY MACBETH. A kind good night to all.

[Exeunt all but MACBETH *and* LADY MACBETH.*]*

MACBETH. It will have blood, they say; blood will have blood.
Stones have been known to move, and trees to speak;
Augures and understood relations have
By maggot pies and choughs and rooks brought forth
The secret'st man of blood. —What is the night?

LADY MACBETH. Almost at odds with morning, which is which.

Peter O'Toole as Macbeth, 1980, Old Vic production, Peter Hirst photographer

125 Stand not...going: Don't bother taking the time to leave in order of your rank.

PERSONA ACTION

Those in the banquet hall rise to leave. In place, all clans discuss what they've seen and heard.

130-132 Soothsayers (**Augures**) have studied the flights of magpies (**maggot pies**), crows (**choughs**), and rooks to reveal (**brought forth**) even the best-concealed murderer (**man of blood**).

132 What is the night?: What time is it?

PERSONA JOURNAL

Have you or anyone you know had spells or fits like Macbeth's?

Macbeth wonders why Macduff has not attended the banquet and reveals that he has a spy in every household. He resolves to visit the witches for clarification of their prophesies.

✱ **MACBETH.** How say'st thou, that Macduff denies his person
At our great bidding?

LADY MACBETH. Did you send to him, sir?

MACBETH. I hear it by the way; but I will send.
There's not a one of them but in his house
I keep a servant fee'd. I will tomorrow,
And betimes I will, to the Weïrd Sisters.
More shall they speak, for now I am bent to know
By the worst means the worst. For mine own good,
All causes shall give way. I am in blood
Stepp'd in so far that, should I wade no more,
Returning were as tedious as go o'er.
Strange things I have in head, that will to hand,
Which must be acted ere they may be scann'd.

LADY MACBETH. You lack the season of all natures, sleep.

MACBETH. Come, we'll to sleep. My strange and self-abuse
Is the initiate fear that wants hard use.
We are yet but young in deed.

[Exeunt.]

134-135 How say'st...bidding?: What do you think about the fact that Macduff refuses to join us?

136-138 I've just heard his absence talked about informally (**by the way**), but I will send for information. There's not one lord's house where I don't have a paid (**fee'd**) servant to spy for me.

139 betimes: early

140 bent: determined

142-146 Nothing will stand in my way. I have waded (**stepp'd**) so far in blood that it's just as easy to go forward (**o'er**) as it is to go back. I have strange plans that demand to be completed and I need to do them before I think too much about them.

? What does Macbeth want to ask the witches?

147 season: refreshment

148 strange and self-abuse: remarkable self-delusion

149-150 It is the fear of a beginner (**initiate**) who does not have (**wants**) the experience that hardens one (**hard use**). We are still new (**young in deed**) at this.

✱ **Bad Blood** "How say'st thou," asks Macbeth, "that Macduff denies his person/ At our great bidding?" This is an early hint of trouble between Macbeth and Macduff. In Shakespeare's historical source, Raphael Holinshed's *Chronicles,* King Macbeth built himself a great castle, ordering all his thanes to take turns helping with its construction. When Macduff's turn came, he sent builders but didn't show up at the site himself. Macbeth took offense, and the Macbeth-Macduff feud was underway.

Setting the Scene

MACBETH

Act III, scenes v and vi *or* Discontent Grows

Critical Query: How is Scotland reacting to Macbeth's rule?

Behind the Scene: Which Witch Sings?

In this scene the witches are asked to dance and sing "Come Away," which is an actual song written by Thomas Middleton (See page 107). Here are some of the lyrics for those who plan to enhance their performance with song.

Witches Come away, come away,
Hecate, Hecate, come away!
Hec. I come, I come, I come,
With all the speed I may,
With all the speed I may
(*A spirit like a cat descends*)
Voice. There's one comes down to
fetch his dues,
A kiss, a coll, a sip of blood;
And why thou stay'st so long,
I muse, I muse,
Since the air's too sweet and good.
Hec. O, art thou come?
What news, what news?
Spirit. All goes still to our delight:
Either come, or else
Refuse, refuse.

Time Capsule: Shakespeare the Collaborator

Traditionally, critics have regarded the Hecate scenes, such as scene v, as an unfortunate addition to the play written by someone else. But in his 1995 book *Witches and Jesuits,* the Pulitzer Prize-winning historian Garry Wills argues differently. The Hecate scenes seem to have been added before 1613, while Shakespeare was still with his theatrical company, the King's Men. According to Wills, this means that Shakespeare must have approved of these revisions, even if he didn't write them himself.

Special Effects

- Thunder
- Music and song

Classroom Set Design

The basic four-clan design will work for both scenes v and vi.

Desk

Acting Area

Warm-up Improv 1	Warm-up Improv 2
Your mom's mad because you and your brother were supposed to clean up your rooms before going out. See if you can sweet-talk her into a good mood.	(Use after page 108.) Someone you work with comes in late, leaves early, and always blames someone else for his/her mistakes. Let this person know he'll/she'll be out of a job if this behavior continues.

The three witches meet Hecate, their superior. She scolds them for meddling in Macbeth's fate without consulting her. They agree to meet Macbeth the next day.

Scene v. A Heath

✱ *[Thunder. Enter the three* WITCHES *meeting* HECATE.*]*

FIRST WITCH. Why, how now, Hecate? You look angerly.

HECATE. Have I not reason, beldams as you are,
Saucy and overbold? How did you dare
To trade and traffic with Macbeth
In riddles and affairs of death,
And I, the mistress of your charms,
The close contriver of all harms,
Was never call'd to bear my part
Or show the glory of our art?
And which is worse, all you have done
Hath been but for a wayward son,
Spiteful and wrathful, who, as others do,
Loves for his own ends, not for you.
But make amends now. Get you gone,
And at the pit of Acheron
Meet me i' th' morning. Thither he
Will come to know his destiny.
Your vessels and your spells provide,
Your charms and everything beside.
I am for th' air. This night I'll spend
Unto a dismal and a fatal end.
Great business must be wrought ere noon.
Upon the corner of the moon
There hangs a vap'rous drop profound.
I'll catch it ere it come to ground,
And that, distill'd by magic sleights,
Shall raise such artificial sprites

2 beldams: hags

7 close: secret; **harms:** evil-deeds

11 wayward son: irresponsible man

13 Loves: works only

? Why is Hecate angry with the witches?

15 Acheron: in Greek mythology, Acheron is a river in the under-world.

20 I am for th' air: I must fly away

24 vap'rous drop profound: a useful drop of moisture

26 sleights: powers

27 artificial sprites: unnatural spirits

✱ **Who Wrote This Scene?** Critics generally agree that Shakespeare did not write this scene, nor Hecate's later appearance in *Macbeth*. So who *did* write these passages? The "song within" mentioned in a stage direction toward the end of this scene might be a clue. The complete text of "Come Away, Come Away" is found in *The Witch*, a play by Shakespeare's colleague Thomas Middleton. Critics suspect that Middleton wrote this scene, and also Hecate's appearance in Act IV.

As they depart, the witches gloat over how they will trick Macbeth into thinking he is secure.

As by the strength of their illusion
Shall draw him on to his confusion.
He shall spurn fate, scorn death, and bear
His hopes 'bove wisdom, grace and fear.
And you all know, security
Is mortals' chiefest enemy.

[Music and a song within: "Come Away, Come Away," etc.]

✱ Hark! I am call'd. My little spirit, see,
Sits in a foggy cloud and stays for me.

*[*HECTATE *exits.]*

FIRST WITCH. Come, let's make haste. She'll soon be back again.

[Exeunt.]

29 confusion: destruction

31 grace: virtue

32 security: overconfidence

PERSONA JOURNAL

Have you or anyone you know ever sought the witches' help or been bothered by them?

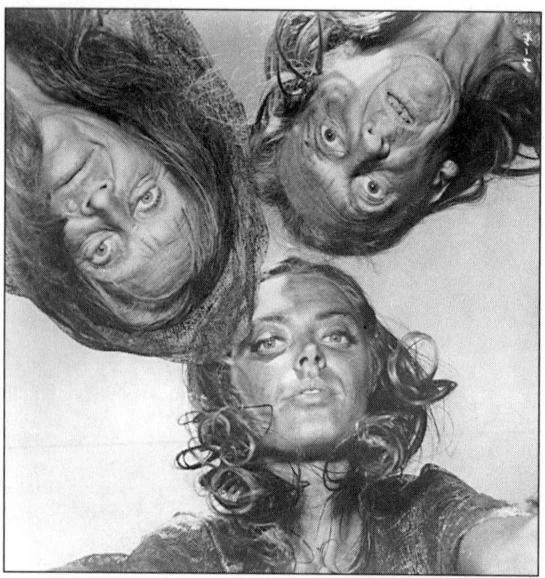

April Olrich, Valerie Taylor, Anita Sharp-Bolster, as the three witches in a 1960 film of *Macbeth*

✱ **Special Effects** Hecate says that her "little spirit" sits waiting for her "in a foggy cloud...." This suggests that she makes an airborne exit to meet her spirit. Originally, Hecate probably was hauled aloft by pulleys in a cloud-shaped wagon. Keep in mind that this sensational stage effect (like the scene itself) was probably not Shakespeare's idea.

Lennox cautiously discusses Macbeth's possible involvement with the deaths of Duncan, Banquo, and the guards. He suggests that Malcolm, Donalbain, and Fleance might also be in danger and notes that Macduff is in disfavor for not attending the banquet.

✱ Scene vi. Forres. A Room in the Palace

[Enter LENNOX *and another* LORD.*]*

LENNOX. My former speeches have but hit your thoughts,
Which can interpret farther. Only I say
Things have been strangely borne. The gracious Duncan
Was pitied of Macbeth; marry, he was dead.
And the right valiant Banquo walk'd too late,
Whom, you may say, if't please you, Fleance kill'd,
For Fleance fled. Men must not walk too late.
Who cannot want the thought, how monstrous
It was for Malcolm and for Donalbain
To kill their gracious father? Damnèd fact!
How it did grieve Macbeth! Did he not straight
In pious rage the two delinquents tear
That were the slaves of drink and thralls of sleep?
Was not that nobly done? Ay, and wisely, too,
For 'twould have anger'd any heart alive
To hear the men deny't. So that I say
He has borne all things well. And I do think
That had he Duncan's sons under his key—
As, an't please heaven, he shall not—they should find
What 'twere to kill a father. So should Fleance.
But, peace. For from broad words and 'cause he fail'd
His presence at the tyrant's feast, I hear
Macduff lives in disgrace. Sir, can you tell
Where he bestows himself?

1-2 hit...farther: echoed what you have been thinking, and you can draw your own conclusions

3 borne: managed (by Macbeth)

4 of: by; **marry:** rightly so

5 walk'd: stayed out

8 want the thought: help thinking

11 straight: immediately

12 delinquents: referring to Duncan's guards; **tear:** kill

13 Who were in a drunken stupor (**slaves of drink**) and enslaved (**thralls**) by sleep

17 He has borne: Macbeth has managed

? Do you think Lennox is being sarcastic here?

19 an't: if it

20 'twere: happens to those who

21-22 because of his unguarded speaking and because he didn't appear at Macbeth's feast

24 bestows himself: has taken refuge

? What do you think Macduff has been saying?

✱ **Out of Order** Critics have pointed out that this scene seems to fall in the wrong place in the play. Chronologically, it should go after Act IV, scene i—and probably did in Shakespeare's original version. But when Act III, scene iv was added, this scene was moved earlier to keep two witch scenes from taking place one after another.

Malcolm has been well received in England, and Macduff has gone to join him in order to raise an army to overthrow Macbeth. Macbeth has heard of this plot and is preparing for war.

LORD. The son of Duncan,
From whom this tyrant holds the due of birth,
Lives in the English court and is received
Of the most pious Edward with such grace
That the malevolence of fortune nothing
Takes from his high respect. Thither Macduff
Is gone to pray the holy king upon his aid
To wake Northumberland and warlike Siward
That, by the help of these—with Him above
To ratify the work—we may again
Give to our tables meat, sleep to our nights,
Free from our feasts and banquets bloody knives,

24 son of Duncan: Malcolm

25 from whom this tyrant withholds (**holds**) his birthright (**due of birth**)

27 Of: by; **Edward:** Edward the Confessor, King of England from 1042-1066

28-29 In spite of Malcolm's bad luck (**malevolence of fortune**) the king still (**nothing takes**) has great respect for him.

30 pray: humbly ask; **upon his aid:** to help him

31 Siward: Earl of Northumberland

33 ratify: bless

? From this unnamed lord's speech, what can you conclude about life in Scotland under Macbeth's rule?

Robert Taber as Macduff, Lyceum Theatre, London 1898

Lennox and another lord discuss the fact that Macduff has refused to support Macbeth. They believe that Macduff is in danger.

Do faithful homage, and receive free honours,
All which we pine for now. And this report
Hath so exasperate the King that he
Prepares for some attempt of war.

LENNOX. Sent he to Macduff?

LORD. He did, and with an absolute 'Sir, not I,'
The cloudy messenger turns me his back
And hums, as who should say 'You'll rue the time
That clogs me with this answer.'

LENNOX. And that well might
Advise him to a caution t' hold what distance
His wisdom can provide. Some holy angel
Fly to the court of England and unfold
His message ere he come, that a swift blessing
May soon return to this our suffering country
Under a hand accurs'd.

LORD. I'll send my prayers with him.

[Exeunt.]

41 cloudy: unhappy

42 hums: mutters

42-43 "You'll regret burdening me with such an answer."

44 him to a caution: Macduff to be careful

46 unfold: reveal

Reacting to Act III

Analysis

1. From the point of view of one of their servants, describe how Macbeth's and Lady Macbeth's behavior has changed since they have become King and Queen.
2. Why isn't Macbeth enjoying being King?
3. How does Macbeth manage to talk the murderers into killing Banquo?
4. How do you think Macbeth treats the murderers when next they meet? Will he continue to have them do his dirty work, or will he consider them a "problem"?
5. What does Macbeth mean when he says, "Blood will have blood" on page 104?
6. Do you think scene vi is important to the play? Why or why not?

Literary Elements

1. Review Hecate's speech on pages 107-108 and compare its **verse structure** to other speeches in the play. Why do you think critics are so sure that someone other than Shakespeare wrote this speech?
2. The **climax** or **turning point** in a play is the event that begins a downward spiral of action that leads to a tragic conclusion. Some readers think that Fleance's escape is the turning point in *Macbeth.* Do you agree, or do you think the climax will occur later in the play? Defend your answer.

Writing

1. Your persona attended the coronation of Macbeth at Scone. Write a diary entry describing the ceremony and the events that occurred. Utilize the language of Shakespeare in writing the diary entry.
2. From the point of view of one of Macbeth's spies in the castles of the Scottish Thanes, write an account of any activities in the household that you think Macbeth would want to know about. Utilize the language of Shakespeare in writing the report to Macbeth.
3. Having attended the banquet where Macbeth has his "fit," write a letter to someone who was not there. In the letter, describe what happened, how you and everyone else reacted to the events of that evening, and what various people said after you left the banquet hall.
4. From what you know about Lady Macbeth so far, make a list of her character traits. Then, list the proof from the text that supports each trait. Finally, write a description of Lady Macbeth based on the first three acts. Use a graphic organizer like the one below to organize your thoughts.

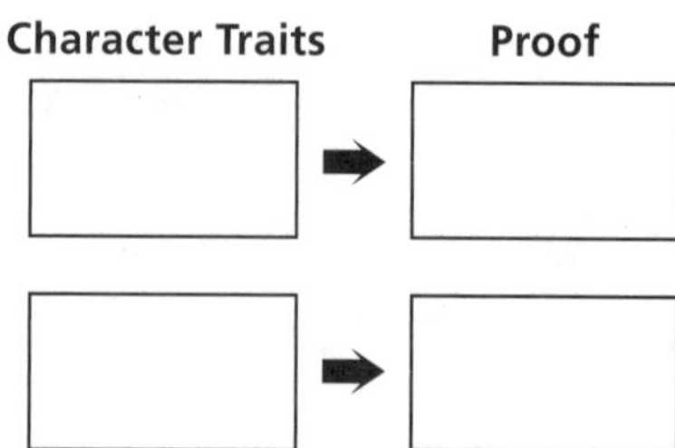

Macbeth Act IV

The Three Witches from *Macbeth*, Alexandre-Marie Colin, 1827

"By the pricking of my thumbs, Something wicked this way comes."

Setting the Scene

MACBETH

Act IV, scene i *or* The Future Foretold

Critical Query: What does Macbeth's future hold?

Special Effects

(Skim pages 118-122 of the following scene. Then brainstorm ways of creating the apparitions.)

- Thunder
- Music & song
- Knocking
- Music of oboes
- 1st apparition – Helmeted head
- 2nd apparition – Bloody child
- 3rd apparition – Crowned child with branch in hand
- Banquo's ghost with kings

Classroom Set Design

Use the standard four-clan seating. The acting area will have a semicircle of desks indicating the witches' dwelling. A wastebasket in the center can serve as a cauldron.

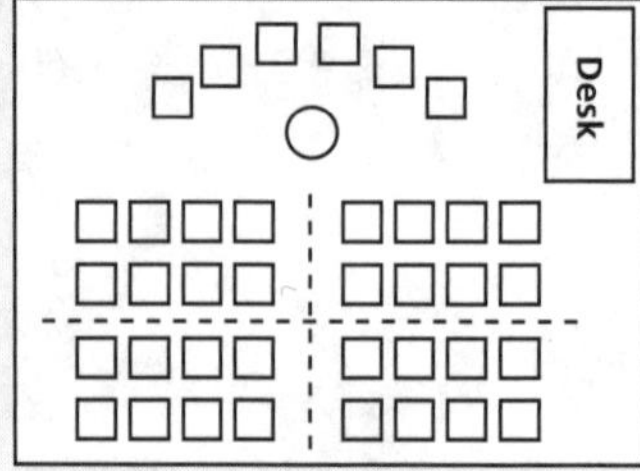

From the Prop Box

- Cauldron (wastebasket)
- Ingredients for the witches' brew
- Hand mirror for Banquo's ghost
- Crowns for Macbeth and apparitions

Famous Quotes from Scene ii

- Double, double, toil and trouble
- Something wicked this way comes

Behind the Scene: Return of the Dancing Witches

As in Act III, the witches perform another dance and song by Thomas Middleton. Here are some of the lyrics.

Hec. Black spirits and white, red spirits and gray,
Mingle, mingle, mingle, you that mingle may!
Round, around, around, about about!
All ill come running in, all good keep out!

Warm-up Improv

You do not want to tell your friend the truth about his/her date for this weekend. Find a way to avoid the truth without being too obvious when your friend asks you.

The three witches have gathered around a boiling cauldron and are casting a spell.

ACT IV

Scene i. A Dark Place. In the Middle a Cauldron Boils

[*Thunder. Enter the three* WITCHES.]

FIRST WITCH. Thrice the brinded cat hath mew'd.

SECOND WITCH. Thrice, and once the hedge-pig whined.

THIRD WITCH. Harpier cries ''Tis time,'tis time!'

FIRST WITCH. Round about the cauldron go;
In the poison'd entrails throw.
Toad, that under cold stone
Days and nights has thirty-one
✱ Swelter'd venom sleeping got,
Boil thou first i' th' charmèd pot.

ALL. Double, double toil and trouble;
Fire burn, and cauldron bubble.

SECOND WITCH. Fillet of a fenny snake
In the cauldron boil and bake.
Eye of newt and toe of frog,
Wool of bat and tongue of dog,
Adder's fork and blindworm's sting,
Lizard's leg and howlet's wing,
For a charm of powerful trouble,
Like a hell-broth boil and bubble.

ALL. Double, double toil and trouble;
Fire burn and cauldron bubble.

1 **brinded:** striped

2 **hedge-pig:** hedgehog

3 **Harpier:** the familiar of the third witch

12 **Fillet:** slice; **fenny:** living in a bog or swamp

16 **Adder's fork:** snake's forked tongue; **blindworm:** harmless, legless lizard, thought to be poisonous in Elizabethan times

17 **howlet:** small owl

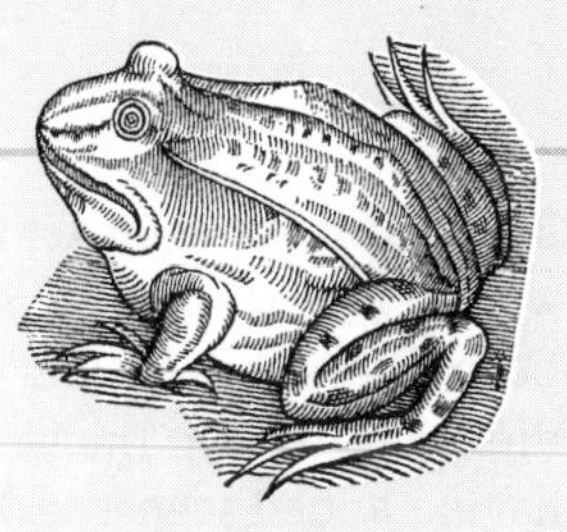

✱ **Secret Ingredient** The first Witch puts the "swelter'd venom" of a toad into cauldron. Toads actually do secrete a venom from their skin, which they use to protect themselves from animal predators. This venom can paralyze and even kill some animals. It's not very harmful to humans, although it can irritate the eyes and tongue.

Hecate and three additional witches enter. All of them sing and dance as they continue to work their magic. Hecate and the second group of witches leave.

THIRD WITCH. Scale of dragon, tooth of wolf,
Witch's mummy, maw and gulf
Of the ravin'd salt-sea shark,
Root of hemlock digg'd i' th' dark,
Liver of blaspheming Jew,
Gall of goat and slips of yew
Silver'd in the moon's eclipse,
Nose of Turk and Tartar's lips,
Finger of birth-strangled babe
Ditch-deliver'd by a drab,
Make the gruel thick and slab.
Add thereto a tiger's chaudron
For th' ingredients of our cauldron.

ALL. Double, double toil and trouble;
Fire burn, and cauldron bubble.

SECOND WITCH. Cool it with a baboon's blood.
Then the charm is firm and good.

✱ *[Enter* HECATE *and three other* WITCHES.*]*

HECATE. O well done! I commend your pains,
And every one shall share i' th' gains.
And now about the cauldron sing
Like elves and fairies in a ring,
Enchanting all that you put in.

[Music and a song: "Black Spirits," etc.]

*[*HECATE *and the second group of* WITCHES *exit.]*

23 Witch's mummy: mummified human flesh; **maw and gulf:** stomach and throat

24 ravin'd: ravenous

25 hemlock: a poisonous herb

26 blaspheming: god-insulting

27 yew: poisonous evergreen

30 birth-strangled: killed at birth

31 drab: prostitute

32 gruel: soup; **slab:** sticky or thick

33 chaudron: stomach

? As director, what would you do about the witches' dance and song? Would they be elaborate or simple?

✱ **Black Spirits** As in Act III, scene v, Hecate's appearance here was probably not written by Shakespeare. Again, Thomas Middleton may have been the culprit behind these crude lines of verse. The song "Black Spirits" referred to in the stage directions is from Thomas Middleton's play *The Witch*—which is one reason scholars suspect Middleton of having added scenes to *Macbeth*.

The second witch senses the arrival of Macbeth. Macbeth demands that the witches answer his questions. They ask if he prefers answers from them or from their masters.

SECOND WITCH. By the pricking of my thumbs,
Something wicked this way comes.
Open, locks,
Whoever knocks.

✱ *[Enter* MACBETH.*]*

MACBETH. How now, you secret, black, and midnight hags?
What is 't you do?

ALL. A deed without a name.

MACBETH. I conjure you by that which you profess
Howe'er you come to know it, answer me.
Though you untie the winds and let them fight
Against the churches, though the yeasty waves
Confound and swallow navigation up,
Though bladed corn be lodg'd and trees blown down,
Though castles topple on their warders' heads,
Though palaces and pyramids do slope
Their heads to their foundations, though the treasure
Of nature's germens tumble all together
Even till destruction sicken, answer me
To what I ask you.

FIRST WITCH. Speak.

SECOND WITCH. Demand.

THIRD WITCH. We'll answer.

FIRST WITCH. Say, if th' hadst rather hear it from our mouths,
Or from our masters'.

53 yeasty: foamy

54 Confound: destroy; **navigation:** ships

55 lodg'd: flattened

56 warders': watchmen's

59 nature's germens: the seeds from which all life grows

60 sicken: becomes sick of its own work

? How has Macbeth's attitude toward the witches changed since their earlier meeting?

✱ TALES FROM THE STAGE

As Macbeth, the actor John Wilkes Booth made a spectacular entrance in this scene. He leaped off a 12-foot platform onto the stage amid the witches. The athletic Booth never injured himself doing this stunt. On April 14, 1865, during a performance of a play at Ford's Theatre in Washington, Booth fatally shot Abraham Lincoln in the president's box. Booth then leaped from the box to the stage—but this time, he broke his leg.

BOSTON MUSEUM

ACTING AND STAGE MANAGER.......................Mr E. F. KEACH

SECOND WEEK OF

J. WILKES

BOOTH

IN VIEW OF THE CONTINUED RUSH TO WITNESS THE EFFORTS OF THE YOUNG AMERICAN TRAGEDIAN, APPLICATIONS FOR RESERVED SEATS WILL STILL BE RECEIVED ANY NUMBER OF DAYS IN ADVANCE.

Mr. Booth will appear, this Evening, in Shakspere's Great Dramatic Creation,

MACBETH!

It being his first assumption of that Character in Boston.

Lady Macbeth.......................Kate Reignolds
Macduff.......................Mr. Wm. Whalley

THE CAPITAL FARCE,

POODLE VS. ST. BERNARD!

Timothy Poodle.......................Mr. W. Warren

On Monday Evening, Jan. 26th, 1863,

The Performance will commence with the Overture, "Angel of Midnight," [illegible]

Leader and Musical Director, JULIUS EICHBERG.

After which, the Celebrated Tragedy, in 5 acts, entitled

Macbeth theatre bill from Bollinger Lincoln Collection, University of Iowa

Macbeth asks to hear from their masters. The witches call forth the first apparition—a helmeted head. Macbeth begins to speak, but is cautioned to be silent.

MACBETH. Call 'em. Let me see 'em.

FIRST WITCH. Pour in sow's blood that hath eaten
Her nine farrow; grease that's sweaten
From the murderer's gibbet throw
Into the flame.

ALL. Come high or low;
Thyself and office deftly show!

[Thunder. FIRST APPARITION: *an armed* HEAD.*]*

MACBETH. Tell me, thou unknown power—

FIRST WITCH. He knows thy thought.
Hear his speech, but say thou nought.

65 farrows: piglets; **sweaten:** sweated

66 gibbet: gallows

68 Show yourselves and skillfully (**deftly**) display your function (**office**).

[*stage directions*] armed head: head in a helmet

? What might the helmeted head represent?

75 harp'd: guessed

Edmund Dulac's *Poster for Macbeth*, 1911
His Majesty's Theatre

The first apparition warns Macbeth to beware of Macduff. The second apparition, a bloody child, tells Macbeth that no man born of woman can harm him. A third apparition appears as a crowned child with a tree branch in its hand.

FIRST APPARITION. Macbeth! Macbeth! Macbeth!
Beware Macduff;
Beware the Thane of Fife. Dismiss me. Enough.

[Descends.]

MACBETH. Whate'er thou art, for thy good caution, thanks.
Thou hast harp'd my fear aright. But one
word more—

FIRST WITCH. He will not be commanded. Here's another
More potent than the first.

[Thunder. SECOND APPARITION*: A bloody* CHILD.*]*

SECOND APPARITION. Macbeth! Macbeth! Macbeth!—

MACBETH. Had I three ears, I'd hear thee.

SECOND APPARITION. Be bloody, bold, and resolute. Laugh
to scorn
The power of man, for none of woman born
Shall harm Macbeth.

[Descends.]

MACBETH. Then live, Macduff: what need I fear of thee?
But yet I'll make assurance double sure
And take a bond of fate. Thou shalt not live,
That I may tell pale-hearted fear it lies,
And sleep in spite of thunder.

[Thunder. THIRD APPARITION: *a* CHILD *crowned, with a tree in his hand]*

What is this
That rises like the issue of a king,

82-83 How might Macbeth be hurt if "no man of woman born" can harm him?

86 take a bond of fate: guarantee

87 tell...lies: tell my fears that they are false

89 like the issue of a king: looking like a king's son

Why do you think Macbeth decides to kill Macduff even though the apparition says he has nothing to fear?

The third apparition tells Macbeth that he will never be conquered until the trees in Birnam forest march the twelve miles to Dunsinane Hill. Macbeth is relieved by the predictions, which seem to guarantee him safety and long life. Yet, he has one more question. He demands to know if Banquo's descendants will ever rule Scotland.

And wears upon his baby brow the round
And top of sovereignty?

ALL. Listen but speak not to't

THIRD APPARITION. Be lion-mettled, proud, and take no care
Who chafes, who frets, or where conspirers are.
Macbeth shall never vanquish'd be until
Great Birnam Wood to high Dunsinane Hill
Shall come against him.

[Descends.]

MACBETH. That will never be.
Who can impress the forest, bid the tree
Unfix his earthbound root? Sweet bodements, good!
Rise never, rebellious dead, till the wood
Of Birnam rise, and our high-placed Macbeth
Shall live the lease of nature, pay his breath
To time and mortal custom. Yet my heart
Throbs to know one thing. Tell me, if your art
Can tell so much: shall Banquo's issue ever
Reign in this kingdom?

ALL. Seek to know no more.

MACBETH. I will be satisfied. Deny me this,
And an eternal curse fall on you! Let me know!

[Cauldron sinks. Hautboys.]

✱ Why sinks that cauldron? And what noise is this?

90-91 round/And top: crown

92 lion-mettled: fierce as a lion

93 chafes: becomes angry

97 impress: compel

98 his: its; **bodements:** prophecies

99 rebellious: perhaps referring to Banquo's ghost

101 live the lease of nature: live out his natural life

102 mortal custom: customary death

? What is Macbeth's mood after hearing from the first three apparitions?

✱ **Special Effects** The cauldron used by the witches was lowered through a trapdoor in the center of the stage to give the sinking effect called for in the stage directions. The space below the trapdoor was known as "Hell" because ghosts and other supernatural beings waited there before rising up to make their appearance on stage. (See the theatre diagram on page 182.)

The witches call forth the last apparition — a line of eight kings followed by the ghost of Banquo, who indicates that the kings are his descendants. The last king has a mirror in his hand that signifies many more kings to come.

FIRST WITCH. Show!

SECOND WITCH. Show!

THIRD WITCH. Show!

ALL. Show his eyes and grieve his heart.
Come like shadows; so depart.

✱ *[A show of* EIGHT KINGS, *the last with a glass in his hand;* GHOST OF BANQUO *following.]*

? What might the witches be doing during the parade of ghostly kings?

Scene from *Macbeth and the Witches*, by Cattermole, The Folger Shakespeare Library, Washington, D.C.

✱ **Parade of Kings** *Macbeth* was written during the reign of King James I and possibly played for him in a royal performance. In this play, Shakespeare went to unusual lengths to flatter the monarch. For example, James considered himself a direct descendant of the mythical Banquo. So the parade of kings across the stage consists of James' Scottish ancestors. Some scholars have suggested that the "glass" (mirror) carried by the last king actually showed King James' reflection as he sat in the audience.

Macbeth is infuriated by this last display and demands to know if it is really true. The witches affirm the vision. They begin to sing and dance once more and then vanish. Macbeth is shaken and calls Lennox who has been waiting for him.

MACBETH. Thou art too like the spirit of Banquo. Down!
Thy crown does sear mine eyeballs. And thy hair,
Thou other gold-bound brow, is like the first.
A third is like the former. —Filthy hags,
Why do you show me this? —A fourth! Start, eyes!
What, will the line stretch out to th' crack of doom?
Another yet? A seventh! I'll see no more.
And yet the eighth appears, who bears a glass
Which shows me many more, and some I see
* That twofold balls and treble scepters carry.
Horrible sight! Now, I see,'tis true,
For the blood-bolter'd Banquo smiles upon me
And points at them for his.

*[*APPARITIONS *vanish.]*

What, is this so?

FIRST WITCH. Ay, sir, all this is so. But why
Stands Macbeth thus amazedly?
Come, sisters, cheer we up his sprites
And show the best of our delights.
I'll charm the air to give a sound
While you perform your antic round,
That this great king may kindly say,
Our duties did his welcome pay.

[Music. The WITCHES *dance and then vanish.]*

MACBETH. Where are they? Gone? Let this pernicious hour
Stand aye accursèd in the calendar!
Come in, without there.

115 sear: burn

116 other: second

118 Start: fall from their sockets

119 th' crack of doom: the thunder crash of Judgment Day

121 glass: mirror

125 blood-bolter'd: blood splattered

126 his: his descendants

? How does Macbeth's mental state change as each image appears?

128 amazedly: in a trance

129 sprites: spirits

132 antic round: strange dance

135 pernicious: evil

136 aye: forever

137 without there: you, out there!

* **That twofold ... carry:** The balls are usually taken to refer to the double coronation of James I in Scotland and in England. The treble scepters refer to the two used in the English coronation and the one used in the Scottish coronation. The passage is clearly a tribute to James I and the union of Great Britain under him.

Lennox tells Macbeth that Macduff has fled to England. Macbeth makes plans to attack Macduff's castle and kill anyone related to him.

[Enter LENNOX.*]*

LENNOX. What's your Grace's will?

MACBETH. Saw you the Weïrd Sisters?

LENNOX. No, my lord.

MACBETH. Came they not by you?

LENNOX. No, indeed, my lord.

MACBETH. Infected be the air whereon they ride,
And damn'd all those that trust them! I did hear
The galloping of horse. Who was't came by?

LENNOX. 'Tis two or three, my lord, that bring you word
Macduff is fled to England.

MACBETH. Fled to England?

LENNOX. Ay, my good lord.

MACBETH. *[Aside.]* Time, thou anticipat'st my dread exploits:
The flighty purpose never is o'ertook
Unless the deed go with it. From this moment
The very firstlings of my heart shall be
The firstlings of my hand. And even now,
To crown my thoughts with acts, be it thought and done:
The castle of Macduff I will surprise,
Seize upon Fife; give to th' edge o' th' sword
His wife, his babes, and all unfortunate souls
That trace him in his line. No boasting like a fool:
This deed I'll do before this purpose cool.
But no more sights!—Where are these gentlemen?
Come, bring me where they are.

[Exeunt.]

PERSONA JOURNAL

What kind of person is Lennox? Tell what you know about him. Where do his loyalties lie?

146–148 Time, thou...it: Time, you foresee (**anticipat'st**) my dreadful (**dread**) deeds (**exploits**). A quickly conceived plan (**flighty purpose**) is never fulfilled (**o'ertook**) unless the deed follows right after the thought.

149 firstlings: firstborn

155 trace him in his line: are his descendants

? What does Macbeth say about his future thoughts and actions?

? How has Macbeth's ability to commit murder changed since the death of Duncan?

TALES FROM THE STAGE

Macbeth!—The Musical

The 17th-century poet and playwright Sir William Davenant claimed to be Shakespeare's son out of wedlock. So he felt fully qualified to revise Shakespeare's plays, including *Macbeth*. Davenant's 1672 version cut out the Porter's scene from Act II and the doctor from Act IV. Along with deletions, there were additions. He had Lady Macbeth and Lady Macduff meet for a chat and expanded the role of Macduff, eventually having the witches take his side against Macbeth. Davenant's version of *Macbeth* added so many songs and dances that it was described as an opera containing elaborate sets, lavish costumes, and spectacular stage effects.

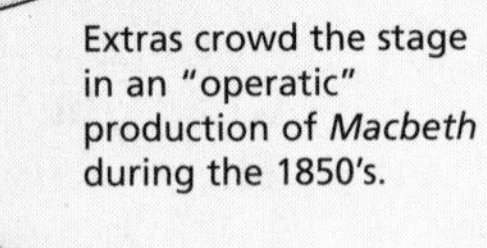

Extras crowd the stage in an "operatic" production of *Macbeth* during the 1850's.

The witches actually flew on broomsticks, and Hecate descended from the sky on a cloud! In his memoirs published in 1708, company prompter John Downes recalled the details of this profitable production:

"*The Tragedy of Macbeth,* altered by Sir William Davenant, being dressed all in its Finery, as new Clothes, new Scenes, Machines, as flyings for the Witches; with all the Singing and Dancing in it: The first Composed by Mr. Locke, the other by Mr. Channel and Mr. Priest; it being all Excellently performed, being in the nature of an Opera, it Recompensed double the Expense; it proves still a lasting Play."

MACBETH,
A
TRAGEDY:
With all the
ALTERATIONS,
AMENDMENTS,
ADDITIONS,
AND
NEW SONGS.

As it is now Acted at the Dukes Theatre.

LONDON:
Printed for *A. Clark*, and are to be sold by most Booksellers, 1674.

Title page of Davenant's adaptation of *Macbeth*, 1674

Sir William Davenant

For many years, Davenant's version of *Macbeth* was the only one produced, and Shakespeare's original was all but forgotten.

Setting the Scene

MACBETH

Act IV, scene ii or Macduff's Punishment

Critical Query: Is this slaughter necessary?

Word Play: Extended Metaphor

A **metaphor** makes a direct comparison between two unlike things that nevertheless have something in common. An **extended metaphor** continues the comparison for some length and in various ways. Read the upcoming scene and look for the extended metaphors based on flight and birds.

From the Prop Box

- Swords (plastic or foam)
- Daggers (plastic or foam)

Classroom Set Design

Use the basic four-clan set with a chair in the acting area for Lady Macduff.

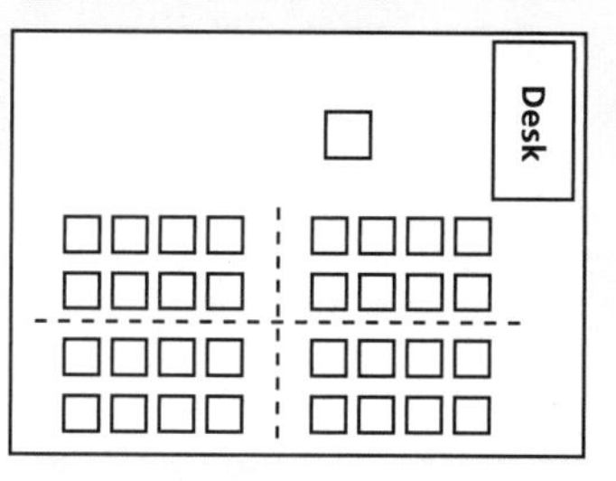

Behind the Scene: Doubling

Shakespeare's company was fairly small, so roles were often "doubled" in his original productions—meaning that a single actor played more than one part. At least one scholar has suggested that the young male actor who played Lady Macbeth also played Lady Macduff.

Warm-up Improv

Your father has been accused of taking a bribe. He is out-of-the-country for three weeks. You don't believe it is true. Defend him to a neighbor.

At Macduff's castle, Lady Macduff learns from Ross that her husband has gone to England. She is angry that he would abandon her and their children. Ross tries to calm her and assures her that Macduff is wise and knows what is best.

Scene ii. A Room in Macduff's Castle

[Enter LADY MACDUFF, *her* SON, *and* ROSS.*]*

LADY MACDUFF. What had he done, to make him fly the land?

ROSS. You must have patience, madam.

LADY MACDUFF. He had none.
His flight was madness. When our actions do not,
Our fears do make us traitors.

ROSS. You know not
Whether it was his wisdom or his fear.

LADY MACDUFF. Wisdom? To leave his wife, to leave his babes,
His mansion and his titles in a place
From whence himself does fly? He loves us not;
He wants the natural touch; for the poor wren,
The most diminutive of birds, will fight,
Her young ones in her nest, against the owl.
All is the fear and nothing is the love;
As little is the wisdom, where the flight
So runs against all reason.

ROSS. My dearest coz,
I pray you, school yourself. But for your husband,
He is noble, wise, judicious, and best knows
The fits o' th' season. I dare not speak much further;
But cruel are the times when we are traitors
✱ And do not know ourselves; when we hold rumour
From what we fear, yet know not what we fear,

PERSONA ACTION

Representatives of the Macduff clan are in the room as the scene opens. They watch and respond appropriately as events unfold.

4 Our fears...traitors: Macduff's fear made him flee Scotland for the English court, thus making him seem like a traitor.

7 his titles: hereditary possessions
9 He wants...touch: lacks the normal protective instincts
11 Her young...nest: when her young are in the nest
14 coz: cousin
15 school: control; **for:** as for
17 The fits o' th' season: how the wind is blowing
18-19 we are...ourselves: we are judged traitors while being unaware of our treason

19-20 hold rumour/From what we fear: believe rumors because we are afraid

PERSONA JOURNAL

What is your reaction to the news that Macduff has gone to England?

✱ **The Rumor Mill** In March, 1606, word spread through England that King James had been assassinated with "an envenomed knife." Considerable panic arose from this false rumor. Ross may be referring to this recent event when he says, "we hold rumour / From what we fear, yet know not what we fear ..."

Ross leaves. Lady Macduff and her son begin to talk about their situation.

But float upon a wild and violent sea
Each way and move.—I take my leave of you.
Shall not be long but I'll be here again.
Things at the worst will cease or else climb upward
To what they were before.—My pretty cousin,
Blessing upon you.

LADY MACDUFF. Father'd he is, and yet he's fatherless.

ROSS. I am so much a fool, should I stay longer
It would be my disgrace and your discomfort.
I take my leave at once.

[Exit.]

LADY MACDUFF. Sirrah, your father's dead.
And what will you do now? How will you live?

SON. As birds do, mother.

LADY MACDUFF. What, with worms and flies?

SON. With what I get, I mean; and so do they.

✱ **LADY MACDUFF.** Poor bird, thou'dst never fear the net nor lime,
The pitfall nor the gin.

SON. Why should I, mother? Poor birds they are not set for.
My father is not dead, for all your saying.

LADY MACDUFF. Yes, he is dead. How wilt thou do for a father?

SON. Nay, how will you do for a husband?

LADY MACDUFF. Why, I can buy me twenty at any market.

SON. Then you'll buy 'em to sell again.

PERSONA JOURNAL

What kind of person is Ross? Where do his loyalties lie?

29 It: my tears. (Apparently, Ross is close to tears.)

PERSONA JOURNAL

Macduff clan: What do you think of the Macduffs and their children? Tell about an encounter you've had with one of them.

35 pitfall: trap; **gin:** snare

36 Poor birds … for: People do not set traps for ordinary birds.

38 How wilt thou do: What will you do?

? Why does Lady Macduff say her husband is dead?

✱ **Bird Bait** By "lime," Lady Macduff means birdlime, a sticky substance spread on branches to catch birds. It is usually made from holly bark.

Macduff's son asks if his father is a traitor. Lady Macduff replies that anyone who swears an oath and breaks it is a traitor and deserves to die. Her son questions this logic and asks whether or not his father is truly dead.

LADY MACDUFF. Thou speak'st with all thy wit,
And yet, i' faith, with wit enough for thee.

SON. Was my father a traitor, mother?

LADY MACDUFF. Ay, that he was.

SON. What is a traitor?

LADY MACDUFF. Why, one that swears and lies.

SON. And be all traitors that do so?

LADY MACDUFF. Every one that does so is a traitor and must be hanged.

✱ **SON.** And must they all be hanged that swear and lie?

LADY MACDUFF. Every one.

SON. Who must hang them?

LADY MACDUFF. Why, the honest men.

SON. Then the liars and swearers are fools, for there are liars and swearers enow to beat the honest men and hang up them.

LADY MACDUFF. Now, God help thee, poor monkey!
But how wilt thou do for a father?

SON. If he were dead, you'd weep for him. If you would not, it were a good sign that I should quickly have a new father.

LADY MACDUFF. Poor prattler, how thou talk'st!

[Enter a MESSENGER.*]*

? What is the tone of the conversation between Lady Macduff and her son? From what you can tell, what kind of relationship do they have?

42 wit: intelligence

43 for thee: for a child

47 swears and lies: makes a promise and breaks it

? Why is Macduff's son so sure that his father is not dead?

56 enow: enough

Father Henry Garnet

✱ **Liar, Liar** "And must they all be hanged that swear and lie?" asks Lady Macduff's son. This is probably a reference to Father Henry Garnet, the alleged mastermind of the Gunpowder Plot to overthrow the British government (See page 7.) Because Garnet argued that Catholics needed not tell the truth under oath, he was also probably the "equivocator" ridiculed by the Porter in Act II, scene iii.

A messenger warns Lady Macduff that she and her children are in danger and must flee immediately. Lady Macduff is questioning the need to run just as murderers enter the room.

MESSENGER. Bless you, fair dame. I am not to you known,
Though in your state of honour I am perfect.
I doubt some danger does approach you nearly:
If you will take a homely man's advice,
Be not found here. Hence with your little ones!
To fright you thus methinks I am too savage;
To do worse to you were fell cruelty,
Which is too nigh your person. Heaven preserve you!
I dare abide no longer.

[Exit.]

LADY MACDUFF. Whither should I fly?
I have done no harm. But I remember now
I am in this earthly world; where to do harm
Is often laudable, to do good sometime
Accounted dangerous folly. Why then, alas,
Do I put up that womanly defense,
To say I have done no harm?

[Enter MURDERERS.*]*

What are these faces?

FIRST MURDERER. Where is your husband?

LADY MACDUFF. I hope, in no place so unsanctified

65 Though in...perfect: though I am fully aware of your honorable rank

66 doubt: fear; **nearly:** very soon

67 homely: plain or humble

70–71 To do...person: But it would be an even greater cruelty not to warn you of the terrible danger which is already near.

? Some readers have suggested that Lady Macbeth might have sent or might actually *be* the messenger. What is your opinion of these interpretations?

72 whither: where

75 laudable: praiseworthy

? How will Lady Macduff and her son react when they see the murderers?

80 unsanctified: godless

PERSONA JOURNAL

Macduff clan: From what you can tell, who is the messenger; who are the murderers?

Lady Macduff and child.
The Granger Collection

Macduff's son defends his father's reputation and is killed. Lady Macduff flees, followed by the murderers.

Where such as thou may'st find him.

FIRST MURDERER. He's a traitor.

SON. Thou liest, thou shag-hair'd villain!

FIRST MURDERER. What, you egg?

[Stabbing him.]

Young fry of treachery!

SON. He has kill'd me, mother:
Run away, I pray you!

[Dies.]

[Exit LADY MACDUFF, *crying "Murder!"]*

[Exeunt MURDERERS, *following her.]*

82 egg: brat

83 fry: spawn

PERSONA ACTION

Macduff representatives scatter as the murderers enter.

PERSONA JOURNAL

Macduff clan: What did you do as the murderers began their rampage? Did anything happen to you or others that you know?

PERSONA JOURNAL

All clans except Macduff: What have you heard about the murders at Macduff's castle?

Setting the Scene

MACBETH

Act IV, scene iii *or* Who Do You Trust?

Critical Query: Is Malcolm the right man for the job?

Behind the Scene

So how do you really feel about Malcolm? At the end of this scene the actor playing Malcolm gets to sit in the hot seat and answer questions about his ability to be king and lead an army against Macbeth. Imagine that you are his potential subjects. What do you want to know before you give him your support? What do you think about the way he treats Macduff in this scene?

In Character: Things Are Tough for Macduff

Macduff takes an emotional roller coaster ride through this scene, beginning with Malcolm's distrust in him and ending with tragic news about his family. Plot his emotions on a graph like the one below using line numbers to indicate mood changes from high to low.

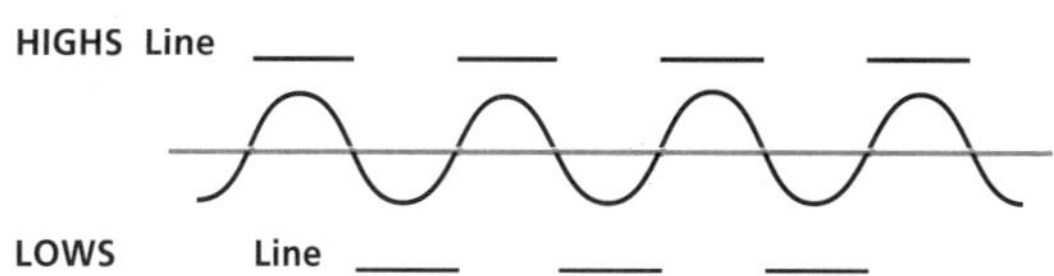

Acting Area

Desk

Classroom Set Design

Use the standard four-clan arrangement.

Warm-up Improv 1	Warm-up Improv 2
Many employees at a fast-food restaurant have complained about their boss. The company has sent someone to calm things down. Improvise the meeting between this person and the employees.	You were supposed to be watching your little sister, but she tripped and fell down some stairs while you were on the phone with a friend. She needed several stitches and may have a permanent scar on her face. Talk this over with your parents.

In England, Macduff describes to Malcolm the terrible state of affairs in Scotland and urges him to take action against Macbeth. Malcolm does not fully trust Macduff and questions his loyalty.

Scene iii. England. Before the King's Palace

[Enter MALCOLM *and* MACDUFF.*]*

✱ **MALCOLM.** Let us seek out some desolate shade and there
Weep our sad bosoms empty.

MACDUFF. Let us rather
Hold fast the mortal sword and, like good men,
Bestride our downfall'n birthdom: Each new morn
New widows howl, new orphans cry, new sorrows
Strike heaven on the face, that it resounds
As if it felt with Scotland, and yell'd out
Like syllable of dolour.

MALCOLM. What I believe, I'll wail;
What know, believe; and what I can redress,
As I shall find the time to friend, I will.
What you have spoke, it may be so, perchance.
This tyrant, whose sole name blisters our tongues,
Was once thought honest: you have loved him well.
He hath not touch'd you yet. I am young, but something
You may deserve of him through me, and wisdom
To offer up a weak, poor, innocent lamb
T' appease an angry god.

MACDUFF. I am not treacherous.

MALCOLM. But Macbeth is.
A good and virtuous nature may recoil
In an imperial charge. But I shall crave your pardon.
That which you are, my thoughts cannot transpose:

PERSONA ACTION

Representatives from Canmore and Macduff clans enter as this scene begins. They listen and react appropriately to all that happens.

3 mortal: deadly

4 Bestride our...birthdom: stand guard over our fallen native country

6 that: so that

8 syllable of dolour: sounds of grief

9 redress: put right

10 As I...friend: when the time is right

12 sole: mere

14 touch'd: hurt

14-15 something...me: You might betray me to win back Macbeth's favor.

15 deserve: gain; **and wisdom:** you may think it wise

19-20 recoil /In...charge: give in under pressure from a king

21 That which...transpose: Whatever your nature is cannot be changed by what I think of you.

✱ **A Little Ray of Sunshine?** "Let us seek out some desolate shade," Malcolm suggests to Macduff. Does this mean that the sun is shining in this scene? If so, this is a rare moment of light in a play otherwise filled with darkness. Perhaps Shakespeare is suggesting a contrast between England under the kindly rule of King Edward, and Scotland under the evil rule of Macbeth. Remember that in Scotland, the sun cannot be seen, for "dark night strangles the travelling lamp" (page 77).

Angels are bright still, though the brightest fell.
Though all things foul would wear the brows of grace,
Yet grace must still look so.

MACDUFF. I have lost my hopes.

MALCOLM. Perchance even there where I did find my doubts.
Why in that rawness left you wife and child,
Those precious motives, those strong knots of love,
Without leave-taking? I pray you,
Let not my jealousies be your dishonours,
But mine own safeties. You may be rightly just,
Whatever I shall think.

MACDUFF. Bleed, bleed, poor country!
Great tyranny, lay thou thy basis sure,
For goodness dare not check thee. Wear thou thy wrongs;
The title is affeer'd.— Fare thee well, lord.
I would not be the villain that thou think'st
For the whole space that's in the tyrant's grasp,
And the rich East to boot.

MALCOLM. Be not offended:
I speak not as in absolute fear of you.
I think our country sinks beneath the yoke.
It weeps, it bleeds, and each new day a gash
Is added to her wounds. I think withal
There would be hands uplifted in my right;
And here from gracious England have I offer
Of goodly thousands. But, for all this,
When I shall tread upon the tyrant's head
Or wear it on my sword, yet my poor country

22 the brightest: reference to Lucifer

23-24 Though all evil **(foul)** things would like to look virtuous **(wear the bows of grace)**, only virtue can look like virtue.

26 rawness: vulnerable position

27 motives: reasons for living

28 leave-taking: even saying goodbye

? What reasons does Malcolm give for not trusting Macduff?

29-30 Don't let my suspicions **(jealousies)** seem like reflections on your honor **(dishonours)**, but take them only as precautions that I must use for my own safety.

32 basis sure: secure foundation

33 check: restrain; **Wear thou thy wrongs:** Display your crimes openly.

34 Your crown **(title)** is legally confirmed **(affeer'd)**.

38 absolute fear: complete mistrust

43 gracious England: the gracious King of England

44 for all this: in spite of this

Surprisingly, Malcolm states that even with all his evils, Macbeth may be a better ruler than he, Malcolm, would be. Malcolm then confides that he possesses the vice of lust and that no woman in Scotland would be safe under his rule. Macduff is taken aback, but says that surely Malcolm's needs could be met discreetly.

Shall have more vices than it had before,
More suffer, and more sundry ways than ever,
By him that shall succeed.

MACDUFF. What should he be?

MALCOLM. It is myself I mean, in whom I know
All the particulars of vice so grafted
That, when they shall be open'd, black Macbeth
Will seem as pure as snow, and the poor state
Esteem him as a lamb, being compared
With my confineless harms.

MACDUFF. Not in the legions
Of horrid hell can come a devil more damn'd
In evils to top Macbeth.

MALCOLM. I grant him bloody,
Luxurious, avaricious, false, deceitful,
Sudden, malicious, smacking of every sin
That has a name. But there's no bottom, none,
In my voluptuousness. Your wives, your daughters,
Your matrons, and your maids, could not fill up
The cistern of my lust, and my desire
All continent impediments would o'erbear
That did oppose my will. Better Macbeth
Than such an one to reign.

MACDUFF. Boundless intemperance
In nature is a tyranny. It hath been
Th' untimely emptying of the happy throne
And fall of many kings. But fear not yet
To take upon you what is yours. You may
Convey your pleasures in a spacious plenty

49 shall succeed. What...be?: shall be Macbeth's successor. How can anyone be worse than Macbeth?

51 particulars: various kinds; **grafted:** implanted

55 confineless: limitless

58 Luxurious: lustful; **avaricious:** greedy

59 Sudden: violent

61 voluptuousness: lust

63 cistern: vessel or container

64 continent impediments: restraining limits

? How does Macduff react to Malcolm's description of his lust?

66 Boundless intemperance: unlimited lust

68 untimely emptying: premature loss

71 secretly fulfill **(convey)** your needs **(pleasures)** abundantly **(spacious plenty)**

Malcolm continues with a list of all his vices and says they would be uncontrollable if he were king.

And yet seem cold— the time you may so hoodwink.
We have willing dames enough. There cannot be
That vulture in you, to devour so many
As will to greatness dedicate themselves,
Finding it so inclined.

MALCOLM. With this there grows
In my most ill-compos'd affection such
A stanchless avarice that, were I king,
I should cut off the nobles for their lands,
Desire his jewels and this other's house;
And my more-having would be as a sauce
To make me hunger more, that I should forge
Quarrels unjust against the good and loyal,
Destroying them for wealth.

MACDUFF. This avarice
Sticks deeper, grows with more pernicious root
Than summer-seeming lust, and it hath been
The sword of our slain kings. Yet do not fear.
Scotland hath foisons to fill up your will
Of your mere own. All these are portable,
With other graces weigh'd.

✱ **MALCOLM.** But I have none. The king-becoming graces,
As justice, verity, temp'rance, stableness,
Bounty, perseverance, mercy, lowliness,
Devotion, patience, courage, fortitude,
I have no relish of them but abound
In the division of each several crime,
Acting it many ways. Nay, had I power, I should
Pour the sweet milk of concord into hell,

72 cold: chaste; **time:** people; **hoodwink:** fool

75 dedicate: offer up

77 ill-composed affection: unbalanced character

78 stanchless avarice: insatiable greed

82 forge: create

? What are the vices Malcolm claims to have? How would he deliver these lines?

86 summer-seeming: only appropriate in the summer of life and therefore of short duration; **it:** greed

87 sword: killer

88 foisons: plentiful resources

89 Of your mere own: entirely from your royal properties alone; **these:** vices; **portable:** bearable

90 With other graces weigh'd: balanced against your other virtues

92 As: Such as

95 relish of: taste for

96 division: different forms; **several:** distinct

98 concord: harmony

✱ **Kingly Graces** The dialogue in which Malcolm accuses himself of horrible vices is very close to Shakespeare's historical source, Holinshed's *Chronicles*. Some critics consider this passage dull and tedious, and it is often cut from productions. Others consider it crucial to the play's concept of what makes a good king—for here Malcolm lists the kingly graces even as he denies having them: "justice, verity, temp'rance, stableness, / Bounty, perseverance, mercy, lowliness, / Devotion, patience, courage, fortitude ..."

Macduff laments the state of his poor country with neither Macbeth nor Malcolm fit to rule. Malcolm then reveals that his self-incrimination was only a test of Macduff's honor and loyalty. He asks for Macduff's guidance and retracts the things he said about himself.

Uproar the universal peace, confound
All unity on earth.

MACDUFF. O Scotland, Scotland!

MALCOLM. If such a one be fit to govern, speak.
I am as I have spoken.

MACDUFF. Fit to govern?
No, not to live.— O nation miserable,
With an untitled tyrant bloody-scepter'd,
When shalt thou see thy wholesome days again,
Since that the truest issue of thy throne
By his own interdiction stands accurs'd,
And does blaspheme his breed? —Thy royal father
Was a most sainted king. The queen that bore thee,
Oft'ner upon her knees than on her feet,
Died every day she lived. Fare thee well.
These evils thou repeat'st upon thyself
Have banished me from Scotland.—O my breast,
Thy hope ends here!

MALCOLM. Macduff, this noble passion,
Child of integrity, hath from my soul
Wiped the black scruples, reconcil'd my thoughts
To thy good truth and honour. Devilish Macbeth
By many of these trains hath sought to win me
Into his power, and modest wisdom plucks me
From over-credulous haste. But God above
Deal between thee and me, for even now
I put myself to thy direction and
Unspeak mine own detraction, here abjure
* The taints and blames I laid upon myself

99 **confound:** destroy

104 **untitled:** illegitimate; **bloody-scepter'd:** holding a scepter won by bloodshed

106 **truest issue:** rightful heir

107 **interdiction:** judgment

108 **blaspheme his breed:** slander his own heritage

111 **Died:** prepared herself to enter heaven

? Do you think Macduff has ever thought of himself as king? From what you know, would he be a good ruler?

114 **passion:** display of feelings

115 **Child of:** born of your

116 **black scruples:** dark suspicions

118 **trains:** lures or traps

119 **modest wisdom plucks me:** prudent caution has rescued me

121 **Deal between thee and me:** oversee our dealings

122 **to thy direction:** under your guidance

123 **abjure:** renounce

* **This Is a Test** You might have trouble making sense of Malcolm's "test" of Macduff. What does Malcolm actually learn about Macduff from this test? Historian Garry Wills has suggested that Malcolm's speeches about his own pretended evils are really a sham recruitment. He is testing Macduff by tempting him toward evil, as if to say, "I am worse than Macbeth—will you follow me?" In expressing his horror at Malcolm's "vices," Macduff proves his virtue and gains Malcolm's trust.

Malcolm insists that he is truly without vice and ready to retake Scotland from Macbeth.

For strangers to my nature. I am yet
Unknown to woman, never was forsworn,
Scarcely have coveted what was mine own,
At no time broke my faith, would not betray
The devil to his fellow, and delight
No less in truth than life. My first false speaking
Was this upon myself. What I am truly,
Is thine and my poor country's to command—
Whither indeed, before thy here-approach,
Old Siward with ten thousand warlike men,
Already at a point, was setting forth.
Now we'll together; and the chance of goodness
Be like our warranted quarrel. Why are you silent?

125 For strangers to my nature: as being alien to me

126 Unknown to...forsworn,: a virgin, never committed perjury,

131 upon: about

133 Whither indeed: in fact; **thy here-approach:** you arrived

135 at a point: in readiness

136-137 and the...quarrel: May our chance of success be as good as our cause is just.

How might Macduff react to Malcolm's sudden reversal?

Roddy McDowall as Malcolm, Welles film, 1948

As Macduff is considering what Malcolm has said, a doctor announces that the King of England is coming. The King has the power to heal, and many are waiting to be cured.

MACDUFF. Such welcome and unwelcome things at once
'Tis hard to reconcile.

[Enter a DOCTOR.*]*

MALCOLM. Well, more anon.—Comes the King forth, I pray you?

DOCTOR. Ay, sir. There are a crew of wretched souls
That stay his cure. Their malady convinces
The great assay of art, but at his touch—
Such sanctity hath heaven given his hand—
They presently amend.

MALCOLM. I thank you, doctor.

[Exit DOCTOR.*]*

MACDUFF. What's the disease he means?

MALCOLM. 'Tis call'd the evil:
A most miraculous work in this good king,
Which often, since my here-remain in England
I have seen him do. How he solicits heaven
Himself best knows, but strangely visited people,
All swoll'n and ulcerous, pitiful to the eye,
The mere despair of surgery, he cures,
Hanging a golden stamp about their necks,
Put on with holy prayers; and 'tis spoken,
To the succeeding royalty he leaves
* The healing benediction. With this strange virtue,
He hath a heavenly gift of prophecy,
And sundry blessings hang about his throne
That speak him full of grace.

142 stay: await

142–143 Their illness (**malady**) defeats (**convinces**) all efforts of medical science (**great assay of art**).

145 presently amend: immediately are cured

146 the evil: "the King's evil," scrofula, frequently characterized by an enlarged degeneration of lymphatic glands in the neck. The disease was thought to be curable at the touch of any king descended from Edward, the Confessor.

148 my here-remain: my stay here

150 visited: diseased

152 mere: total

153 stamp: a coin given by the King to those he cures

156 virtue: power

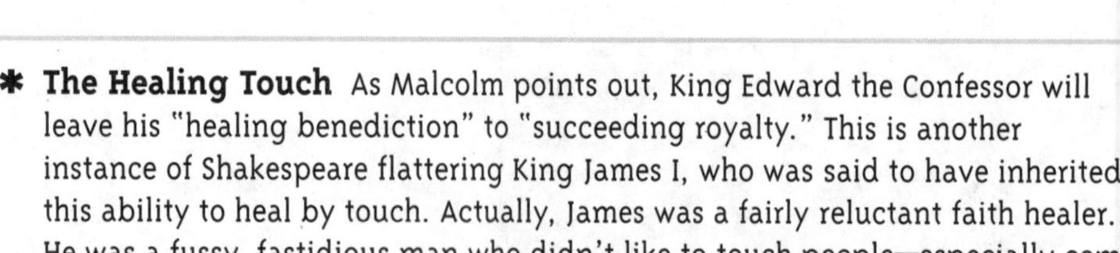

King James I

* **The Healing Touch** As Malcolm points out, King Edward the Confessor will leave his "healing benediction" to "succeeding royalty." This is another instance of Shakespeare flattering King James I, who was said to have inherited this ability to heal by touch. Actually, James was a fairly reluctant faith healer. He was a fussy, fastidious man who didn't like to touch people—especially commoners.

Ross arrives to report that the situation in Scotland continues to deteriorate. Macduff asks for news of his wife and children.

[Enter ROSS.*]*

MACDUFF. See who comes here.

* **MALCOLM.** My countryman, but yet I know him not.

MACDUFF. My ever-gentle cousin, welcome hither.

MALCOLM. I know him now. —Good God, betimes remove
The means that makes us strangers!

ROSS. Sir, amen.

MACDUFF. Stands Scotland where it did?

ROSS. Alas, poor country,
Almost afraid to know itself. It cannot
Be call'd our mother, but our grave; where nothing
But who knows nothing is once seen to smile;
Where sighs and groans and shrieks that rent the air
Are made, not mark'd; where violent sorrow seems
A modern ecstasy. The dead man's knell
Is there scarce ask'd for who; and good men's lives
Expire before the flowers in their caps,
Dying or ere they sicken.

MACDUFF. O, relation
Too nice and yet too true!

MALCOLM. What's the newest grief?

ROSS. That of an hour's age doth hiss the speaker.
Each minute teems a new one.

MACDUFF. How does my wife?

ROSS. Why, well.

162 betimes: soon

163 The means: refers to Macbeth

167 But who: except someone who; **once:** ever

168 rent: pierce

169 made, not mark'd: sounded, but go unnoticed

170 A modern ecstasy: like a routine emotion

173 or ere they: before they ever; **relation:** report

PERSONA JOURNAL

All personas except those in this scene: Describe something that's happened to you that illustrates what life is currently like in Scotland.

174 nice: exact

175 That of...speaker: Any report more than an hour old will get the speaker hissed off the stage for bringing stale news.

176 teems: produces

177 well: meaning "at peace" when spoken of the dead

* **"My countryman, but yet I know him not."** If Malcolm recognizes Ross as his countryman, why doesn't he also recognize Ross himself? Perhaps Ross is wearing clothing that marks him as a Scotsman. And yet, in Shakespeare's original production of *Macbeth*, there was probably little attempt to costume characters according to period or locale. One critic has suggested that Malcolm snubs Ross when he first enters. After all, Ross has been loyal to Macbeth until recently.

Ross says when he last saw Macduff's wife and children they were safe. He urges Malcolm to attack Macbeth, since many men and even women would be willing to join in the fight. Malcolm is ready and has support from the English. Ross reluctantly says he has some bad news.

MACDUFF. And all my children?

ROSS. Well too.

MACDUFF. The tyrant has not batter'd at their peace?

ROSS. No; they were well at peace when I did leave 'em.

MACDUFF. Be not a niggard of your speech. How goes't?

ROSS. When I came hither to transport the tidings
Which I have heavily borne, there ran a rumour
Of many worthy fellows that were out;
Which was to my belief witness'd the rather
For that I saw the tyrant's power afoot.
Now is the time of help. Your eye in Scotland
Would create soldiers, make our women fight,
To doff their dire distresses.

MALCOLM. Be't their comfort
We are coming thither. Gracious England hath
Lent us good Siward and ten thousand men;
An older and a better soldier none
That Christendom gives out.

ROSS. Would I could answer
This comfort with the like. But I have words
That would be howl'd out in the desert air,
Where hearing should not latch them.

MACDUFF. What concern they?
The general cause or is it a fee-grief
Due to some single breast?

? **179** What two meanings does this line have?

180 Don't be stingy (**niggard**) with your words (**speech**). What's going on?

182 heavily: sadly

183 out: ready for battle

184 witness'd the rather: confirmed for me all the more

185 For that: for when; **power afoot:** troops stirring

186 of: for; **eye:** presence

188 doff: rid

189 England: the King of England

192 gives out: proclaims

194 would: ought to

195 latch: catch the sound of

196-197 a fee-grief...breast: a particular sorrow (**fee-grief**) belonging (**due to**) a single heart (**breast**)

Ross reveals the murder of Macduff's wife, children, and servants. Macduff is stunned. Malcolm promises that he will have revenge.

ROSS. No mind that's honest
But in it shares some woe, though the main part
Pertains to you alone.

MACDUFF. If it be mine,
Keep it not from me. Quickly let me have it.

ROSS. Let not your ears despise my tongue forever,
Which shall possess them with the heaviest sound
That ever yet they heard.

MACDUFF. Hum! I guess at it.

ROSS. Your castle is surpris'd, your wife and babes
Savagely slaughter'd. To relate the manner
Were on the quarry of these murder'd deer
To add the death of you.

MALCOLM. Merciful heaven!
What, man, ne'er pull your hat upon your brows.
Give sorrow words. The grief that does not speak
Whispers the o'erfraught heart and bids it break.

MACDUFF. My children too?

ROSS. Wife, children, servants, all
That could be found.

MACDUFF. And I must be from thence?
My wife kill'd too?

ROSS. I have said.

MALCOLM. Be comforted.
Let's make us med'cines of our great revenge
To cure this deadly grief.

202 heaviest: saddest

204 surpris'd: attacked without warning

205–207 To relate...you: To give you the details would, in the face of those slaughtered, kill you too.

210 whispers to the overburdened **(o'erfraught)** heart and tells **(bids)** it to break

212 from thence: away from there

? How will Macduff express his anguish? In a loud or soft voice? With large gestures or small? Moving or still?

Still in shock, Macduff asks again if any one of his children has survived. He blames himself for being away and grieves for his family.

MACDUFF. He has no children. All my pretty ones?
Did you say "all"? O hell-kite! All?
What, all my pretty chickens and their dam
At one fell swoop?

MALCOLM. Dispute it like a man.

MACDUFF. I shall do so,
But I must also feel it as a man.
I cannot but remember such things were,
That were most precious to me. Did heaven look on
And would not take their part? Sinful Macduff,
They were all struck for thee! Naught that I am,
Not for their own demerits, but for mine,
Fell slaughter on their souls. Heaven rest them now.

216 He: Macbeth

217 hell-kite: evil bird of prey

218 dam: mother

220 Dispute: avenge

PERSONA JOURNAL

Do you blame Macduff for the murders of his wife, children, and servants?

225 Naught that I am: I'm the wicked one.

226 demerits: faults

Ross tells of the murder of Macduff's family. Production photo from Shakespeare Centre Library, Stratford-Upon-Avon

Malcolm advises Macduff to turn his grief into anger to avenge his family. Macduff vows to kill Macbeth. They leave to plan their attack.

MALCOLM. Be this the whetstone of your sword. Let grief
Convert to anger. Blunt not the heart; enrage it.

MACDUFF. O, I could play the woman with mine eyes
And braggart with my tongue! But, gentle heavens,
Cut short all intermission! Front to front
Bring thou this fiend of Scotland and myself.
✱ Within my sword's length set him. If he 'scape,
Heaven forgive him too.

MALCOLM. This tune goes manly.
Come, go we to the King. Our power is ready;
Our lack is nothing but our leave. Macbeth
Is ripe for shaking, and the powers above
Put on their instruments. Receive what cheer you may:
The night is long that never finds the day.

[Exeunt.]

228 whetstone of: sharpening stone for

230 play the...eyes: weep

232 intermission: delay; **Front to front:** face to face

235 goes manly: has a manly sound

237 Our lack...leave: We only need to say goodbye.

239 Put on their instruments: urge us on as their agents

Woodcut of Macduff's murdered family, Holinshed's *Chronicles*, 1577

✱ **Royal Censorship** "If he 'scape, / Heaven forgive him too," says Macduff of Macbeth. Critics suspect that Shakespeare original words were something like, "May God forgive him too." But in 1606, the year *Macbeth* was probably first performed, King James passed a law forbidding playwrights to mention God at all. So Shakespeare had to use the word *heaven* instead.

Reacting to Act IV

Analysis

1. Refer back to Act III, scene iv and now Act IV, scene i. What do you think of Lennox?
2. Remember that Ross was the person in Act I who told Macbeth that he had been named the new Thane of Cawdor. Now, look at Act IV, scene ii and scene iii. What is your opinion of Ross?
3. Why does Macbeth decide to kill Macduff's family?
4. List the people Macbeth has killed or has had killed and note which ones were murdered onstage and which offstage. Do you think the locations were random decisions by Shakespeare or are there dramatic reasons involved?
5. How does Malcolm test Macduff's loyalty?
6. Why do you think Shakespeare included the discussion about the King of England and his special talents in Act IV, scene iii?
7. What do you think will happen in Act V, the final act of the play?

Literary Elements

1. The term **foreshadowing** refers to hints about what might happen at a later point in the plot. Find at least three examples of foreshadowing in Act IV.
2. Review the ingredients that the witches put into their cauldron. What might this repulsive stew **symbolize**?

Writing

1. At the bottom of page 135, Malcolm lists the qualities of a good king. Create a chart with the qualities listed down the left side of your paper. Create four more columns labeled *Macbeth, Duncan, Malcolm,* and *Macduff.* Analyze which character would make the best king by checking off the qualities each candidate has demonstrated. For Macbeth, consider his character BEFORE the murder of Duncan. Compare your results with those of your classmates.
2. Imagine that after Lady Macduff discovers that her husband has fled to England, she writes to him expressing her concerns and fears. Write that letter, utilizing the language of Shakespeare.
3. Imagine that you are a reporter for a tabloid newspaper that is known for sensational writing and/or questionable sources. You are assigned to report on the murders that took place at Macduff's castle. Write an article explaining what happened. Be sure to include a headline for the article.

Macbeth

Act V

Isuzu Yamada as Asaji in *The Throne of Blood*, 1957

"Out, damned spot! out, I say!"

Setting the Scene

MACBETH

Act V, scene i *or* Deep Sleep

Critical Query: What's troubling Lady Macbeth?

Classroom Set Design

Use the regular four-clan arrangement with an entrance for Lady Macbeth as shown.

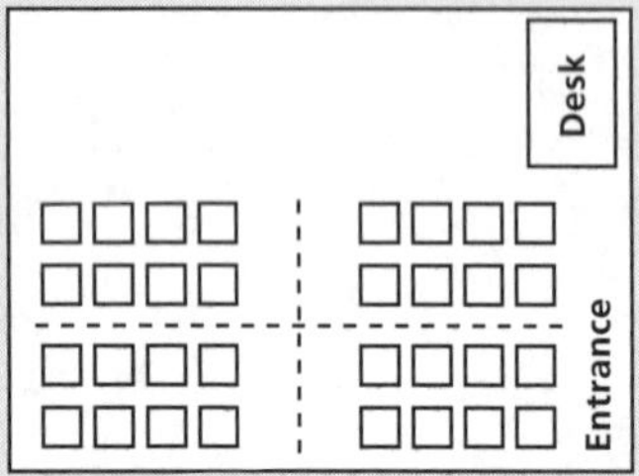

On Location: Dunsinane

According to Holinshed's *Chronicles*, Macbeth "builded a strong castle on the top of a high hill called Dunsinane" after he became king. Dunsinane is a hill in central Scotland. Upon its 1,012-foot summit stand the ruins of a stone fort that was already ancient in Macbeth's time. According to tradition, Macbeth fought and lost a battle against Duncan's son Malcolm at Dunsinane in 1054, but he didn't die there. He was slain in a later battle against Malcolm in 1057.

From the Prop Box

- Candle with holder for Lady Macbeth
- Writing materials for the doctor

Famous Quotes from Scene ii

- Out, damned spot! out, I say!
- All the perfumes of Arabia will not sweeten this little hand.

The More You Know: Sleepwalking

Coming up is a famous scene in which Lady Macbeth walks in her sleep. The medical term for this activity is *somnabulism*, and it really happens. Perhaps you or somebody you know has sleepwalked at one time or another. In addition to getting up and walking around (like Lady Macbeth, with their eyes open), somnambulists sometimes talk, dress, eat, go to the bathroom, leave the house, and even drive a car. They seldom remember these episodes when they awake. As in the case of Lady Macbeth, sleepwalking is sometimes triggered by stress and anxiety.

Warm-up Improv

Your brainy brother has been sleepwalking. You and your parents stay up one night to watch. It turns out that he not only walks in his sleep, he also talks, and from what he says, he has apparently cheated on a recent exam! You are all shocked. What do you do next?

At Dunsinane castle, one of Lady Macbeth's ladies-in-waiting, or gentlewomen, is discussing Lady Macbeth's sleepwalking with a doctor. The doctor has waited for two evenings to see if the report is true. During the conversation, Lady Macbeth, fast asleep, enters with a candle in her hand.

ACT V.

Scene i. Dunsinane. Anteroom in the Castle

[Enter a DOCTOR of Physic and a waiting GENTLEWOMAN.]

DOCTOR. I have two nights watched with you, but can perceive no truth in your report. When was it she last walked?

GENTLEWOMAN. Since his majesty went into the field, I have seen her rise from her bed, throw her night-gown upon her, unlock her closet, take forth paper, fold it, write upon't, read it, afterwards seal it, and again return to bed; yet all this while in a most fast sleep.

DOCTOR. A great perturbation in nature, to receive at once the benefit of sleep and do the effects of watching! In this slumb'ry agitation, beside her walking and other actual performances, what at any time, have you heard her say?

GENTLEWOMAN. That, sir, which I will not report after her.

DOCTOR. You may to me, and 'tis most meet you should.

GENTLEWOMAN. Neither to you nor anyone, having no witness to confirm my speech.

✱ *[Enter* LADY MACBETH, *with a taper.]*

Lo you, here she comes. This is her very guise and, upon my life, fast asleep. Observe her, stand close.

DOCTOR. How came she by that light?

[*stage directions*] Physic: medicine; **waiting gentlewoman:** a lady of nobility, who is a companion to the Queen

3 field: battlefield

? What do you think Lady Macbeth writes on the paper?

8 great perturbation: serious disturbance

9–10 do the effects of watching: act like a person awake

10 slumb'ry agitation: actions while asleep

14 meet: proper

[*stage directions*] taper: a thin candle

17 very guise: usual behavior

18 stand close: keep hidden

PERSONA JOURNAL

What have you seen or heard about the change in Lady Macbeth's behavior?

✱ **Where's She Been?** It's been a long time since we've seen Lady Macbeth. In fact, she hasn't appeared since Act III, scene iv. Lady Macbeth's absence through most of the play's last two acts adds to the difficulty of performing *Macbeth*. Much of the excitement of the first three acts comes from the emotionally charged scenes between Lady Macbeth and her husband. Audiences tend to miss her once she disappears.

The gentlewoman reports that Lady Macbeth goes through the motions of washing her hands for up to 15 minutes at a time.

GENTLEWOMAN. Why, it stood by her. She has light by her continually; 'tis her command.

DOCTOR. You see her eyes are open.

GENTLEWOMAN. Ay, but their sense are shut.

DOCTOR. What is it she does now? Look how she rubs her hands.

GENTLEWOMAN. It is an accustomed action with her to seem thus washing her hands. I have known her continue in this a quarter of an hour.

LADY MACBETH. Yet here's a spot.

DOCTOR. Hark, she speaks. I will set down what comes from her, to satisfy my remembrance the more strongly.

Francesca Annis
Polanski film, 1972

PERSONA JOURNAL

Who do you know that has suffered from sleepwalking and/or delusions? Provide some details of this person's illness.

? Why do you think Lady Macbeth insists on having light around her at all times?

25 an accustomed action: a habit

29 set: write

? How do you think the gentlewoman feels about Lady Macbeth?

Lady Macbeth continues to talk in her sleep about the murders of Duncan and Lady Macduff. The doctor watches as Lady Macbeth tries and tries to rub the "blood" from her hands.

LADY MACBETH. Out, damned spot! out, I say! One. Two. Why then, 'tis time to do't. Hell is murky. Fie, my lord, fie, a soldier, and afeard? What need we fear who knows it, when none can call our power to account? Yet who would have thought the old man to have had so much blood in him?

DOCTOR. Do you mark that?

LADY MACBETH. The Thane of Fife had a wife. Where is she now? What, will these hands ne'er be clean? No more o' lord, no more o' that. You mar all with this starting.

DOCTOR. Go to, go to. You have known what you should not.

GENTLEWOMAN. She has spoke what she should not, I am sure of that. Heaven knows what she has known.

LADY MACBETH. Here's the smell of the blood still. All the perfumes of Arabia will not sweeten this little hand. O, O, O!

DOCTOR. What a sigh is there! The heart is sorely charged.

GENTLEWOMAN. I would not have such a heart in my bosom for the dignity of the whole body.

DOCTOR. Well, well, well.

GENTLEWOMAN. Pray God it be, sir.

31 One. Two: a reference to the striking of the hour the night when Duncan was murdered

33 lord: Macbeth

32 Fie: shame on you

35 old man: Duncan

37 mark: hear

38 Thane of Fife: Macduff

40–41 You mar…starting: You will spoil everything (**mar all**) with your nervousness (**starting**).

42 Go to: for shame

48 sorely charged: extremely burdened

50 the dignity: all of the nobility

? This famous scene has been performed in many ways. What choices would you make with movement and voice to show Lady Macbeth's mental state?

TALES FROM THE STAGE

Shakespeare makes things tough for the actress playing Lady Macbeth during the sleepwalking scene. She enters carrying a candle, and she also tries to rub an imaginary spot of blood off her hands. How is she supposed to do both of those things at once? Traditionally, actresses were expected to hold the candle throughout the scene. However, the famous 18th-century actress Sarah Siddons came up with a simple solution. She set the candle down on a table, *then* pantomimed washing her hands. Audiences were shocked, but the actress received critical aclaim.

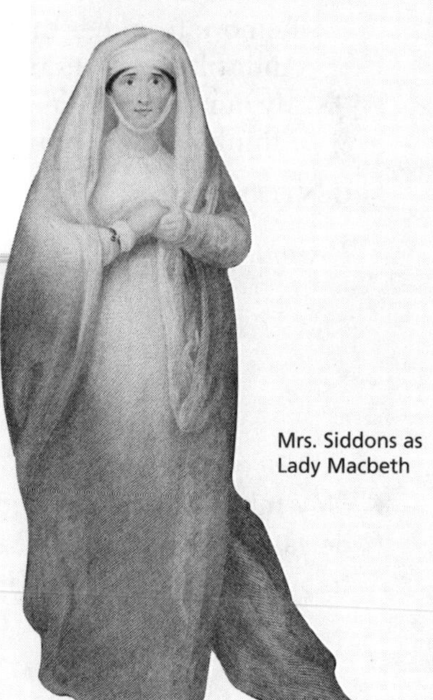

Mrs. Siddons as Lady Macbeth

The doctor says that Lady Macbeth's illness is beyond his powers to cure. He instructs the gentlewoman to watch her mistress carefully and to keep anything dangerous away from her.

DOCTOR. This disease is beyond my practice. Yet I have known those which have walked in their sleep who have died holily in their beds.

LADY MACBETH. Wash your hands. Put on your nightgown. Look not so pale. I tell you yet again, Banquo's buried; he cannot come out on's grave.

DOCTOR. Even so?

LADY MACBETH. To bed, to bed. There's knocking at the gate. Come, come, come, come. Give me your hand. What's done cannot be undone. To bed, to bed, to bed.

[Exit.]

DOCTOR. Will she go now to bed?

GENTLEWOMAN. Directly.

DOCTOR. Foul whisp'rings are abroad. Unnatural deeds
Do breed unnatural troubles. Infected minds
To their deaf pillows will discharge their secrets.
More needs she the divine than the physician.
God, God forgive us all. Look after her.
Remove from her the means of all annoyance
And still keep eyes upon her. So, good night.
✱ My mind she has mated, and amazed my sight.
I think but dare not speak.

GENTLEWOMAN. Good night, good doctor.

[Exeunt.]

55 holily: at peace with God

58 on's: of his

59 Even so?: That too!

65 Ugly **(foul)** rumors **(whisp'rings)** are flying about **(abroad)**.

68 the divine: a priest

70 the means of all annoyance: anything dangerous

? Why is the gentlewoman told to keep dangerous things away from Lady Macbeth?

? What does the doctor "think but dare not speak"?

✱ **"My mind she has mated..."** In Shakespeare's time, the verb "mate" meant to confuse, perplex, or defeat. This is the origin of the term "checkmate" in the game of chess—a move in which the king is trapped and unable to escape.

Setting the Scene

MACBETH

Act V, scene ii, iii, and iv *or* Branching Out

Critical Query: How is the battle going?

Classroom Set Design

The standard four-clan arrangement should work for all three scenes. A bench might be added for scene iii.

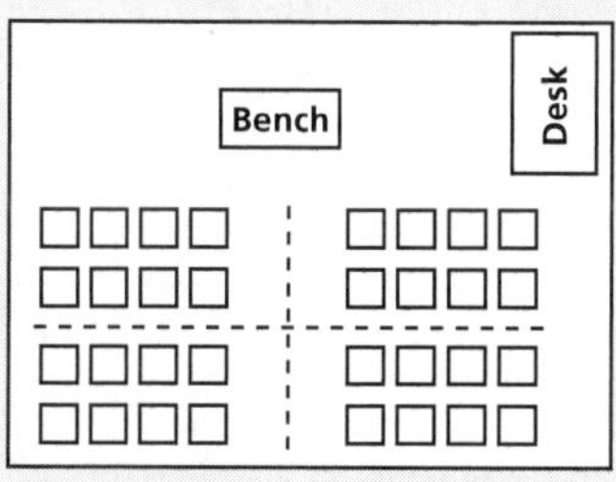

The More You Know: Medieval Medicine

Shakespeare based the doctor in *Macbeth* on the physicians of his own time. But medical practices hadn't changed much in the five and a half centuries since Macbeth's time. Ever since the Greek physician Hippocrates (460-377 B.C.), physicians had believed in the "humors theory." According to this theory, the human body contained four fluids called "humors." These were blood, phlegm, yellow bile, and black bile. Good mental and physical health meant that these fluids were well balanced. If a patient became ill or insane, a doctor assumed that there was too much of one fluid. The doctor purged the patient of the excess humor by means of bleeding, vomiting, and enemas. A doctor making a house (or castle) call would come prepared with razors, enemas, and purgative plants like rhubarb and senna. He also might have live leeches handy to suck out nasty humors through a patient's skin. Today's medical science rejects the humors theory. In fact, doctors in the days of Macbeth and Shakespeare generally did more harm than good.

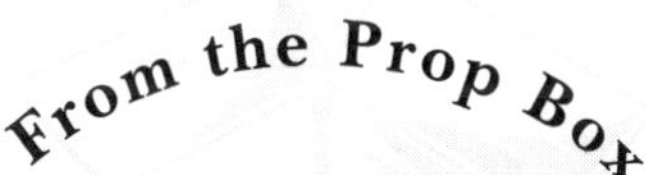

- Flags and/or banners
- Swords (plastic or foam)
- Armor pieces for Macbeth (plastic or foam)
- Staff for Macbeth
- Crown for Macbeth
- Branches for the soldiers (brooms or umbrellas are two possibilities)

Special Effects Drums

Warm-up Improv

(Use after page 153) You are riding in a car with your friend's cousins. These cousins take risks and have you somewhat concerned. You want out of the car.

In the countryside near Dunsinane, Macbeth's enemies gather to discuss their plans. Macbeth is preparing for battle, but his troops have little loyalty towards him.

Scene ii. The Country near Dunsinane

[Drum and colours. Enter MENTEITH, CAITHNESS, ANGUS, LENNOX, *and* SOLDIERS.*]*

MENTEITH. The English power is near, led on by Malcolm,
✱ His uncle Siward and the good Macduff.
Revenges burn in them, for their dear causes
Would to the bleeding and the grim alarm
Excite the mortified man.

ANGUS. Near Birnam Wood
Shall we well meet them; that way are they coming.

CAITHNESS. Who knows if Donalbain be with his brother?

LENNOX. For certain, sir, he is not. I have a file
Of all the gentry. There is Siward's son
And many unrough youths that even now
Protest their first of manhood.

MENTEITH. What does the tyrant?

CAITHNESS. Great Dunsinane he strongly fortifies.
Some say he's mad; others that lesser hate him
Do call it valiant fury: but for certain
He cannot buckle his distemper'd cause
Within the belt of rule.

ANGUS. Now does he feel
His secret murders sticking on his hands.
Now minutely revolts upbraid his faith-breach.
Those he commands move only in command,
Nothing in love. Now does he feel his title

[*stage directions*] colours: flags or banners

PERSONA ACTION

A representative army of Stuarts, Macduffs, Canmores, and a few Macbeths who have switched sides should gather at one end of the room and react physically and verbally throughout scenes ii, iv, vi, vii, and viii.

3 dear: deeply felt

4-5 Would to...man: would call even a dead man to bloody and terrifying battle

? Why do you think Donalbain has not joined his brother Malcolm in the fight against Macbeth?

8 file: list

10 unrough: beardless

11 Protest their...manhood: will declare their passage into manhood

15-16 He...rule: His kingdom is diseased and he can no longer control it.

18 Now every minute (**minutely**) there are new uprisings to protest (**upbraid**) his treachery (**faith-breach**).

✱ **Family Matters** Here Siward is referred to as Malcolm's uncle. But according to Shakespeare's historical source, Holinshed's *Chronicles*, Siward was actually Malcolm's grandfather. In Shakespeare's time, "uncle" sometimes meant "grandfather." But since Shakespeare suggests that Siward is at least as young as the late King Duncan, Shakespeare probably meant "uncle" as we understand the word today. He didn't mind changing history to suit his dramatic purposes.

The opposition leaders resolve to unite behind Malcolm and join together at Birnam Woods.

Hang loose about him, like a giant's robe
Upon a dwarfish thief.

MENTEITH. Who, then, shall blame
His pester'd senses to recoil and start
When all that is within him does condemn
Itself for being there?

CAITHNESS. Well, march we on
To give obedience where 'tis truly owed.
Meet we the med'cine of the sickly weal,
And with him pour we in our country's purge
Each drop of us.

LENNOX. Or so much as it needs
To dew the sovereign flower and drown the weeds.
Make we our march towards Birnam.

[Exeunt, marching.]

22 his tormented **(pester'd)** senses for being jumpy **(recoil)** and easily startled **(start)**

27 weal: population

? What is the "med'cine" that Caithness refers to in line 27? Who or what are the "weeds" in line 30?

29 Each drop of us: every drop of our blood.

PERSONA JOURNAL

To whom are you loyal in this conflict? Why are you sure you've made the right choice? Explain.

Because of the witches' prophesies, Macbeth is confident that he can withstand any threat. He has heard that many Scottish thanes have abandoned him and joined Malcolm. A frightened servant enters with a report that 10,000 English soldiers are gathering to attack.

Scene iii. Dunsinane. A Room in the Castle

[Enter MACBETH, DOCTOR, *and* ATTENDANTS.*]*

MACBETH. Bring me no more reports. Let them fly all.
Till Birnam Wood remove to Dunsinane
I cannot taint with fear. What's the boy Malcolm?
Was he not born of woman? The spirits that know
All mortal consequences have pronounced me thus:
'Fear not, Macbeth. No man that's born of woman
Shall e'er have power upon thee.' Then fly, false thanes,
And mingle with the English epicures.
The mind I sway by and the heart I bear
Shall never sag with doubt nor shake with fear.

[Enter a SERVANT.*]*

The devil damn thee black, thou cream-fac'd loon!
✱ Where got'st thou that goose-look?

SERVANT. There is ten thousand—

MACBETH. Geese, villain?

SERVANT. Soldiers, sir.

MACBETH. Go prick thy face and over-red thy fear,
Thou lily-liver'd boy. What soldiers, patch?
Death of thy soul! Those linen cheeks of thine
Are counselors to fear. What soldiers, whey-face?

SERVANT. The English force, so please you.

MACBETH. Take thy face hence.

PERSONA ACTION

Representative Clan Macbeth servants should be in the acting area to help Macbeth on and off with his armor.

1 them: the thanes (who are deserting Macbeth)

3 taint: be infected

5 All mortal consequences: the fate of all humans

8 epicures: lovers of luxury (and therefore soft)

9 sway: am governed

10 sag with: give in

11 loon: lunatic

14 prick: scratch; **over-red:** let blood cover

15 lily-liver'd: cowardly; **patch:** fool

16 of thy: on your

? Why is Macbeth so angry with the servant? How could you show the King's agitation to the audience?

17 Are counselors: teach others

PERSONA JOURNAL

Clan Macbeth: Has Macbeth always treated his servants this way? Explain.

✱ **"Where got'st thou that goose-look?"** Shakespeare wrote his plays on white paper with a black goose-quill pen. In this scene, Macbeth damns his servant "black" for his "goose look." One Shakespeare scholar has suggested that he might have gotten this image from the writing utensils right in front of him!

Macbeth is anxious for the battle that will decide his fate and vows to fight to the end. He learns from the doctor that Lady Macbeth is mentally ill.

[Exit SERVANT.*]*

Seyton!—I am sick at heart,
When I behold—Seyton, I say!—This push
Will cheer me ever or disseat me now.
I have lived long enough. My way of life
Is fall'n into the sere, the yellow leaf,
And that which should accompany old age,
As honour, love, obedience, troops of friends,
I must not look to have, but, in their stead
Curses, not loud but deep, mouth-honour, breath,
Which the poor heart would fain deny, and dare not.—
Seyton!

[Enter SEYTON.*]*

SEYTON. What is your gracious pleasure?

MACBETH. What news more?

SEYTON. All is confirm'd, my lord, which was reported.

MACBETH. I'll fight till from my bones my flesh be hack'd.
✱ Give me my armour.

SEYTON. 'Tis not needed yet.

MACBETH. I'll put it on.
Send out more horses. Skirr the country round.
Hang those that talk of fear. Give me mine armour.—
How does your patient, doctor?

DOCTOR. Not so sick, my lord,
As she is troubled with thick-coming fancies,
That keep her from her rest.

20 push: attack

21 disseat: unthrone

23 the sere, the yellow: shriveled and faded

27 mouth-honour: false compliments

28 fain: gladly

? How do you think Seyton feels about Macbeth?

35 Skirr: search

38 thick-coming fancies: many hallucinations

PERSONA JOURNAL

The threat of war is growing. Are you and your family safe? Explain your situation.

✱ **On Again, Off Again** Shakespeare wrote few stage directions, but often peppered his dialogue with clues about stage action. For example, Macbeth calls out, "Give me my armour." The armor is brought to him, and he proceeds to put it on. Once he has his armor at least partly on, he changes his mind: "Pull't off, I say." Then he commands, "Bring it after me," and the armor is carried after him when he exits.

Macbeth demands that the doctor cure Lady Macbeth, but the doctor replies that she must cure herself. As Macbeth dons his armor, he shouts orders to his servants and sarcastically asks the doctor to find a cure for his kingdom.

MACBETH. Cure her of that.
Canst thou not minister to a mind diseased,
Pluck from the memory a rooted sorrow,
Raze out the written troubles of the brain,
And with some sweet oblivious antidote
Cleanse the stuff'd bosom of that perilous stuff
Which weighs upon the heart?

DOCTOR. Therein the patient
Must minister to himself.

MACBETH. Throw physic to the dogs. I'll none of it.
Come, put mine armour on. Give me my staff.

[ATTENDANTS *begin to arm him.]*

Seyton, send out.—Doctor, the thanes fly from me.—
* Come, sir, dispatch. —If thou couldst, doctor, cast
The water of my land, find her disease,
And purge it to a sound and pristine health,
I would applaud thee to the very echo
That should applaud again.—Pull't off, I say.—
What rhubarb, senna, or what purgative drug,
Would scour these English hence? Hear'st thou of them?

DOCTOR. Ay, my good lord. Your royal preparation
Makes us hear something.

MACBETH. Bring it after me.—
I will not be afraid of death and bane
Till Birnam Forest come to Dunsinane.

DOCTOR. *[Aside.]* Were I from Dunsinane away and clear,
Profit again should hardly draw me here.

[Exeunt.]

42 Raze out: erase

43 oblivious: tranquilizing

44 stuff'd: over-full

50 dispatch: make haste

50–51 Cast...land: Analyze my kingdom.

54 Pull't off, I say: to a servant, referring to a piece of armor

? Why can't Macbeth decide whether he wants his armor on or off?

55 purgative: laxative

56 scour: rid; **them:** English

58 Bring it after me: to a servant, again referring to armor

59 bane: ruin

? **61–62** What does the doctor mean as he mutters these lines?

* **Lab Work** Just like today, doctors of Shakespeare's time tested people's urine to find out what made them sick. When Macbeth tells the Doctor to "cast / The water of my land," he's ambitiously proposing a urine test for all of Scotland.

Malcolm meets with his allies near Birnam forest. He commands every soldier to cut down a tree branch and carry it in order to camouflage the army's advance on the castle.

Scene iv. Country near Birnam Wood

[Drum and colours. Enter MALCOLM, SIWARD *and* YOUNG SIWARD, MACDUFF, MENTEITH, CAITHNESS, ANGUS, LENNOX, ROSS, *and* SOLDIERS, *marching.]*

MALCOLM. Cousins, I hope the days are near at hand
That chambers will be safe.

MENTEITH. We doubt it nothing.

SIWARD. What wood is this before us?

MENTEITH. The wood of Birnam.

MALCOLM. Let every soldier hew him down a bough
And bear't before him. Thereby shall we shadow
The numbers of our host and make discovery
Err in report of us.

SOLDIERS. It shall be done.

SIWARD. We learn no other but the confident tyrant
Keeps still in Dunsinane and will endure
Our setting down before 't.

MALCOLM. 'Tis his main hope;
For, where there is advantage to be given,
Both more and less have given him the revolt,
And none serve with him but constrainèd things
Whose hearts are absent too.

MACDUFF. Let our just censures
Attend the true event, and put we on
Industrious soldiership.

PERSONA ACTION

All of Malcom's forces should be on one side of the room and should pantomime the cutting of tree branches when called for.

1 Cousins: kinsmen

2 That chambers will be safe: when a man will be safe in his own home

2 We doubt it nothing: We have no doubt that it will be so.

4 hew: cut

? Why does Malcolm have the soldiers cut tree branches? What effect will this action have on Macbeth?

5 shadow: conceal

6 host: army; **discovery:** Macbeth's scouts

8 no other but: nothing except that

10 Our setting...before 't: our setting siege in front of it

11 where there...given: wherever opportunity is offered

12 more and less: nobles and commoners

13 but constrainèd things: unless they are forced to

14 censures: judgments

15 Attend the true event: await the actual outcome

SIWARD. The time approaches
That will with due decision make us know
What we shall say we have and what we owe.
Thoughts speculative their unsure hopes relate,
But certain issue strokes must arbitrate;
Towards which, advance the war.

[Exeunt, marching.]

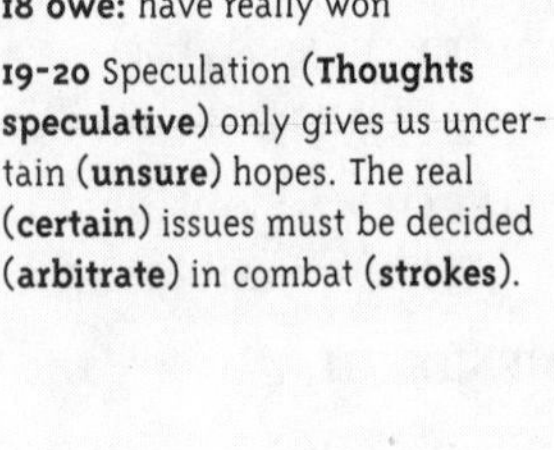

18 owe: have really won

19-20 Speculation (**Thoughts speculative**) only gives us uncertain (**unsure**) hopes. The real (**certain**) issues must be decided (**arbitrate**) in combat (**strokes**).

Gustave Doré: das graphische Werks, v. 2, p. 1052
courtesy of the Faculty of Architecture and History of Art Library, University of Cambridge

Setting the Scene

MACBETH

Act V, scene v and vi *or* How Does Your Battle Grow?

Critical Query: Is there any way out for Macbeth?

The More You Know: Sieges

"Our castle's strength / Will laugh a siege to scorn," says Macbeth. This is no idle boast. Although the actual forts of Macbeth's time were not very impressive, the feudal castles that Shakespeare imagined were very hard to enter. First, the attackers had to cross the moat—a broad, protective ditch. They usually did this by filling in part of it with stones and dirt. But then how were they to get past the castle walls? Soldiers sometimes scaled the walls with ladders, but this was dangerous. Castle defenders on tops of the walls could throw rocks down at the attackers or shoot at them with crossbows. Sometimes attacking armies used huge towers on wheels to bring them level with the tops of the walls. Attackers also tried to break down walls with massive, rock-throwing machines.

Classroom Set Design

Use the standard arrangement for all three scenes with a bench added for scene v.

Bench

Desk

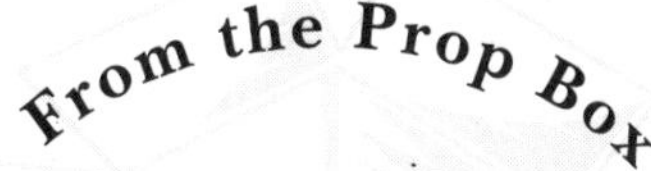

- Flags and/or banners
- Swords (plastic or foam)
- Branches for the soldiers

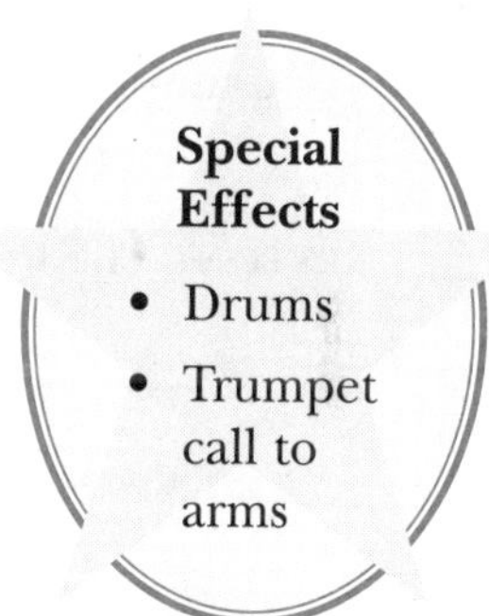

Warm-up Improv 1	Warm-up Improv 2
You want a car and you work very hard to get one. After you have it, you discover the burden of insurance, gas, maintenance, tires, etc. Talk to your friend about your disappointment in how much trouble owning a car can be.	Your pet of 15 years dies this morning as you are leaving for school. You have two final exams and they cannot be made up. Talk to your mom about this before you leave for school.

Within the castle, Macbeth gives orders and prepares for a siege. After hearing women scream, a servant enters to announce that Lady Macbeth is dead.

Scene v. Dunsinane. Within the Castle

[Enter MACBETH, SEYTON, *and* SOLDIERS, *with drum and colours]*

MACBETH. Hang out our banners on the outward walls.
The cry is still 'They come!' Our castle's strength
Will laugh a siege to scorn. Here let them lie
Till famine and the ague eat them up.
Were they not forc'd with those that should be ours,
We might have met them dareful, beard to beard,
And beat them backward home. *[A cry of women within.]*
What is that noise?

SEYTON. It is the cry of women, my good lord. *[Exit.]*

MACBETH. I have almost forgot the taste of fears.
The time has been my senses would have cool'd
To hear a night-shriek, and my fell of hair
Would at a dismal treatise rouse and stir
As life were in't. I have supp'd full with horrors.
Direness, familiar to my slaughterous thoughts
Cannot once start me. *[Reenter* SEYTON.*]*
Wherefore was that cry?

SEYTON. The Queen, my lord, is dead.

PERSONA ACTION

Clan Macbeth forces enter with Macbeth, and line up at the opposite end of the room from Malcolm's forces. You will be on stage for the rest of the play.

3 **lie:** stay

4 **ague:** fever or disease

5 **forced:** reinforced; **those that... ours:** our deserters

6 **met them dareful:** fought them in the field boldly

? Why is Macbeth forced to try and outlast a siege instead of engaging in face to face combat with Malcolm's forces?

10-15 There was a time when I would have felt a cold chill to hear a scream in the night and my hair would stand on end as if it were alive. Since then, I've seen so much horror and have had so many murderous thoughts that they no longer bother me.

TALES FROM THE STAGE

Revenge Is Sweet

An ambitious but not overly talented young actor was employed in Sir Donald Wolfit's traveling Shakespeare company as the final messenger in *Macbeth* who has to run on the stage, stammer out "My Lord, the queen is dead," and then run away. For many seasons he did just this, and then he became bored and asked Sir Donald if he could play a larger part. Wolfit refused. The actor continued to ask and Wolfit continued to refuse. The young actor became increasingly depressed and the matter developed into an obsession. Thoughts of revenge filled his waking hours and one evening he decided to sabotage the play. That night he ran onto the stage. "My Lord," he shouted, "the queen is *much better and is even now at dinner*." He then ran off, leaving the astonished actor-manager to deal with the situation as best he could. —from *Theatrical Anecdotes*, by Peter Hay

✱ **MACBETH.** She should have died hereafter.
There would have been a time for such a word.
Tomorrow and tomorrow and tomorrow
Creeps in this petty pace from day to day
To the last syllable of recorded time,
And all our yesterdays have lighted fools
The way to dusty death. Out, out, brief candle!
Life's but a walking shadow, a poor player
That struts and frets his hour upon the stage
And then is heard no more. It is a tale
Told by an idiot, full of sound and fury,
Signifying nothing.

17 hereafter: later

18 for such a word: to grieve

20 petty: slow

24 player: actor

? How would you describe Macbeth's state of mind as he performs this famous soliloquy?

Sir Herbert Beerbohm Tree as Macbeth

✱ **What Does He Mean?** "She should have died hereafter," says Macbeth upon learning of Lady Macbeth's death; "There would have been a time for such a word." These lines have puzzled critics for hundreds of years. Is this all Macbeth has to say about the loss of his beloved wife? And what does he mean, by "should" and "hereafter"? By "should," Macbeth might either mean "ought to" or "would." And by "hereafter," he might either mean the future or some mysterious, timeless moment.

A messenger arrives to report the astonishing news that a forest is advancing toward the castle. A furious Macbeth begins to realize that there might be double meanings to the witches' predictions. He sounds the alarm for his army to attack.

[Enter a MESSENGER.*]*

Thou com'st to use thy tongue; thy story quickly.

MESSENGER. Gracious my lord,
I should report that which I say I saw,
But know not how to do 't.

MACBETH. Well, say, sir.

MESSENGER. As I did stand my watch upon the hill,
I look'd toward Birnam, and anon methought,
The wood began to move.

MACBETH. Liar and slave!

MESSENGER. Let me endure your wrath, if't be not so.
Within this three mile may you see it coming.
I say, a moving grove.

MACBETH. If thou speak'st false,
Upon the next tree shalt thou hang alive
Till famine cling thee. If thy speech be sooth,
I care not if thou dost for me as much.—
I pull in resolution and begin
To doubt th' equivocation of the fiend,
That lies like truth. 'Fear not, till Birnam Wood
Do come to Dunsinane,' and now a wood
Comes toward Dunsinane.— Arm, arm, and out!—
If this which he avouches does appear,
There is nor flying hence nor tarrying here.
I 'gin to be aweary of the sun
And wish th' estate o' th' world were now undone.—
Ring the alarum bell!—Blow wind, come wrack,
At least we'll die with harness on our back.

[Exeunt.]

PERSONA ACTION

All of Malcolm's forces should carry "tree branches" as they slowly advance toward the other side of the room during this scene.

34 anon: soon

40 cling: shrivel; **speech be sooth:** story is true

42 I pull in resolution: I'm losing my confidence.

43 To doubt...fiend: suspect the double meanings of that devil

47 avouches: say it is true

48 nor flying hence: neither fleeing

49 'gin: begin

50 th' estate o' th' world: the orderly structure of the world; **undone:** destroyed

51 alarum bell: call to battle; **wrack:** destruction

52 harness: armor

Outside the castle, Malcolm commands that the tree branches now be cast aside. A trumpet is sounded for the battle to begin.

Scene vi. Dunsinane. Before the Castle

[Drum and colours. Enter MALCOLM, SIWARD, MACDUFF, *and their Army, with boughs.]*

MALCOLM. Now near enough. Your leafy screens throw down,
And show like those you are.— You, worthy uncle,
Shall, with my cousin, your right noble son,
Lead our first battle. Worthy Macduff and we
Shall take upon's what else remains to do,
According to our order.

SIWARD. Fare you well.
Do we but find the tyrant's power tonight,
Let us be beaten if we cannot fight.

MACDUFF. Make all our trumpets speak; give them all breath,
Those clamorous harbingers of blood and death.

[Exeunt. Alarums continue.]

2 uncle: refers to Siward

4 battle: battalion; **we:** I (the royal we)

6 order: plan

7 power: army

10 harbingers: announcers

Soldiers abandoning their tree branches and charging the castle.
Schaefer film, 1961

Setting the Scene

MACBETH

Act V, scene vii and viii *or* End Game

Critical Query: Did Macbeth have to die?

Classroom Set Design

This scene can best be played in the round, with chairs and personas situated on all four sides of the room. This will leave a large open space for swordplay. Leave at least two openings for characters entering and exiting.

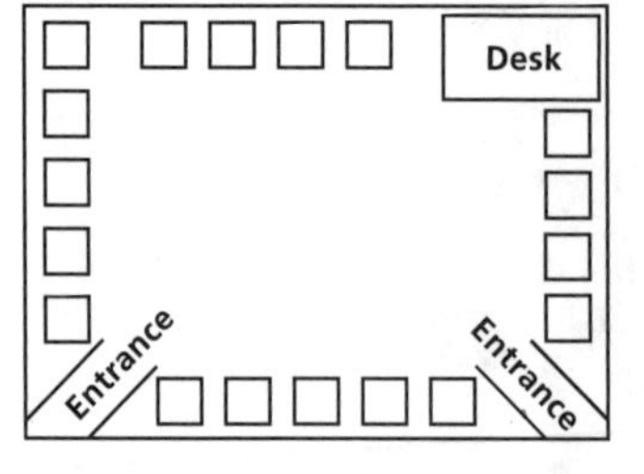

Special Effects

- Fighting sounds
- Trumpet call to arms
- Retreat sound
- Trumpet flourish

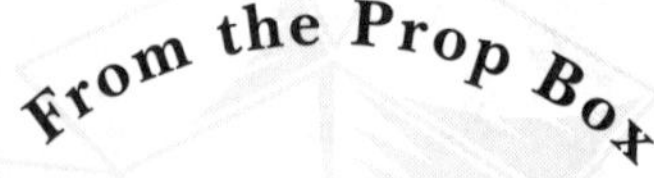

- Flags and/or banners
- Swords (plastic or foam)
- Macbeth's "head"
- Crown for Malcolm

Plan the Fight Scene

In lieu of an improvisation for these scenes, time should be spent with the class assisting in the planning and practice of the sword fights.

The More You Know: Stage Fights

This action-filled scene requires extra preparation for those involved in the sword fights that occur. Detailed choreography and practice are necessary for combat scenes to be effective and safe.

- Actors should decide what type of fight is best suited for this scene—a violent brawl, a by-the-books fencing duel, or something in between.
- Plan each part of the fight scene step-by-step and move-by-move.
- Write down the movements for reference as you prepare.
- Rehearse the movements in slow motion. Remember to practice falls as well as fighting. It may be easier to divide the fight into segments, practicing each segment until all parties are confident of their moves.
- Most importantly, as you plan and rehearse, rule one is safety. No one should be hurt in a stage fight.

On the battlefield, Macbeth is fearless and continues to believe he cannot be harmed. He encounters Young Siward and slays him.

Scene vii. Another Part of the Field

[Enter MACBETH.*]*

* **MACBETH.** They have tied me to a stake. I cannot fly,
But, bear-like, I must fight the course. What's he
That was not born of woman? Such a one
Am I to fear, or none.

[Enter YOUNG SIWARD.*]*

YOUNG SIWARD. What is thy name?

MACBETH. Thou'lt be afraid to hear it.

YOUNG SIWARD. No, though thou call'st thyself a hotter name
Than any is in hell.

MACBETH. My name's Macbeth.

YOUNG SIWARD. The devil himself could not pronounce a title
More hateful to mine ear.

MACBETH. No, nor more fearful.

YOUNG SIWARD. Thou liest, abhorrèd tyrant. With my sword
I'll prove the lie thou speak'st.

[They fight, and YOUNG SIWARD *is slain.]*

MACBETH. Thou wast born of woman.
But swords I smile at, weapons laugh to scorn,
Brandish'd by man that's of a woman born.

[Exit.]

[Alarums. Enter MACDUFF.*]*

PERSONA ACTION

Some of the fighting force should mime the fighting of the battle on the sides of the acting area during this scene.

5 Thou'lt: you will

8 title: name

11 prove: prove that you are lying

? Do you think Macbeth still believes in the witches' predictions?

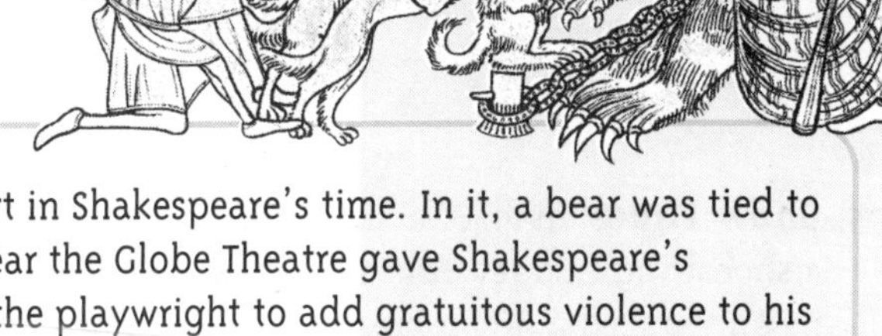

* **Bear-baiting** Bear-baiting was a cruel but popular sport in Shakespeare's time. In it, a bear was tied to a stake and attacked by vicious dogs. A "bear garden" near the Globe Theatre gave Shakespeare's company considerable competition, possibly prompting the playwright to add gratuitous violence to his plays. Here, Macbeth compares himself to a baited bear. A "course" was a bout or round of bear-baiting.

Macduff is intent on finding and killing Macbeth to avenge the deaths of his wife and children. The castle has surrendered, Macbeth's men are deserting, and the battle is almost won.

MACDUFF. That way the noise is. Tyrant, show thy face!
If thou be'st slain, and with no stroke of mine,
My wife and children's ghosts will haunt me still.
I cannot strike at wretched kerns, whose arms
Are hired to bear their staves. Either thou, Macbeth,
Or else my sword with an unbatter'd edge
I sheathe again undeeded. There thou shouldst be;
By this great clatter, one of greatest note
Seems bruited. Let me find him, Fortune!
And more I beg not.

[Exit. Alarums.]

✱ *[Enter* MALCOLM *and* SIWARD.*]*

SIWARD. This way, my lord. The castle's gently render'd:
The tyrant's people on both sides do fight,
The noble thanes do bravely in the war,
The day almost itself professes yours,
And little is to do.

MALCOLM. We have met with foes
That strike beside us.

SIWARD. Enter, sir, the castle.

[Exeunt. Alarums.]

16 still: forever

18 staves: weapons; **Either thou:** either I find you

20 undeeded: unused

21–22 one of…bruited: someone of the highest rank seems to be announced (**bruited**)

24 gently render'd: surrendered without a fight

27 itself professes: declares itself

28 We: I

29 That strike beside us: who have deliberately avoided hitting me

✱ **Chow Time!** In 1948, actor-director Orson Welles made a movie version of *Macbeth* in a mere 21 days on a shoestring budget. For the climax, he needed footage of Malcolm's army charging Macbeth's castle. So he announced a lunch break to his costumed extras (anonymous actors who appear in crowd scenes), then filmed their hungry stampede to the studio cafeteria.

Macbeth is still fighting fiercely when Macduff appears to challenge him.

Scene viii. Another Part of the Field

[Enter MACBETH.*]*

MACBETH. Why should I play the Roman fool and die
On mine own sword? Whiles I see lives, the gashes
Do better upon them.

[Enter MACDUFF.*]*

MACDUFF. Turn, hellhound, turn!

MACBETH. Of all men else I have avoided thee:
But get thee back. My soul is too much charg'd
With blood of thine already.

MACDUFF. I have no words;
My voice is in my sword, thou bloodier villain
Than terms can give thee out.

[They fight. Alarum.]

PERSONA ACTION

The rest of the fighting forces should join the battle pantomime along the sides of the acting area.

1 Roman: Roman gentlemen traditionally committed suicide to avoid dishonor in defeat.

2 lives: the enemy

5 charg'd: burdened

? Why has Macbeth been avoiding an encounter with Macduff?

8 Than terms...out: than words can describe

Macbeth finally comes face to face with his nemesis.
Royal Shakespeare Company, 1982
Shakespeare Centre Library,
Stratford-Upon-Avon: Joe Cocks Studio Collection

Macbeth tells Macduff of the witches' protective prophesy and learns that Macduff was not born naturally, but rather taken prematurely from his mother's womb. Macbeth at last realizes the full extent of the witches' treachery. Nevertheless, he fights on.

MACBETH. Thou losest labour.
As easy may'st thou the intrenchant air
With thy keen sword impress as make me bleed.
Let fall thy blade on vulnerable crests;
I bear a charmèd life, which must not yield,
To one of woman born.

MACDUFF. Despair thy charm,
And let the angel whom thou still hast serv'd
Tell thee Macduff was from his mother's womb
Untimely ripp'd.

MACBETH. Accursèd be that tongue that tells me so,
For it hath cow'd my better part of man!
And be these juggling fiends no more believed
That palter with us in a double sense,
That keep the word of promise to our ear
And break it to our hope. I'll not fight with thee.

MACDUFF. Then yield thee, coward,
And live to be the show and gaze o' th' time.
We'll have thee, as our rarer monsters are,
Painted on a pole, and underwrit
'Here may you see the tyrant.'

MACBETH. I will not yield
To kiss the ground before young Malcolm's feet
And to be baited with the rabble's curse.
Though Birnam Wood be come to Dunsinane,
And thou oppos'd, being of no woman born,
Yet I will try the last. Before my body

8 Thou losest labour: You are wasting your energy.

9 As easy...air: You can as easily cut the impenetrable air.

11 crests: armour

14 angel: evil spirit

16 Untimely ripp'd: prematurely delivered (cesarean section)

18 cow'd my...man: drained me of my manliness

19 juggling fiends: deceiving witches

20 That palter...sense: who trick us with their double meanings

? What does Macduff threaten to do with Macbeth if he refuses to fight?

24 gaze: spectacle

26 underwrit: written underneath

29 baited: taunted; **rabble's:** mob's

31 oppos'd: my opponent

Macbeth and Macduff continue to battle until Macduff kills Macbeth and carries his body away. Malcolm, Siward, and Ross enter.

I throw my warlike shield. Lay on, Macduff,
And damn'd be him that first cries, "Hold, enough!"

33 Lay on: strike hard

✱ *[Exeunt, fighting. Alarums.]*

[They reenter fighting. MACBETH *is slain.* MACDUFF *exits carrying off* MACBETH*'s body. Retreat. Flourish. Enter, with drum and colours,* MALCOLM, SIWARD, ROSS, *the other* THANES, *and* SOLDIERS.*]*

MALCOLM. I would the friends we miss were safe arrived.

35 miss: lack

SIWARD. Some must go off; and yet by these I see
So great a day as this is cheaply bought.

36 go off: die; **by these I see:** to look at those here

MALCOLM. Macduff is missing, and your noble son.

Toshiro Mifune as Macbeth in *The Thone of Blood*, 1957

✱ **A Japanese Macbeth** In 1957, director Akira Kurosawa filmed a Japanese version of *Macbeth*. Titled *Kumonosu-Jo* ("Cobweb Castle"), it is known in English as *The Throne of Blood*. Although Kurosawa reset the story in medieval Japan, he followed the plot of *Macbeth* closely. But in the end, the film's Samurai protagonist does not fight a duel with a Macduff-like character. Instead, his own soldiers turn against him and shoot him full of arrows when they see the forest marching toward the castle. (Another image from this film can be found on page 145.)

Ross informs Siward that his son was killed in battle. Siward asks if his son's wounds were on the front of his body. Ross confirms that they were and that Young Siward died bravely. Macduff enters with Macbeth's head. All hail Malcolm as the new King of Scotland.

ROSS. Your son, my lord, has paid a soldier's debt.
He only liv'd but till he was a man,
The which no sooner had his prowess confirm'd
In the unshrinking station where he fought,
But like a man he died.

SIWARD. Then he is dead?

ROSS. Ay, and brought off the field. Your cause of sorrow
Must not be measur'd by his worth, for then
It hath no end.

SIWARD. Had he his hurts before?

ROSS. Ay, on the front.

SIWARD. Why then, God's soldier be he!
Had I as many sons as I have hairs,
I would not wish them to a fairer death;
And so, his knell is knoll'd.

MALCOLM. He's worth more sorrow,
And that I'll spend for him.

SIWARD. He's worth no more.
They say he parted well and paid his score,
And so, God be with him. Here comes newer comfort.

[Reenter MACDUFF, *with* MACBETH*'s head.]*

MACDUFF. Hail, King! for so thou art. Behold where stands
Th' usurper's curs'd head. The time is free.
I see thee compass'd with thy kingdom's pearl,
That speak my salutation in their minds,
Whose voices I desire aloud with mine.
Hail, King of Scotland!

ALL. Hail, King of Scotland!

[Flourish.]

PERSONA ACTION

With the slaying of Macbeth, all clans gradually move to the center of the acting area while listening to Malcolm, Ross, and Siward. When Macduff enters with Macbeth's head, cheers begin to grow and all repeat after Macduff, "Hail King of Scotland!"

39 paid a soldier's debt: has died in battle

42 In the...fought: by standing his ground where he fought

44 cause: reason

46 before: on the front of his body

50 knell is knoll'd: The funeral bell has rung for him.

? What do you think of the way Siward speaks of his son?

55 free: meaning from tyranny

56 thee compass'd...pearl: that you are surrounded by the best subjects in your kingdom

PERSONA JOURNAL

Macbeth Clan: What are your thoughts about Macbeth's death and Malcolm becoming king? Do you fear reprisals and punishment for having fought on the losing side?

Malcolm thanks his loyal supporters, rewarding them with the title of Earl. He reports that Lady Macbeth has committed suicide and vows to correct the wrongs that the Macbeths have committed. He invites everyone to attend his crowning at Scone.

MALCOLM. We shall not spend a large expense of time
Before we reckon with your several loves
✱ And make us even with you. My thanes and kinsmen,
Henceforth be earls, the first that ever Scotland
In such an honour nam'd. What's more to do,
Which would be planted newly with the time,
As calling home our exil'd friends abroad
That fled the snares of watchful tyranny,
Producing forth the cruel ministers
Of this dead butcher and his fiend-like queen
Who, as 'tis thought, by self and violent hands,
Took off her life—this, and what needful else
That calls upon us, by the grace of grace,
We will perform in measure, time, and place.
So thanks to all at once and to each one,
Whom we invite to see us crown'd at Scone.

[Flourish. Exeunt.]

61-62 we reckon...you: I reward the loyalty of each of you and repay my debt to you.

64-65 What's more...time: whatever else should be done, whatever else ought to be started at this time

66 As: such as

68 Producing forth...ministers: bringing forward and exposing the ruthless agents

70 self: her own

? Do you think "butcher" and "fiend" are fair descriptions of the Macbeths?

PERSONA JOURNAL

The battle and the hostilities are over. How was your family impacted? How do you expect your life to change now that Scotland is at peace?

✱ **"My thanes and kinsmen, / Henceforth be earls..."** Here as elsewhere, Shakespeare echoes his historical source, Holinshed's *Chronicles*. Of Malcolm's succession to the throne, Holinshed wrote, "Many of them that before were thanes, were at this time made earls...These were the first earls that have been heard of among the Scottishmen..."

The three witches,
Polanski film, 1971

The Royal Concentration Span So ends Shakespeare's shortest tragedy and third shortest play. Why is *Macbeth* so short? Some scholars suggest that the original play was drastically cut, perhaps because of censorship. Another possibility has to do with kingly taste. *Macbeth* is so full of royal flattery that it may have been written especially for King James I—who was easily bored and disliked long plays.

Reacting to Act V

Analysis

1. Describe Lady Macbeth's mental state at the beginning of this act.
2. What do you suppose prompted the gentlewoman to go to the doctor for help?
3. The gentlewoman appears to be very loyal to Lady Macbeth. Does this surprise you? Why or why not?
4. Does Lady Macbeth's mental condition come as a surprise, or was this possibility part of her character from the beginning? Explain.
5. Review Macbeth's speech at the top of page 155. What are the things that Macbeth thinks should accompany old age? What does he think will happen to him instead?
6. How does Macbeth react to the news that his wife is dead?
7. Explain how Macbeth is lulled into a false sense of security by the witches' predictions and how the truth of the predictions leads to his downfall.
8. Is there any point in this act at which you feel sympathy for Macbeth? Explain your answer.

Literary Elements

1. A **metaphor** is a figure of speech that makes a comparison between things that are not truly alike. An **extended metaphor** is a complex comparison that goes on for several lines, comparing the unlike things point by point. Explain the extended metaphor on page 153 involving medicine.
2. **Dramatic irony** occurs when the audience knows something that the characters on stage do not. Explain the irony on page 157 when the soldiers are ordered to cut down tree branches.

Writing

1. Write a dialogue that might occur between Lady Macbeth and a therapist.
2. Write a paraphrase of Macbeth's "Tomorrow and tomorrow and tomorrow" soliloquy on page 161 (lines 19-28).
3. Review the Venn diagram that you completed after Act I, where you compared your persona with a major character. Write a short essay on the changes and growth of both your persona and the major character that you selected.
4. As the new head of the Macbeth clan, write a eulogy for your dead kinsman. Utilize the language of Shakespeare in your writing.

Reacting to the Play

Analysis

1. Why do you think the witches chose Macbeth for their victim? Would Banquo have served their purpose just as well?
2. Throughout the text, there are references to double meanings and opposites. In Act I, scene i, the witches say "Fair is foul, and foul is fair." In Act I, scene iii, Macbeth echoes that with "So foul and fair a day I have not seen." Find more examples of double meanings and opposites in the text. Why do you think Shakespeare carefully weaves these references throughout the play?
3. If Macbeth had not killed Duncan, do you think that he would still have become king?
4. Did the Macbeths really care for each other or were they only interested in themselves? Defend your answer with examples from the play.
5. Where is Fleance? What do you think happened to him?
6. Review your answer to the first writing activity on page 144. By the end of the play, do you think that Scotland is being ruled by the person best suited to be king? Explain your answer.
7. What do you think was Macbeth's biggest mistake?
8. In your opinion, who or what is ultimately responsible for Macbeth's death?
9. Identify some situations in today's world where the struggle for power has led to violence. Can you name some world leaders, past or present, that resemble Macbeth in their methods to gain control and remain in power?

Literary Elements

1. What do you think is the overriding message, or **theme**, of the play?
2. Along with blood and darkness, what other strands of **imagery** do you find in the play? Give examples to support your answer.
3. Review the definition of the **tragic hero** on page 23. How does Macbeth fit this definition? What is his tragic flaw?

Writing

1. Write a short parody of Macbeth.
2. Choose one scene from the play and rewrite the dialogue in modern English.
3. Who is the stronger character, Macbeth or Lady Macbeth? Write an opinion essay that explains your choice.
4. Who would get your vote to be the next King of Scotland after Macbeth? Write an essay explaining your preference.
5. Examine Macbeth's downfall by writing an essay comparing Macbeth's reputation in Act I with his reputation at the end of the play.

Life in 11th-Century Scotland

Shakespeare played fast and loose with historical facts in *Macbeth.* Almost nothing in the "Scots tragedy" actually happened as Shakespeare wrote it. Still, the real Scotland of Macbeth's time was as troubled, violent, and fascinating as anything the Bard dreamed up. The following account is how things *really* occurred.

Scotland is divided into three main regions—the rocky, mountainous Highlands to the north, the hilly Southern Uplands, and the Lowlands between them. Macbeth himself was a Highlander, possibly of Viking (Scandinavian) ancestry. As King, he completed the job of uniting these regions into a single Scottish nation.

If you lived in any of these regions during the 11th century, you wouldn't have spoken Shakespeare's English. You probably would have spoken Gaelic, a language that came to Scotland from Ireland. A few Scottish Highlanders still speak Gaelic today. Some of today's English words come from Gaelic—including *bog, slogan,* and *whisky.*

Since the Romans had brought Christianity to Scotland many centuries before, you would probably have been a Christian—a member of the Celtic Christian church. On the other hand, you might have believed in a pagan religion instead. Macbeth himself worshipped the gods of Scandinavia before he converted to Christianity.

In Macbeth's Scotland, you would have belonged to one of several classes. Nobles were divided in family groups called clans. The highest nobles, of course, were the king and queen. Next in line were lords called mormaers, who ruled vast territories. Macbeth was the mormaer of the province of Moray before he became king.

Ranking below the nobility were free commoners and people who lived in virtual slavery.

Being the King of Scotland was a dangerous job. During one period before Macbeth was king, seven Scottish kings in a row were murdered. When a king died (rarely of natural causes), the new king was elected by a rather confusing custom called tanistry. In order to be elected king under tanistry, a nobleman had to be liked and respected by his peers. It helped to be a good warrior. A reputation for ruthlessness didn't hurt either.

For example, Macbeth is thought to have avenged his father's murder by burning a treacherous cousin to death. He later slew King Duncan in battle (not in his sleep) in order to get himself elected king. Such violent deeds were considered quite proper in 11th century Scotland. In fact, Macbeth was regarded as a just and peaceable king.

Even so, King Macbeth had plenty of worries. Scotland was constantly under threat of invasion from Norsemen, Danes, and the English. Macbeth also lived in danger of rebellion among his own subjects—a quarrelsome mix of peoples that included Picts, Scots, and Celts.

So kings and nobles always had to be ready to fight. Medieval warfare required physical strength as well as skill. Soldiers wore heavy suits of mail—flexible, cloth-like armor made from tiny loops of iron. They carried massive, double-edged, iron swords perfected by the Vikings. These swords were used for slashing, not thrusting or stabbing—which was a good thing, since mail was easily pierced by a direct stab.

Bagpipes, which had been played for many centuries before Macbeth's time, were great spirit-raisers for Scottish warriors. The pipes' shrill martial music stirred the blood and readied men for battle. In fact, the bagpipe itself has sometimes been called a weapon of war.

If you were a commoner or peasant, you had other things to think about than war. Just surviving in the rugged Scottish countryside was no easy task. People mined, did metalwork and blacksmithing, fished, and raised large flocks of sheep and cattle.

If you were a woman, you would have spent a lot of your time spinning thread from wool or linen. Since spinning wheels had not yet come to Scotland, you would have used a tool called a drop spindle. First, you would pull out strands of wool or linen, then attach them to the spindle. Then you would drop the spinning spindle so that the strands twisted together into thread.

This was a time-consuming task because a lot of thread was needed. Miles of it were used to make even a simple jacket. So spinning was an important activity that wasn't restricted to women or commoners. Even some noblemen are said to have done it.

The Scottish were also skilled weavers and embroiderers, and made attractive, patterned clothing from the thread they spun. Not much is known about Scottish clothing of this period, since no examples have survived. Nobles of the time might have worn plaid to show what clan they belonged to. But the famous Highland kilt would not appear for several more centuries.

Jewelry, very important in Scottish life, was made by both male and female commoners. Handsome brooches were used to fasten clothing, and both men and women wore necklaces.

Along with semi-precious jewels, necklaces were strung with amber, bits of bone, and glass beads. Depending on your religion, you might have worn either a Christian crucifix or the image of a Norse god on a necklace. You might even have worn both if you believed in both the Christian and Norse religions—as Macbeth himself may have done during part of his life.

If you were a commoner, making clothes and jewelry could be a source of income. But you wouldn't sell your wares for money. Coins wouldn't be used in Scotland until the 12th century. Instead, you would have traded or bartered your crafted goods.

You also would have done most of your cooking out-of-doors. A cauldron of pottery or metal (not unlike the one used by the witches in *Macbeth*) was held by chains over a bed of embers. To adjust the heat, you raised or lowered the cauldron.

You could cook several things at once in a cauldron. While you were boiling or roasting meat, you could also cook vegetables—either by putting them in a cloth bag and into the cauldron, or by steaming them above the cauldron.

Commoners' ovens were also out-of-doors. The walls of these ovens were made of stones, with a single slab of rock across the top. Grassy soil was piled around the stone walls for insulation. The top slab was either covered with soil or left bare for use as a stove. Kings and nobles had similar ovens inside their castles.

Despite all his historical inaccuracies, Shakespeare did get one thing right. At the end of *Macbeth,* he hints that Scotland is in for some serious changes now that Malcolm has become king. Indeed, Scotland changed a great deal after Macbeth's death.

Macbeth's successor, Malcolm III, had lived for many years in England and was married to an English princess named Margaret. Even though Malcolm frequently raided and invaded England, Malcolm and his queen began to bring English ways and customs to Scotland. Little by little, English would replace Gaelic as Scotland's first language. As the centuries passed, Scotland would struggle and often fight to maintain its separate identity—both culturally and politically.

By Shakesepare's time, Scotland and England were coming closer together—especially when a Scotsman named James became King of England in 1603. In 1707, after centuries of war and bloodshed, Scotland, England, and Wales all became part of a single nation called the Kingdom of Great Britain. Scottish independence had come to an end.

Shakespeare's Life

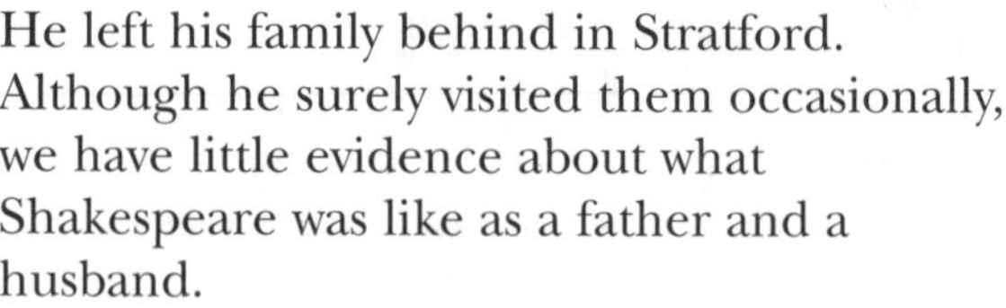

Many great authors can be imagined as living among the characters in their works. Historical records reveal how these writers spoke, felt, and thought. But Shakespeare is more mysterious. He never gave an interview or wrote an autobiography—not even one of his letters survives. What we know about his life can be told very briefly.

Shakespeare was born in April 1564. The exact date of his birth is unknown, but he was baptized on April 26 in the Stratford-upon-Avon church. His father, John, was a prominent local man who served as town chamberlain and mayor. Young William attended grammar school in Stratford, where he would have learned Latin—a requirement for a professional career—and some Greek.

Shakespeare's schoolroom

In 1582, William married Anne Hathaway. He was eighteen; she was twenty-six. At the time of their marriage, Anne was already three months pregnant with their first daughter, Susanna. In 1585, the couple had twins, Judith and Hamnet. Hamnet died before reaching adulthood, leaving Shakespeare no male heir.

Even less than usual is known about Shakespeare's life between 1585 and 1592. During that time, he moved to London and became an actor and playwright. He left his family behind in Stratford. Although he surely visited them occasionally, we have little evidence about what Shakespeare was like as a father and a husband.

Several of his early plays were written during this time, including *The Comedy of Errors, Titus Andronicus,* and the three parts of *Henry VI.* In those days, working in the theatre was rather like acting in soap operas today—the results may be popular, but daytime serials aren't recognized as serious art. In fact, many people were opposed to even allowing plays to be performed. Ministers warned their congregations of the dangers of going to plays.

But Shakespeare and his friends were lucky. Queen Elizabeth I loved plays. She protected acting companies from restrictive laws and gave them her permission to perform.

Queen Elizabeth I

Shakespeare wrote several plays to be performed for the queen, including *Twelfth Night.*

After Elizabeth's death in 1603, Shakespeare's company became known as the King's Men. This group of actors performed for James I, who had ruled Scotland before becoming King of England. Perhaps to thank James for his patronage, Shakespeare wrote *Macbeth,* which included two topics of strong interest to the King—Scottish royalty and witchcraft.

Unlike many theatre people, Shakespeare actually earned a good living. By 1599, he was part-owner of the Globe, one of the newest theatres in London. Such plays as *Othello, Hamlet,* and *King Lear* were first performed there.

In 1610 or 1611, Shakespeare moved back to the familiar surroundings of Stratford-upon-Avon. He was almost fifty years old, well past middle age by 17th-century standards. Over the years, he'd invested in property around Stratford, acquiring a comfortable estate and a family coat of arms.

But Shakespeare didn't give up writing. In 1611, his new play *The Tempest* was performed at Court. In 1613, his play *Henry VIII* premiered. This performance was more dramatic than anyone had expected. The stage directions called for a cannon to be fired when "King Henry" came on stage. The explosion set the stage on fire, and the entire theatre burned to the ground.

Shakespeare died in 1616 at the age of fifty-two. Scholars have wondered why he willed his "second-best bed" to his widow, but he also left Anne his plays and a comfortable income. His gravestone carried this inscription:

Good friend for Jesus sake forbear
To dig the dust enclosed here!
Blest be the man that spares these stones,
And curst be he that moves my bones.

Shakespeare's Theatre

In Shakespeare's London, a day's entertainment often began with a favorite amusement, bearbaiting. A bear would be captured and chained to a stake inside a pit. A pack of dogs would be released, and they would attack the bear. Spectators placed bets on which would die first. Admission to these pits cost only a penny, so they were very popular with working-class Londoners.

After the bearbaiting was over, another penny purchased admission to a play. Each theatre had its own company of actors, often supported by a nobleman or a member of the royal family.

As part-owner of the Globe Theatre, Shakespeare wrote plays, hired actors, and paid the bills. Since the Globe presented a new play every three weeks, Shakespeare and his actors had little time to rehearse or polish their productions. To complicate matters even more, most actors played more than one part in a play.

Boys played all the female roles. Most acting companies had three or four youths who were practically raised in the theatre. They started acting as early as age seven and played female roles until they began shaving. Actresses would not become part of the English theatre for another fifty years.

The audience crowded into the theatre at about 2 p.m. The cheapest seats weren't seats at all but standing room in front of the stage. This area, known as the "pit," was occupied by "groundlings" or "penny knaves," who could be more trouble to the actors than they were worth. If the play was boring, the groundlings would throw rotten eggs or vegetables. They talked loudly to their friends, played cards, and even picked fights with each other. One theatre was set on fire by audience members who didn't like the play.

The Swan Theatre in London, drawn by Arend van Buchell in 1596.

The theatre was open to the sky, so rain or snow presented a problem. However, the actors were partially protected by a roof known as the "heavens," and wealthier patrons sat in three stories of sheltered galleries that surrounded the pit and most of the main stage.

The main stage, about twenty-five feet deep and forty-five feet wide, projected into

Richard Tarleton, comedian

the audience, so spectators were closely involved in the action. This stage was rather bare, with only a few pieces of furniture. But this simplicity allowed for flexible and fluid staging. Unlike too many later productions, plays at the Globe did not grind to a halt for scene changes. When one group of actors exited through a doorway and a new group entered through another, Shakespeare's audience understood that a new location was probably being represented.

So the action of the plays was exciting and swift. The Chorus of *Romeo and Juliet* speaks of "the two hours' traffic of our stage," which suggests a rate of performance and delivery that today's actors would find nearly impossible.

Behind the main stage was the "tiring-house" where the actors changed costumes. Above the stage was a gallery that, when it wasn't occupied by musicians or wealthy patrons, could suggest any kind of high place—castle ramparts, a cliff, or a balcony. In his book *Witches and Jesuits,* the scholar Garry Wills suggests that the three witches "hovered" at such an upper level.

Special effects were common. A trap door in the main stage allowed ghosts to appear, as the three apparitions do to Macbeth in Act IV, scene i. Even more spectacularly, supernatural beings could be lowered from above the stage; the witch-goddess Hecate may have come and gone in this manner. For added realism, actors hid bags of pig's blood and guts under their stage doublets. When pierced with a sword, the bags spilled out over the stage and produced a gory effect.

All these staging methods and design elements greatly appealed to Elizabethan audiences and made plays increasingly popular. By the time Shakespeare died in 1616, there were more than 30 theaters in and around London.

What would Shakespeare, so accustomed to the rough-and-tumble stagecraft of the Globe, think of the theaters where his plays are performed today? He would probably miss some of the vitality of the Globe. For centuries now, his plays have been most often performed on stages with a frame called the "proscenium arch," which cleanly separates the audience from the performers. This barrier tends to cast a peculiar shroud of privacy over his plays so that his characters do not seem to quite enter our world.

But with greater and greater frequency, Shakespeare's plays are being performed out-of-doors or in theaters with three- or four-sided stages. And a replica of the Globe Theatre itself opened in London in 1996, only about 200 yards from the site of the original. This new Globe may prove an exciting laboratory where directors and actors can test ideas about Elizabethan staging. Their experiments may change our ideas about how Shakespeare's plays were performed and give new insights into their meaning.

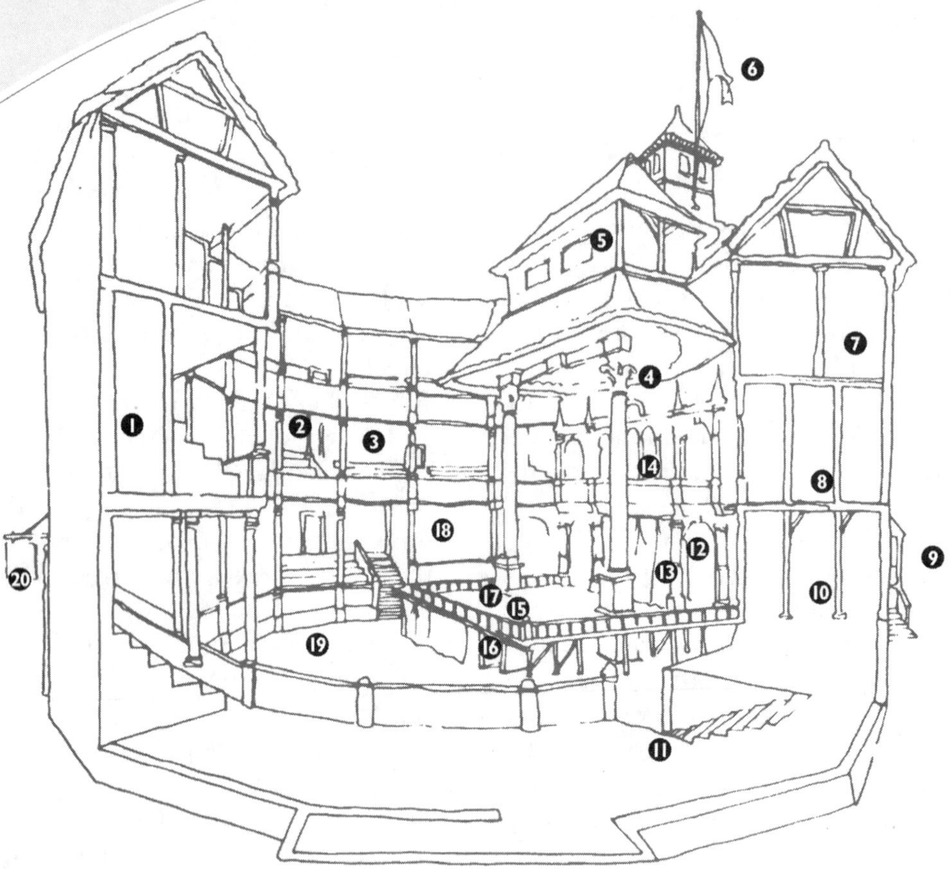

1 Corridor A passageway serving the middle gallery.

2 Entrance Point leading to the staircase and upper galleries.

3 Middle Gallery The seats here were higher priced.

4 The Heavens So identified by being painted with the zodiac signs.

5 Hut A storage area that also held a winch system for lowering characters to the stage.

6 Flag A white flag above the theatre meant a show that day.

7 Wardrobe A storage area for costumes and props.

8 Dressing Rooms Rooms where actors were "attired" and awaited their cues.

9 Tiring-House Door The rear entrance or "stage door" for actors or privileged spectators.

10 Tiring-House Backstage area providing space for storage and business.

11 Stairs Theatregoers reached the galleries by staircases enclosed by stairwells.

12 Stage Doors Doors opening into the Tiring-House.

13 Inner Stage A recessed playing area often curtained off except as needed.

14 Gallery Located above the stage to house musicians or spectators.

15 Trap Door Leading to the Hell area where a winch elevator was located.

16 Hell The area under the stage, used for ghostly comings and goings or for storage.

17 Stage Major playing area jutting into the Pit, creating a sense of intimacy.

18 Lords Rooms or private galleries. Six pennies let a viewer sit here, or sometimes on stage.

19 The Pit Sometimes referred to as "The Yard," where the "groundlings" watched.

20 Main Entrance Here the doorkeeper collected admission.

Shakespeare's Sources: The Legend of Macbeth

The overwhelming presence of evil in *Macbeth* raises an interesting question: Just how wicked was the historical Macbeth? Shakespeare was not a writer to let the facts stand in the way of a good story; the real Macbeth was not the murderous tyrant portrayed in his play.

According to less biased accounts, Macbeth ruled Scotland wisely and effectively from 1040 to 1057. His people prospered during his reign, and he brought an end to a long conflict between the Scottish Church and the Pope. Macbeth and his wife generously supported monasteries, and he even made a pilgrimage to Rome. Perhaps most significantly, he was the last Scottish king to devote himself to the language and traditions of the Celts, a people who periodically dominated the British Isles throughout antiquity.

rnament from a Celtic illuminated
anuscript

Macbeth *did* kill his predecessor Duncan. But he did so in open combat, not while Duncan lay asleep. Moreover, Duncan was not the pious and kind ruler Shakespeare made him out to be. He ruled for only six years, and according to contemporary accounts, he did so very badly. He was cruel and aggressive, involving Scotland in a long war that caused his people great suffering. Perhaps worst of all, he was simply not very capable. When Macbeth defeated Duncan and assumed the throne, the Scottish people rightly expected better times.

So Shakespeare did with Macbeth as he had already done with Richard III—he took a basically decent ruler and demonized him. But Shakespeare did not create this murderous, tyrannical Macbeth from scratch. Much of the legend had been around for many years. Why and how did it come about?

According to a familiar saying, history is always written by victors. When Macbeth was killed by Malcolm, Duncan's family was permanently restored to the throne. Not surprisingly, this line of royalty was anxious to have its legitimacy honored. Any kind words historians had to say about Macbeth were repressed. Even Shakespeare had political reasons for giving a negative portrayal of Macbeth. King James I traced his lineage back not only to the mythical Banquo but also to Duncan himself.

The story of Macbeth's meeting with the three witches was probably invented by the historian Hector Boece (ca. 1465–1536). By Shakespeare's time, the story was accepted as historical fact.

Holinshed's *Chronicles* (1577)

Three centuries after Macbeth's reign, a historian named Hector Boece described Macbeth as a bloodthirsty monster. This account was largely accepted by Raphael Holinshed in his 1587 book *Chronicles of England, Scotlande, and Ireland.*

Shakespeare used Holinshed's *Chronicles* as a source of information for all his plays dealing with British history, and *Macbeth* was no exception. Holinshed told of the witches' prophecies and the accession of Banquo's descendants to the throne of Scotland. But as dramatists will, Shakespeare took liberties with his source. He combined Holinshed's account of Macbeth's rise to power with the story of Donwald, an earlier Scottish tyrant who murdered King Duffe.

Macbeth Timeline

1039	King Duncan marches north to put down Tofin's rebellion; Macbeth kills Duncan at Bothgowanan
1050	Macbeth and his wife are the first Scottish rulers to make a large gift to the Church
1054	Siward defeats Macbeth in battle; Macbeth flees to the north
1056	Macduff slays Macbeth
1057	Malcolm Canmore becomes King of Scotland

There Shakespeare found some of the most gripping elements of his drama. Like Shakespeare's Macbeth, Donwald committed his initial crime by night while the King was a guest in his castle—a violation of the sacred rules of hospitality. Like Macbeth, Donwald was goaded to action by his ambitious and iron-willed wife.

A Scottish king is crowned at Scone, where the country's Celtic ruler traditionally assumed the throne.

Holinshed's *Chronicles* (1577)

However freely Shakespeare may have played with historical facts, he was reasonably faithful to the feudal, Celtic politics of Macbeth's time. Today's audiences may be surprised by Macbeth's alarm in Act I when he hears Duncan declare his own eldest son, Malcolm, the heir to the Scottish throne. We are used to royal succession by *primogeniture.* This system automatically makes the eldest child (typically a male) the heir to all of a parent's property—including a crown. So why *wouldn't* Malcolm rule after his father's death?

In Scotland, the kingship was *elective.* A group of nobles (called *thanes*) were eligible to rule because they were descendants of Kenneth Mac Alpine. This was the man who, in the 9th century, united Scotland and became its first king. When a king died, a new ruler was elected from among the thanes. This system, while simple, seldom ran smoothly. Rebellion and assassination were common. Few Scottish kings died of old age.

So when Shakespeare's Duncan names Malcolm the Prince of Cumberland, he ignores the normal process of succession. According to both history and legend, Macbeth had a stronger claim to the throne than young Malcolm. Assassination would have been an acceptable means of correcting this wrong—although the deceitful murder in Shakespeare's play would certainly have offended the Celtic warrior spirit.

Shakespeare was also correct in suggesting that an era of Scottish history ended with Macbeth's death. His successor Malcolm III was educated in England and sought military alliances with the English. After England was defeated by Normandy's William the Conqueror in 1066, Malcolm replaced the old Celtic ways with the new Anglo-Norman culture. Eventually, his successors thought of themselves as more French than Celt. And with the accession of James I to the English throne in 1603, Scotland finally became part of Great Britain.

:tish castle with moat, vbridge, and towers

Excerpt from Holinshed's *Chronicles*

Meeting the Witches

[It happened that] as Makbeth and Banquho journied towards Fores, where the king [Duncan] then laie, they went sporting by the waie togither without other company, save onlie themselves, passing thorough the woods and fields, when suddenlie in the middest of a laund, there met them three women in strange and wild apparell, resembling creatures of elder world, whome when they attentivelie beheld, woodering much at the sight, the first of them spake and said; All haile Makbeth, thane of Glammis (for he had latelie entered into that dignitie and office by the death of his father Sinell). The second of them said; Haile Makbeth thane of Cawder. But the third said; All haile Makbeth that heereafter shalt be king of Scotland.

Murdering the King

Donwald...conceived such an inward malice towards the king (though he shewed it not outwardlie at the first), that the same continued still boiling in his stomach, and ceased not, till through setting on of his wife...hee found meanes to murther the king within the forsaid castell of Fores where he used to sojourne. For the king being in that countrie, was accustomed to lie most commonlie within the same castell, having a speciall trust in Donwald, as a man whom he never suspected.

Of Witches and Witchcraft

Poor King James had a lot of trouble with witches.

His first run-in was in 1590. He was then Scotland's King James VI and hadn't yet become England's King James I. While he was sailing home from Denmark with his new wife, Queen Anne, a group of witches supposedly conjured up a storm to sink his ship. When he and the queen survived, the witches allegedly used a wax doll to cast a fatal spell on him. Again, they failed.

More and more plots against his life followed—and most of them were said to involve witchcraft.

Things didn't settle down when he became the king of England. In 1605 came the notorious Gunpowder Plot. In it, Catholic conspirators almost succeeded in blowing up King James and the entire English government with explosives. (See page 7.)

Now, using gunpowder to commit assassination may not exactly sound supernatural. But gunpowder itself was believed to be invented by the devil. And the plot was said to be hatched during a Black Mass.

Small wonder that James I was obsessed by witchcraft. He even wrote a book about it called *Demonology*.

Witches were nothing new in the times of King James. Nor were they to be found only in the British Isles. Stories of people—especially women—with dangerous, supernatural powers can be found in all places and cultures. And they go all the way back to ancient times.

The Ancient Greeks told the story of a beautiful witch named Medea. Medea used magic against her own father and brothers to save the life of her lover, the hero Jason. Later, when Jason wanted to marry another woman, Medea slew his would-be bride with a magical dress and crown.

The Old Testament also contains many references to witches. According to the book of 1 Samuel, King Saul went to the Witch of Endor to summon a spirit for advice. And the book of Exodus includes the famous commandment, "Thou shalt not suffer a witch to live."

But it was only with the coming of Christianity that fear of witches became widespread. The leaders of the early Christian church assured their followers that witches were powerless and not to be feared. Even so, uneducated Christians grew more and more fearful of witches as their religion spread through Europe. Between the 12th and 15th centuries, the church itself was determined to stamp out witchcraft.

Accused witches were thought to commit all kinds of unholy crimes, including the worship of Satan and the practice of necromancy. Necromancy involved the use of human corpses or body parts to cast spells.

King James wrote about necromancy in *Demonology*. He said that witches dismembered "dead corpses…to make powders thereof, mixing such other things there-amongst as he gives unto them."

Shakespeare had read James' book and refers to necromancy in *Macbeth*. On page 31 the second witch boasts, "Here I have a pilot's thumb, / Wrack'd as homeward he did come." And of course, it was typically witch-like behavior to hang around a battlefield, where human corpses were in hearty supply.

The very idea of such practices terrified ordinary people. Unfortunately, they resorted to equally terrifying practices to get rid of witches.

Imagine yourself a European peasant during medieval times or the Renaissance. You're walking down the road one day, and a grouchy old neighbor woman says something nasty to you. Then, a day or two later, one of your children takes sick. You come to the conclusion that the woman's nasty remark was some kind of evil spell.

If you told all this to the proper authorities, the woman might very well be charged with witchcraft—and possibly tortured and executed.

Of course, she might first be tested for innocence or guilt. But such tests were often quite horrible. In a trial by fire, a suspected witch had to walk a distance of nine feet while carrying a red-hot iron in her bare hand. Her hand would then be bandaged, and the bandage removed after three days. If the hand was badly scarred, this would be proof of witchcraft.

In a trial by water, a suspected witch was bound hand and foot and thrown into a river. Water was thought to be holy and pure. So if the suspect floated, it meant that the water had rejected her as something evil. Therefore, she was truly a witch, and deserved to be killed.

If she sank, it meant that the water had accepted her, which proved her innocence. Of course, this wasn't much help if the suspect happened to drown.

Many people were executed for witchcraft—sometimes by hanging, sometimes by burning at the stake. By far the majority of those were women.

Why were women so much more often accused of witchcraft than men? "The reason is easy," wrote King James, "for as that sex is frailer than man is, so is it easier to be entrapped in those gross snares of the Devil …"

The last great outburst of witch hysteria took place in Salem, Massachusetts, in 1692. This became the topic of another important play, Arthur Miller's *The Crucible.* Thirty people were convicted of witchcraft, and nineteen were hanged.

During the three centuries since then, executions for witchcraft have become almost unheard-of. People tend to be increasingly wary of weird accusations based on superstitious beliefs.

Late in life, King James himself came to doubt the reality of witchcraft and black magic. Even so, he continued to believe that the very *idea* of witchcraft held tremendous power over the human imagination. Today, we can still feel some of that awful power in Shakespeare's *Macbeth.*

Themes and Imagery

THEMES IN MACBETH

A **theme** is an author's ongoing topic, idea, or concern. Below is just a sampling of three themes (the problem of evil; the power of guilt and fear; illusion and reality) that Shakespeare deals with in this thematically rich play.

The Problem of Evil

In his four greatest tragedies—*Hamlet, Othello, King Lear,* and *Macbeth*—Shakespeare seems obsessed with the problem of evil, and asks the sorts of questions we all ask about it: Why is there evil in the world? What drives people to commit evil deeds? Is good stronger than evil? By taking us into the mind of a murderer, *Macbeth* explores such questions with great intensity.

What starts Macbeth and Lady Macbeth on their murderous careers? Ambition is the trigger. Their dialogue hints that they discussed the possibility of killing Duncan even before the action of the play began.

Macbeth may yield to evil, but he is not a completely evil man. So before he kills Duncan, he hopes that one murder will fulfill his ambitions. Then he can be a good king and a good man.

But evil doesn't work that way. The Elizabethans believed in a "chain of vice," by which crime leads to more crime, and murder leads to more murder. Macbeth fully realizes this after he's seen Banquo's ghost: "It will have blood, they say; blood will have blood" (III, iv).

From that time on, Macbeth's evil deeds seem to have a will of their own. He can't stop himself from carrying out ever more monstrous crimes: "I am in blood / Stepp'd in so far that, should I wade no more, / Returning were as tedious as go o'er" (III, iv). And Macbeth's crimes grow worse and worse. He begins by slaying a king in his sleep, and eventually orders the deaths of women and children. Late in the play, characters hint that Macbeth has committed atrocities too horrible to describe: "Each new morn / New widows howl, new orphans cry, new sorrows / Strike heaven on the face…" (IV, iii).

The Power of Guilt and Fear

Elizabethans believed that the "chain of vice" led to "remorse of conscience." And it's something of a scholarly cliché that Macbeth is tortured by a bad conscience.

There can be no doubt that Macbeth is tortured by his own evil deeds. He cannot sleep, and he becomes desperately lonely. Late in the play, he can trust no one, and complains that "honour, love, obedience, troops of friends, / I must not look to have …" (V, iii). He becomes increasingly estranged even from his wife, until he finally lacks the capacity to even grieve at the news of her death: "She should have died hereafter" (V, v).

What of Lady Macbeth? As tough and ruthless as she seems at the beginning of the play, Macbeth's wife is capable of genuine compassion. In II, ii, she can't bring herself to murder Duncan because he looks like her father. And as she slips into madness later in the play, she is haunted by pity for her husband's victims: "The Thane of Fife had a wife. Where is she now?" (V, i). Less imaginative than her husband, Lady Macbeth is nevertheless more vulnerable than he is to "remorse of conscience."

Illusion and Reality

In life, things are often not what they seem. Shakespeare's *Macbeth* is one of the world's great artistic statements of this idea.

In the very first scene, the witches tell us exactly what to expect: "Fair is foul, and foul is fair…" Illusion and paradox will abound in the world of this play. (A **paradox** is when a statement or idea seems contradictory and impossible—and yet, somehow, might really be true.) Macbeth eerily echoes the witches' words with his very first line: "So foul and fair a day I have not seen."

Illusions and deceptions keep piling up after that. In Act I, King Duncan learns that his trusted friend, the Thane of Cawdor, has rebelled against him. "There's no art / To find the mind's construction in the face," sighs Duncan (I, iv). Or as the old saying puts it, "Don't judge a book by its cover." Duncan doesn't learn this lesson well enough to save himself from the seemingly trustworthy Macbeth.

Even Macbeth's castle is deceptive in appearance. Far from being dank, gloomy, and forbidding (as it is often designed—incorrectly—in productions), it is actually a cheerful place—at least at first. "This castle hath a pleasant seat," (I, iv) observes Duncan.

Who would guess that those walls harbor a diabolical plot? And who would guess that Macbeth and his wife—the perfect host and hostess—are planning to murder their royal guest?

Even before he murders Duncan, the hyper-imaginative Macbeth has trouble telling illusion from reality, complaining that "nothing is but what is not" (I, iii). And is that a real knife hovering in the air before he murders Duncan, or just a "dagger of the mind" (II, i)? And is that really the slain Banquo at his feast, or just a hallucination?

Macbeth is goaded on by the witches, who are agents of illusion as well as evil. They assure Macbeth that his downfall will come only with two miracles. They promise that "none of woman born / Shall harm Macbeth"—and also, that "Macbeth shall never vanquish'd be until / Great Birnam Wood to high Dunsinane Hill / Shall come against him" (IV, i).

Neither of these "miracles" really happens. Birnam Wood only appears to move toward Dunsinane when Malcolm's soldiers carry branches from its trees. And the other prophecy is but a trick with words. Macduff, who kills Macbeth, is not the offspring of some goddess or monster, but an ordinary mortal who was from his "mother's womb / Untimely ripp'd" (V, vii). In our own time, countless babies come into the world by cesarean section; nobody claims that they are not "of woman born." The witches use illusions, half-truths, and outright lies to spread evil in the world.

By the end of the play, Macbeth is a mystery even to himself. The one thing he knows for certain is that he is lost in a world of lies and illusions: "Life's but a walking shadow, a poor player / That struts and frets his hour upon the stage / And then is heard no more" (V, v).

IMAGERY

Imagery refers to sensory language. Shakespeare often uses vivid imagery to develop his thematic ideas. Consider how the following images (night and darkness; sleep and death; clothing; violence and bloodshed) reflect on the themes discussed above.

Macbeth is full of images of night and darkness. Both Macbeth and Lady Macbeth summon darkness to hide their misdeeds. Upon receiving news of the witches' prophecies, Lady Macbeth exclaims, "Come, thick night, / And pall thee in the dunnest smoke of hell, / That my keen knife see not the wound it makes ..." (I, v). "Stars, hide your fires," cries Macbeth, soon after meeting the witches—for he desperately hopes that darkness can hide his crimes even from himself: "The eye wink at the hand, yet let that be, / Which the eye fears, when it is done, to see" (I, iv).

As if obeying Macbeth and his wife, darkness descends with a vengeance after Duncan's death. As Ross observes, "By th' clock, 'tis day, / And yet dark night strangles the travelling lamp" (II, iv). Scotland will not see daylight again until Macbeth's violent rule has ended.

Sleep and Death

Upon killing Duncan, Macbeth hears a voice exclaim, "Sleep no more! / Macbeth does murder sleep" (II, ii). And from that time on, Macbeth sleeps little if at all, as Lady Macbeth observes after the banquet scene: "You lack the season of all natures, sleep" (III, iv).

Like all insomniacs, Macbeth can't stop thinking and talking about sleep. Perversely, he hopes that his next crime will make it possible for him to sleep again. "Thou shalt not live," he says of Macduff, "That I may tell pale-hearted fear it lies, / And sleep in spite of thunder" (IV, i).

The imagery of the play often links sleep with death. After Lady Macbeth drugs Duncan's guards, they sleep so soundly "That death and nature do contend about them / Whether they live or die" (I, ii). When Macbeth is afraid to return to the scene of Duncan's murder, Lady Macbeth scolds him, "The sleeping and the dead / Are but as pictures" (II, ii). And after finding Duncan's corpse, Macduff cries out to everybody in the castle, "Shake off this downy sleep, death's counterfeit, / And look on death itself!" (II, iii).

Clothing

Macbeth is a usurper and tyrant at heart, even before he becomes king. So the titles and honors that come to him during the play don't suit him well. Shakespeare suggests this with images of ill-fitting clothing.

In I, iii, when Ross and Angus arrive to tell Macbeth that he is now the Thane of Cawdor, Macbeth replies, "Why do you dress me / In borrow'd robes?" In the same scene, Banquo observes of Macbeth, "New honours come upon him, / Like our strange garments, cleave not to their mould / But with the aid of use." And as the rebel armies close in on Macbeth, Angus observes, "Now does he feel his title / Hang loose about him, like a giant's robe / Upon a dwarfish thief" (V, ii).

In an odd episode late in the play, Macbeth has trouble deciding what clothes to wear. He asks an attendant bring him his armor so he can go into the battle, then begins to put it on over his regal clothing. But when he's partly dressed in his armor, he commands, "Pull't off, I say," then, "Bring it after me" (V, iii). This indecision suggests Macbeth's discomfort with what he's become—not a king or a soldier, but a vicious killer.

Violence and Bloodshed

Duncan's first line in I, ii ("What bloody man is that?") tips us off that Macbeth is going to be an unusually violent play. Indeed, starting with Duncan's line, the word "blood" occurs in one form or another about 40 times in the text.

Beginning with Duncan's murder, seven characters die violent deaths—including Lady Macbeth, who commits suicide. Appropriately, much of the play's imagery evokes violence and bloodshed.

To fill us with horror at Macbeth's crimes against the innocent, violent imagery is sometimes linked to images of children and babies. For example, Lady Macbeth imagines killing her own infant: "I would, while it was smiling in my face, / Have pluck'd my nipple from his boneless gums / And dash'd the brains out ..." (I, vii).

Macbeth's hyperactive imagination leads him to envision truly apocalyptic bloodshed and violence. (*Apocalyptic* means having to do with the end of the world.) Were he to try to wash his hands clean, he imagines that he would fill the oceans with blood: "This my hand will rather / The multitudinous seas in incarnadine, / Making the green one red" (II, ii).

Near the end of the play, Macbeth is exhausted from his own reign of terror. "I have supp'd full with horrors," he says (V, v). We in the audience may feel that we have, too.

Image Credits Art Today (www.arttoday.com): 6, 30, 58, 78, 92, 115, 116, 120, 127, 138, 155, 178 top, 179, 180, 181. © Bettmann/CORBIS: 64. Bollinger Collection, Special Collections Department, University of Iowa Libraries, Iowa City, Iowa: 117. British Travel Association: 178 center left. Courtesy of Stratford Festival Archives: 25. Donald Cooper/Photostage: 52, 73. Everett Collection: 96. By permission of the Folger Shakespeare Library: 121. THE GRANGER COLLECTION, New York: 129. © Hulton-Deutsch Collection/CORBIS: 104, 161, 165. Joe Cocks Studio Collection at the Shakespeare Centre Library, and the copyright is owned by the Shakespeare Birthplace Trust: 142, 167. John Vickers, London: 28, 102. THE KOBAL COLLECTION / TOHO: 169. Kurt E. Schon, Ltd.: 113. Library of Congress: 7, 48, 50, 68, 178 right. Mary Evans Picture Library: 124. Photofest: 21, 32, 35, 41, 42, 45, 55, 60, 79, 81, 83, 87, 108, 137, 145, 148, 163, 172. University of Cambridge: 158. Victoria & Albert Museum, London/Art Resource, NY: 64, 97, 118, 124, 149.